BUILD YOUR MARRIAGE WITH PRAYER

BRAD & HEIDI MITCHELL

Published by Build Your Marriage®
Editing and layout by Paul Braoudakis
Cover design by Aimee Lindamood

www.buildyourmarriage.org

Printed in the United States of America

ISBN: 978-1-7341588-8-5

DEDICATION

To Our Build Your Marriage Board -

David and Teresa Anderson
Dan and Kay Fekete

Thank you for your prayers. "The earnest prayer of a righteous person has great power and produces wonderful results."

— James 5:16b

CONTENTS

INTRODUCTION

We were speaking at a marriage conference when a pastor walked up to us and said, "Thank you for teaching on prayer last night. My wife and I rarely pray together, and after your session, we decided to pray together. It was amazing. This will revolutionize our marriage. We plan to continue praying together."

Statements admitting a lack of prayer are common even for couples in ministry. The fact is, most couples don't pray *together*. We are passionate about encouraging couples to pray *together*. Yet, as we've spoken to thousands of couples, we realize many couples don't pray because they don't know how. They may feel awkward praying in front of their spouse, or they don't know what to say.

We wrote *Build Your Marriage with Prayer* so that after 40 days of praying together as a couple, you will have more confidence talking to God. Prayer will be an essential, natural conversation between you, your spouse, and God. Prayer will be the foundation upon which your marriage is built. Outside of receiving the gift of salvation, prayer is the most important aspect of your marriage.

Praying together unites you. It creates intimacy. When you pray, God's power infuses your marriage.

Build Your Marriage with Prayer is divided into 40 topics, one for each day. Each day starts with a Bible verse, followed by a reading. Then we include a prayer for you and your spouse to pray together. We want both of you to pray out loud together. Some days we've designated the husband to pray, and other days we've indicated that the wife should pray.

After days 10, 20, 30, and 40, we've incorporated some practical praying exercises so that you can develop your own habit and style of expressing your prayers to God. Remember, there are no right or wrong ways to pray to our heavenly Father.

Finally, after each day, we provide two questions for you to discuss. As you do this, we expect that you will gain a greater love and appreciation for each other and God.

We trust that after 40 days, your marriage is transformed as you Build Your Marriage with Prayer.

WHY SHOULD WE PRAY TOGETHER?

"Then you will call upon me and come and
pray to me, and I will hear you."
— Jeremiah 29:12 (ESV)

The majority of couples don't pray together. It's estimated that only 5-11% of couples do so. We're talking about Christians and missionaries and pastors and … you? Every year, we teach hundreds of couples and are astonished at how few of them pray together. We wrote this 40-day book to help you and your spouse pray together. If you already pray together, then use this devotional to deepen and expand your prayer life. If praying together isn't something you do, we encourage you to start, and we're going to make it easy for you.

Research consistently shows that couples who pray together daily have higher rates of marital satisfaction and decrease their chance of divorce. A Gallup Poll revealed that when couples pray together, their chance of divorce is 1 in 1,152 couples.[1]

Besides reducing your risk for divorce, couples who pray together grow in intimacy as they share their needs and desires with each other. Most married couples can unite their bodies, but uniting their souls is much more difficult. Prayer brings your souls together. It also increases your faith as you focus on God as your leader and provider. When you see your prayer requests answered, it increases your trust and reliance on God. Prayer also drives away Satan, the enemy of your marriage. And it's through prayer that you glorify and worship God. Prayer is the foundation upon which your marriage is built. John Bunyan, the author of *Pilgrim's Progress*, said, "Pray often, for prayer is a shield to the soul, a sacrifice to God, and a scourge to Satan."

Let's get started.

---

1. faithfulfathering.org/dad-talk/view/1431/power-of-prayer

Prayer (Husband prays)

Dear God,

We are committed to prayer. We're excited to start on this journey and see where you lead us. Build in us a strong desire to pray together and help us to find the time each day to pray. Grow our marriage while also increasing our love for you. Deepen our understanding of each other.

In Jesus' name, Amen.

Questions

1. When is the best time for us to pray? We commit to praying together each day at this time.

2. What do we hope to gain from praying together?

DAY TWO

HOME

"For every house is built by someone,
but the builder of all things is God."
— Hebrews 3:4 (ESV)

We've been married for more than 40 years, and we have lived in 13 homes. Each home had its own characteristics. Some were cramped and old; others were new and spacious. Some were a combination of these. But what made each of these houses similar is that God has been at the center. Early in our marriage, we established that the foundation of our home would be Jesus Christ.

When we move into a new place, we dedicate that house to the Lord in prayer. We're mindful of what occurs in our house. We strive to honor God with the music we play, the shows we watch, and the events that happen in our home. We like to host friends and family for overnights and dinners. Our desire is that others feel welcomed and cared for in our home. We want them to experience the love of Jesus.

Some of our best memories are sitting around our dining room table. We've hosted Bible study groups, friends, family, missionaries, pastors, unbelievers, and sometimes even a few strangers. We've grown in our relationships with others and have been challenged in our walk with God.

The Bible mentions several individuals who used their homes to serve others. In 2 Kings 4:8, Elisha was traveling to Shunem, and a wealthy woman encouraged him to come to her and her husband's home for a meal. Elisha took her up on the offer. Whenever he traveled through their area, he ate in their home.

This woman exemplified the love of God to Elisha. We learn in verses 9-10 that she said to her husband, "I am sure this man who stops in from time to time is a holy man from God. Let's build a small room for him on the roof and furnish it with a bed, table, a chair, and a lamp. Then he will have a place to stay whenever he comes by."

This husband and wife went above and beyond in showing hospitality to Elisha. They created a private sleeping space for Elisha and even furnished it to make it comfortable for him.

As believers in Christ, we are called to practice hospitality. 1 Peter 4:9 says, "Cheerfully share your home with those who need a meal or a place to stay." It doesn't mean you have to have a home that is decorated perfectly or be the best cook in the world. What it does mean is that you focus on others. You use your home and share it generously with others as you exemplify Christ to your friends, relatives, and strangers.

Author Elisabeth Elliot knew the true essence of a home. She said, "Our house is something far greater than its walls and its furniture and pictures and books when its foundation is love for God, trust in His providence, and obedience to His Word. When God is there — talked about, talked to, present — a house becomes a home."[2]

Prayer (Wife prays)

Dear God,

Our desire as a couple is not just to have a house, but a godly home. We want a home where you are honored and glorified. As a couple, we repent of anything that has taken place in our home that failed to honor you whether that's the types of shows we've watched, the music we've listened to, or the words we've used with each other.

Open our eyes to ways we can serve you with our home. Give us a heart for our friends, relatives, and even strangers. Help everyone who enters our house to feel your presence and know that, as a couple, we are first and foremost your servants.

In Jesus' name, Amen.

---

2. www.instagram.com/quoteselisabethelliot/p/DEYu9C_yABe/

Questions

1. As a couple, how can we use our home to serve others? What might stretch us?

2. Is there anything we've allowed in our home that we need to repent of? (If so, offer a short prayer asking for forgiveness right now.)

TIME

"For everything there is a season, a time
for every activity under heaven."
— *Ecclesiastes 3:1*

How busy are you? For most couples, time together is a valuable commodity. Between the chores at home, responsibilities with family, expectations at work, friendships to maintain, church involvement, and personal endeavors like hobbies or exercise, there really isn't much margin, is there?

The Apostle Paul wrote that we are to "look carefully then how you walk" and "make the most of every opportunity because the days are evil" (Ephesians 5:15-16 ESV). Our opportunity is to live with intentionality. Being "careful" means being wise and discerning. Before adding something new to your already full schedule, talk about it together. Listen to each other's perspectives. Work toward being unified in the outcome.

Ask questions like these to bring wisdom into how to use the time God has given you: "Is this going to add more stress to our schedule?" "Should we remove something we're currently doing to make room for this new thing?" "Will our being committed to ___ honor God?"

Don't miss Paul's reason for *why* you should be careful how you live and make the most of every opportunity, "because the days are evil." The devil will do all he can to distract you and keep you so busy you won't have time to cultivate your relationship with Jesus *or* each other. If he can get you into spiritual and relational disconnection, he can neutralize your impact and intimacy.

Charles Hummel, in his book *Priorities: Freedom From the Tyranny of the Urgent*, gives this warning about being too busy even with good things:

> *"Tension and frustration mount when we are performing the wrong tasks or trying to cram too many of the right activities into a given period … A critical spirit develops and we begin to judge and condemn others for what they do or don't do."*

Be on guard because your enemy will use your busyness to develop a negative attitude in your marriage.

Remember, while you do your best and work hard, don't stress about what can't be completed. Brad once had a wise mentor ask him, "Well, Brad, do you believe that God is big enough to handle everything you can't do?" By its very nature, that question is asking, "How big is your God?" and, "How big is your faith?"

Ultimately, your time is under your shared control. It's your responsibility to steward it well and with wisdom. Agree today that you will "be careful how you live" and "make the most of every opportunity."

Prayer (Husband prays)

Dear God,

Thank you for entrusting us with time and opportunities. We want wisdom in how we use that time. Guide us as we evaluate our calendar and involvements. Give us insight to know what needs to remain or be eliminated. We desire unity and courage as we make these decisions, ultimately bringing glory to you.

In Jesus' name, Amen.

Questions

1. What makes us nervous or excited about freeing up our calendar from some activities? In the conversations we need to have about our schedules, what creates hesitation for us?

2. Is there anything in our lives that immediately comes to mind that we can eliminate? What difference could that make in our marriage?

COVENANT

"This explains why a man leaves his father and mother and is joined to his wife, and the two are united into one."
— *Genesis 2:24*

"*I*, _____, take you _____, to be my wedded _____. And I promise before God and these witnesses to be your loving and faithful _____, to have and to hold from this day forward, for better, for worse, for richer, for poorer, in sickness and in health, to love, cherish, and serve as long as we both shall live."

Do you remember your wedding vows? Most likely, you repeated the phrases that the pastor or priest said as you declared your commitment to each other. It was at your wedding when you both entered into a marriage covenant.

Many people mistakenly think of a covenant as a contract between two individuals. But it's far more than that. Contracts are an exchange of promises that may or may not be broken. They are time-bound and have specific actions that are expected.

But a covenant is an oath and vow taken between two parties. It's permanent. A covenant is an unconditional promise made for the benefit of the *other* party. In marriage, the covenant is made in the "presence of a God who holds us responsible to keep them." It's God who joined you together.

There's a powerful picture of a covenant in Genesis 15. God was speaking to Abram (his name was later changed by God to Abraham). God promised Abram that his descendants would outnumber the stars of the sky, even though he didn't have any children and was aging. Abram believed God about the descendants, but he wasn't so convinced about God's promise to give him the land of Canaan, the "Promised Land."

So God established a covenant with Abram to assure him that He would keep His word. God had Abram do something that is a bit graphic, but was somewhat common in Abram's culture. God had Abram bring a heifer, a female goat, a ram, a turtledove, and a pigeon. Each animal was killed, cut in two, and placed so that there was a pathway between the pieces.

When two parties were establishing a covenant, they would walk between the pieces. The symbolism was that if either party were to break the covenant, may what happened to the animals happen to them. It's called "cutting a covenant" and signifies how important the vow is.

However, when God promised to give Abram the land of Canaan, it was *only God* who went between the pieces. Abram wasn't required to do so. It was God saying that *He* and *He alone* was responsible for making sure the promise came true for Abram. And He did.

When Jesus taught His disciples to observe The Lord's Supper, or Communion, He said, "This cup" — meaning His blood that was going to be shed and His life that was going to be given — "is the *new covenant* in my blood" (1 Corinthians 11:25). Just as with Abram, God had taken on full responsibility for establishing the *covenant* of our eternal relationship with Him.

So, when you stood up at your wedding and pronounced your vows, "till death us do part," you were saying, "This isn't about our feelings. It isn't about the circumstances of life like a health crisis or financial downturn. It isn't about a lull in our marriage. It isn't about our kids. This is unconditional. It's a binding covenant between *us*. As a result, we are keeping our covenant."

Take a moment to hold hands and say the vows at the top of this devotional to each other before you pray together.

Prayer (Husband prays)

Dear God,

Thank you for setting the example for us of what a covenant means to you. We are grateful for our marriage and the covenant that was established on our wedding day. Continue to remind us, by your Spirit, of the significance of our vows. We choose to live them out in a way that pleases you and is an example to those around us.

In Jesus' name, Amen.

Questions

1. What stands out to us about our wedding vows?

2. What does it mean to keep our covenant of marriage?

COMMUNICATION

"Do not let any unwholesome talk come out of your mouths, but only what is helpful for building others up according to their needs, that it may benefit those who listen."
— Ephesians 4:29 (NIV)

Randy was the best man in our wedding. Many years ago, Randy's mom and his little brother, Philip, attended a grand and elegant wedding reception in the downtown of a large Midwestern city. The reception was held at the fanciest club in the city, and the bride and groom's 400 closest friends were there to celebrate. Everything was spectacular. There was music, a seven-course dinner, and a beautiful, tiered wedding cake.

Randy's mom was enjoying a slice of the delicious white wedding cake while conversing with friends. Suddenly, Philip tapped his mom on her shoulder and started to say something. Randy's mom, the epitome of etiquette, told her son he was interrupting. But Philip paid no attention to his mom. He patted her shoulder again. Again, his mother told him she was busy, and he wasn't using good manners. Philip didn't quit. He tapped his mom and then blurted out, "Mom, there are maggots in the cake!" And sure enough, there were.

Using unwholesome speech, whether it's degrading, sarcastic, mean, or disrespectful, has no place in your marriage. Words like these should be just as repulsive as eating maggots. God's Word gives several principles you should follow as you talk to each other.

One purpose in communicating with your spouse is to understand them. You want to know what they're thinking, what they feel, and why a certain issue is important to them. You can learn about your spouse by asking them key questions, instead of blurting out your own opinions. Proverbs 18:2 reminds us, "Fools have no interest in understanding; they only want to air their own opinions."

It's important to practice self-control as you talk and listen to your spouse. Have you ever been in a conversation together that started off well but escalated into harsh words? We have, and it didn't go well. Proverbs 10:19 says, "Too much talk leads to sin. Be sensible and keep your mouth shut." There's a time to speak up and a time to refrain from voicing your opinion. Use wisdom about when to discuss sensitive topics.

When communicating with your spouse, don't slander them or use obscene language (Colossians 3:8). Instead, treat them with kindness and respect. Ephesians 4:15 emphasizes the importance of speaking the truth to your spouse in love when it says, "Instead, we will speak the truth in love, growing in every way more and more like Christ ... " When you have something difficult to say, tell the truth but do so with the most loving, gentle words possible.

Finally, encourage and build up your spouse (1 Thessalonians 5:11). What does your spouse do well? Tell them. When has your spouse blessed you? Thank them. When has your spouse served your family or someone else selflessly? Affirm them. When has your spouse demonstrated godly characteristics in their life? Acknowledge them.

Prayer (Both pray the first paragraph, wife concludes prayer)

Dear God,

Thank you for _____ (insert spouse's name). He/she does _____ well and is an encouragement to me.

Put a guard over our mouths so that we honor you with our words. Give us the ability to speak the truth in love while also showing respect and honor. Help us to grow in our understanding of each other as we listen and discern when to speak.

In Jesus' name, Amen.

Questions

1. Is there any area in our marriage where we have used unwholesome (degrading, sarcastic, mean, or disrespectful) speech? If so, where?

2. What needs do you have, and how can I encourage you?

GOD'S WORD

"But they delight in the law of the Lord,
meditating on it day and night."
— Psalm 1:2

Our friends, Ron and Lori, experienced incredible pain and heartbreak. Ron was unfaithful to Lori. Lori, who was devastated, decided to pursue a divorce. Ron and Lori's marriage ended. But eventually, God began to work on Ron. He was heartbroken over his sin, over Lori's pain, and the dissolution of their marriage. He repented. Then, he set to work to be the man God called him to be — first and foremost, he chose to grow in his relationship with Jesus.

In the months to come, Lori saw the change in Ron. It wasn't repentance to win her back, it was a redefining for him spiritually. He matured in Christ. Several months passed, and then Ron asked her on a date. When Ron and Lori went on their first date toward restoration, Ron told Lori that he wanted to bring someone with them on the date; someone who would be with them from that point forward in their relationship. He held her hand and prayed to Jesus, declaring that from then on, Jesus would be at the center of all they did.

A few months later, Brad officiated their remarriage. It was a celebration of healing, forgiveness, and restoration. It was an amazing journey, and we walked with them through it all.

Ron and Lori were Christians before their divorce, and they went to church. But they knew their marriage needed to be different. They committed to placing the Word of God at the center of their marriage. The Bible was their instruction manual. Ron was determined to take the initiative. Not only that, but they decided to pray together daily as well. So, every night before bed, they read a portion of the Bible together. In their first year of remarriage, Ron and Lori read the Bible together cover to cover. They loved and delighted in God's Word.

Your delight in God's Word is something that is developed over time. As you read the Bible, you'll discover more of who God is and how much He loves you. Verses like Lamentations 3:22-23, "The faithful love of the Lord never ends! His mercies never cease. Great is his faithfulness; his mercies begin afresh each morning," will encourage you as you begin each day together.

You'll read words that remind you of God's grace and mercy, like Romans 8:1, which says, "So now there is no condemnation for those who belong to Christ Jesus." Or 1 John 1:9, "But if we confess our sins to him, he is faithful and just to forgive us our sins and to cleanse us from all wickedness." Those words are a great comfort in knowing God doesn't shame us, but restores us.

In your marriage, as you take Scriptures and apply them to your relationship, you will appreciate and delight in the power of God's Word. Over time, you will see changes in your patterns of behavior. For example, the Apostle Paul wrote in 1 Thessalonians 5:11, "So encourage each other and build each other up." You will read those words and live them out in your relationship. Because if your faith isn't working in your marriage, then your faith isn't working!

As you read the Bible and think (meditate) about it, you grow in your love for God's Word. Talk about what you read. Let your conversations draw you to how you can apply the Bible to your lives and marriage. As you increasingly do this, you will fall more deeply in love with God and with His words to you!

Prayer (Wife prays)

Dear God,

Thank you for revealing yourself and your plan to us through the Bible. We are grateful for your Word and want to grow in our knowledge and application of what we read. We are choosing to learn from you and further establish our marriage through Scripture. Give us wisdom and insight into what we are reading by your Holy Spirit.

In Jesus' name, Amen.

Questions

1. What is our favorite verse or passage of the Bible and why?

2. What is a good plan for us to begin reading the Bible together?

DAY SEVEN
TRAVEL

*"If I rise on the wings of the dawn, if I settle on the far side of
the sea, even there your hand will guide me,
your right hand will hold me fast."*
— Psalm 139:9-10 (NIV)

We love to travel! One of our goals is to travel to 80 countries together by the time we're 80 years old. We call it "80 by 80." (To date, we've traveled to 65 countries.)

Travel for you might be camping with your kids, going to a state park, visiting Disney, or staying overnight in a hotel. Travel is good for your marriage because it breaks your routine and gives you the opportunity to focus on your spouse. Research shows that couples who travel have happier relationships.[3]

---

3. 10best.usatoday.com/interests/travel-tips/tips-for-couples-traveling-together/

We've discovered that travel unifies us. When we are exploring a new place, we work together to solve problems. We have conversations about what we'd like to experience and places we'd like to visit. We talk about what impacted us each day, the people we met, what we learned, and the food we enjoyed. Sometimes we have to compromise with each other. We decide if we want to sleep in or get up early. Together, we determine how much we want to rest — or not.

On a recent trip overseas, we enjoyed a delightful dinner at a restaurant. After dinner, we were walking back to our hotel when we stumbled upon a small, intimate park with beautiful greenery and nice walking paths. We noticed a bench and decided to sit down. Two hours later, we left the park after having an intimate and memorable conversation about our marriage. When we reflect on that trip, our two hours talking on that park bench is one of our highlights. A conversation like that probably wouldn't have occurred had we been at home.

One of our favorite quotes is attributed to Saint Augustine: "The world is a book, and those who do not travel read only one page." We'd encourage you to build your marriage through travel. Not only will you explore the world, but you will discover more about your spouse.

Prayer (Husband prays)

Dear God,

Thank you for the gift of travel. It's so fun for us to get away and experience your world.

Direct us in our travel planning. Help us choose the right destinations and plans. Then, when we go on our trip, draw us closer together as we relax and unwind. Let us see each other through the eyes of appreciation and amazement. We ask that our shared experiences unite us.

May we be godly witnesses to all those we meet. Direct our conversations and our interactions with others. Help us notice those who need our assistance and show us how to respond to them. When we travel, we ask for your protection over us. Guide us in all aspects of our travel.

In Jesus' name, Amen.

Questions

1. What are two possible destinations we could travel to in the next year? What is our budget and how can we make this a reality?

2. What are our individual priorities when we travel?

INTEGRITY

"May integrity and honesty protect me,
for I put my hope in you."
— Psalm 25:21

W hen we wrote our book, *Ruined to Recovery: Help When the Affair is Discovered*, we wished it were a book that no one would need. Sadly, that hasn't been the case. The reason is obvious: a lack of integrity. Spouses have broken and betrayed the marriage covenant.

Integrity is vital to your marriage because it protects you from unnecessary pain and disaster. You are spared not just from an affair, but from any breach of trust between you and your spouse.

Ted Engstrom gives a simple definition of integrity: "Integrity is doing what you said you would do. Simply put, it is keeping your promises."

Your marriage is only as strong as your integrity, and the foundation of integrity is a deep and abiding trust in God. Why? Because when we trust in God, we are freed from trying to take shortcuts, shading the truth, holding secrets, and engaging in sin. This leads to decisions of integrity like the following:

- We report to the IRS the income we received in cash.
- We keep our commitments even if something "better" comes along.
- We accurately tell a story or account even when it puts us in a bad light.
- We are honest about our sins and failings, even if there are consequences.
- We are faithful to each other regardless of our struggles.
- We are honest about our purchases and financial decisions.
- We choose to keep our word to each other and other people.

Thomas Macauley said, "The measure of a man's real character is what he would do if he would never be found out." A mutual commitment to absolute honesty and integrity deepens your intimacy with each other and with God. The trust you have in each other and in Him is strengthened and emboldened.

Prayer (Wife prays)

Dear God,

Thank you for being the One in whom we can always trust. We never have to doubt your faithfulness to your promises. We commit once again to complete honesty and integrity with each other and in our relationship with you. Continue to grow and develop us as we hope in you.

In Jesus' name, Amen.

Questions

1. How do honesty and integrity protect our marriage?

2. Are there any areas that come to mind where we haven't been living with complete integrity in our marriage? What about with others?

THANKSGIVING

"Then I will praise God's name with singing,
and I will honor him with thanksgiving."
— Psalm 69:30

Thanksgiving is a happy time in our family. Heidi's birthday is near that holiday, and one of our granddaughters was actually born on Thanksgiving Day. Perhaps, like us, it's easy for you to celebrate Thanksgiving Day, but as a couple, do you regularly thank God for His blessings?

One of our favorite Bible stories is found in Luke 17:12-18:

> As he [Jesus] entered a village there, ten men with leprosy stood at a distance, crying out, "Jesus, Master, have mercy on us!"

He looked at them and said, "Go show yourselves to the priests." And as they went, they were cleansed of their leprosy.

One of them, when he saw that he was healed, came back to Jesus, shouting, "Praise God!" He fell to the ground at Jesus' feet, thanking him for what he had done. This man was a Samaritan.

Jesus asked, "Didn't I heal ten men? Where are the other nine? Has no one returned to give glory to God except this foreigner?"

Convicting, isn't it? Ten men are healed, and yet, only *one* returns to thank Jesus for healing him. When God answers a prayer, do you thank Him or simply move on to your next request, sometimes without recognizing the One who answered your prayer?

As a couple, determine today that you will prioritize gratitude to God. Think of the good gifts He has given you and your spouse: your children, home, church, career, possessions, finances, family, education, health, friends, community, and more. Ultimately, the best gift we have received as believers is the gift of God's Son, Jesus Christ, who died on the cross for your sins.

Pastor D.L. Moody understood the profound significance of God's gift when he said, "Even if nothing else called for thankfulness, it would always be an ample cause for it that Jesus Christ loved us, and gave Himself for us." Let that thought sink in, and then thank God for the gift of Jesus Christ.

Prayer (Both pray)

Dear God,

We thank you and praise you for the gift of your Son. Thank you for loving us enough to send Jesus to save us from our sins.

We recognize you have given us many blessings. Today, we want to thank you for _____ and _____. Expand our hearts in gratitude and appreciation towards you for every good gift, and remind us to express our thankfulness to you.

In Jesus' name, Amen.

Questions

1. Are we good at cultivating a thankful heart towards God? How can we improve?

2. How has God blessed our marriage?

DAY 10
PARENTS

*"Honor your father and mother, as the
Lord your God commanded you ... "*
— Deuteronomy 5:16

It was 11:00 p.m. Heidi had worked a 12-hour shift and arrived home late. She called her parents like she did every evening. Her dad, a night owl, answered the phone. After talking for about 30 minutes, he made a request. He wanted her to order some books for him on Amazon. Heidi was put out. She was tired and thought, "Really, Dad. Now? Couldn't you have mentioned this earlier? What about waiting until tomorrow?" But she chose not to say anything and ordered the books. Her dad was thrilled.

Two months later, Heidi's dad passed away. She will tell you she is thankful she made the choice to speak kindly to him and avoid a trivial argument. She honored her aging father.

Honoring your parents may be easy for you, or it may be challenging. If your parents love God like ours, showing them dignity and respect may not involve much effort. However, we also recognize that some parents are difficult. They may be abusive or neglectful. How can you honor your parents throughout your life?

1. Recognize that God's command to honor your parents isn't based on their character. God has given us an authority structure within the family, and we are to respect our parents based on their role. We think of it this way: Every four years, we elect the President of the United States. Our preferred candidate may win, or the other party's nominee gets elected. But either way, we are to respect the person who is elected president because of their position, not their party. It's the same way in the family. Author Tim Keller said, "It's respect for parents that is the basis for every other kind of respect and every other kind of authority."

2. Refrain from degrading your parents in front of other people. Often, the way you treat your parents will be the very way your children treat you. The Bible assumes individuals will esteem their parents. 1 Timothy 5:1 says, "Never speak harshly to an older man, but appeal to him respectfully as you would your own father." We're also told to treat older women as we would our own mother (1 Timothy 5:2).

3. Give them your time. Listen to your parents when they tell stories. Look at photos. Ask them about their interests and their past. Help them do home projects, watch shows with them, or cook with them. As they age, you may need to accompany them on doctor visits or fix something in their home. God's Word tells us to care for our relatives, or we are worse than unbelievers (1 Timothy 5:8).

4. Thank them. Show appreciation to them for gifts. Look for positive character qualities in their lives and tell them you're grateful for their example in those areas.

5. Remember them with cards, pictures, flowers, texts, or gifts.

6. Forgive them. Your only perfect parent is your heavenly Father. Your earthly parents fail and make mistakes. When they do, be quick to forgive them even if they never ask for it. "Get rid of all bitterness, rage, anger, harsh words, and slander, as well as all types of evil behavior. Instead, be kind to each other, tenderhearted, forgiving one another, just as God through Christ has forgiven you." (Ephesians 4:31-32).

Prayer (Husband prays first paragraph, both pray second)

Dear God,

We know our parents aren't perfect and have failed us at times. Grant us the wisdom to discern the good from the bad. As parents, help us grow in the positive traits our parents passed on to us, and to forge a new path where we should.

We thank you that our parents were _____ _____. We ask for the ability to forgive our parents for _____. Give us grace as we navigate how to honor and esteem our parents (or their memory) today.

In Jesus' name, Amen.

Questions

1. What did our parents do well? What would we do differently?

2. How can we honor our parents at this stage in our lives?

PUTTING PRAYER INTO PRACTICE

Learning to Worship God in Prayer

In 1 Chronicles 29, King David uttered a prayer to God. He said:

"O Lord, the God of our ancestor Israel, may you be praised forever and ever! Yours, O Lord, is the greatness, the power, the glory, the victory, and the majesty. Everything in the heavens and on earth is yours, O Lord, and this is your kingdom. We adore you as the one who is over all things. Wealth and honor come from you alone, for you rule over everything. Power and might are in your hand, and at your discretion people are made great and given strength."
— 1 Chronicles 29:10-12

Read David's prayer out loud. What words did David use to praise God? In what ways did he acknowledge God's greatness?

Together, talk about ways you've seen God's power displayed in your marriage. Think of some words to describe God. Then pray together, acknowledging these qualities of God.

You can use phrases like these:

"God, we thank you for your_____."

"We know you are _____ and we've seen this in our marriage when you _____ and _____."

"We praise you because you are the God who _____."

CHURCH

"And let us not neglect our meeting together, as some people do, but encourage one another...."
— Hebrews 10:25a

Do you want to reduce your risk of divorce? Go to church! According to a study by the Harvard School of Public Health, regularly attending church together reduces a couple's risk of divorce by 47%! [4]

Besides avoiding divorce, there are other reasons to attend church. The Bible tells us we need to meet together with other believers. Community with Christ-followers is important so you don't become isolated. Fellowship also provides a degree of accountability.

---

4. www.thepublicdiscourse.com/2018/03/20935/

When you attend church regularly, you and your spouse grow in your faith as you learn about God and read His Word. You worship Him in the presence of other believers. You are part of a community where you are encouraged. You also practice your spiritual gifts (1 Corinthians 12:7-11) and serve others.

So, how do you find a church that's a good fit for you and your spouse? Begin by visiting a church and asking these important questions:

1. Does this church preach the Word of God?

2. Can I listen to the pastor preach each week? Does their style resonate with me?

3. Read the church's doctrinal statement. What is the church's stand on core beliefs like inerrancy of the Bible, the virgin birth, the Trinity, sin, heaven and hell, Jesus Christ's death and resurrection, how a person is saved, Satan, and other non-negotiables? Does the church add or subtract from the Bible? Avoid any church that gives equal or greater authority to teaching outside of the Bible.

4. Is this church a place where my spouse and I can grow spiritually? Does the worship draw us to God? Do we have a passion for the ministries of the church? Can we serve here? Do we trust the church's leadership? Can we support the church with our spiritual gifts and tithes?

5. Can we make good friends who will encourage us in our marriage and our walk with God? Is it a good fit for our family?

If you answered "yes" to the above questions, you just found a church home. If you already attend church regularly, don't become complacent.

Pastor Dwight L. Moody said, "Church attendance is as vital to a disciple as a transfusion of rich, healthy blood to a sick man."

Prayer (Husband prays)

Dear God,

We pray for our church, (church name). We ask that you guide the leadership as they serve you. Give them wisdom, direction, unity, and pure hearts as they seek to honor you. Protect them from selfish desires, and may they not fall into the traps of the enemy.

Provide our church with financial resources so that we can serve the people of our community well. Our desire is to glorify you through the ministries of ___(church name)___.

We also ask that our family would be challenged to grow in our faith. Show us where to practice our spiritual gifts and how we can best serve you as a couple.

Thank you for your Church, God, which represents your bride. May our love for it deepen with every year.

In Jesus' name, Amen.

Questions

1. Are we satisfied with our involvement in our church? Why or why not? (If applicable, how could we improve?)

2. What do we like about our church? How has our church impacted our relationship with God and others?

DAY 12
CONTENTMENT

"Not that I was ever in need, for I have learned how to be content with whatever I have. I know how to live on almost nothing or with everything. I have learned the secret of living in every situation, whether it is with a full stomach or empty, with plenty or little. For I can do everything through Christ, who gives me strength."
— *Philippians 4:11-13*

Several years ago, we traveled to Cambodia. We drove for several miles between soggy rice fields until we finally arrived at a stilt house, which is an elevated hut. It was hot. It was humid. We were sweaty and uncomfortable. The interpreter, who accompanied us, introduced us to the woman who lived in the hut. We sat under her home on a little wooden mat as the woman told us she had been saving money and praying so she could purchase a cow. Yes, a cow! That cow represented financial hope for her and her family. With tears in her eyes, she told us how good God was to provide for her. God had blessed her.

Heidi was stunned. This woman was incredibly content. Yet, she had very little, and none of the conveniences that we take for granted. Later, as we reflected on our visit, we found it insightful that we often compare ourselves to those who have more than we do, not less. Compared to the physical comforts and conveniences this Cambodian woman had, we have so much more. As we heard her story, we were humbled by her joy.

Author Jerry Bridges in his book *The Practice of Godliness,* stated, "The very first temptation in the history of mankind was the temptation to be discontent … that is exactly what discontent(ment) is — a questioning of the goodness of God."

As a couple, you find contentment when you focus on God's goodness, His provisions, and His blessings. Contentment doesn't naturally flow from our hearts. In the Scripture passage above, Paul said he had to *learn* contentment. So, how do you, as a husband and wife, learn to be content?

You reflect on God's goodness. What blessings has He given you? How has God protected you? When did He surprise you with an answered prayer? When did you see His beauty in nature?

Avoid comparisons. When you look at what others have compared to you, it's a breeding ground for envy and jealousy. Be satisfied with what you have. You don't have to own the nicest home on the block or drive the newest car. As a couple, know when enough is enough.

Grow in godliness and rely on the strength of Jesus Christ. The Apostle Paul said, "Godliness with contentment is great gain." (1 Timothy 6:6 ESV). As you mature in your relationship with Jesus, your thoughts naturally turn away from the outward appearances of this world and instead look upward toward the reality of God.

Prayer (Wife prays)

Dear God,

We confess that we haven't always been content. Here are one or two areas in our marriage where we have allowed discontentment to creep in. They are _____ and _____ _____. We repent of nurturing discontentment in our marriage.

Instead of allowing these issues to take root in our lives, help us to focus on your goodness. Grow us in spiritual maturity through your strength by giving us an eternal perspective on our needs, wants, and desires. Guide us to a place of joy and satisfaction that we can only find in you.

In Jesus' name, Amen.

Questions

1. Where in our marriage can we say, "Enough is enough?"

2. Do we agree that we can learn contentment? What is one practice we can implement as a couple to grow in contentment?

DAY 13
REST

Then Jesus said, "Come to me, all of you who are weary and carry heavy burdens, and I will give you rest. Take my yoke upon you. Let me teach you, because I am humble and gentle at heart, and you will find rest for your souls. For my yoke is easy to bear, and the burden I give you is light."
— Matthew 11:28-30

estroom. Rest area. Rest stop. Restaurant. Rest home. We love the *idea* of rest, but do you *actually* find rest? Are you comfortable with the idea of resting? Or, do you identify more with the title of Tim Hansel's book, *When I Relax I Feel Guilty*?

Our culture equates busyness with success. How many sports and activities your kids participate in equates to, "You must love your children." How many hobbies you have equates to, "You are an interesting, well-rounded person." Working lots of hours equates to "You are committed to winning." But is exhausting yourselves (and your family) what it means to be successful?

Jesus knew the importance of rest. He modeled it for His disciples and us. When He heard that John the Baptist had been killed, He pulled away "to a remote area to be alone" (Matthew 14:13). Jesus knew He needed rest for His emotions. Jesus would go to "an isolated place to pray" (Mark 1:35) when He needed rest for His soul. After an intense season of ministry, Jesus said to His disciples, "Let's go off by ourselves to a quiet place and rest awhile" (Mark 6:31). Jesus knew they needed rest for their bodies.

Jesus set the example *for* rest and calls you as a couple *to* rest. It begins with finding your rest in Him. He said, "Come to me, all of you who are weary and carry heavy burdens and I will give you rest." This is an unconditional invitation. It leads to a genuine and authentic prayer you can bring to Him of *"Jesus, help us."*

The word "weary" in the original Greek language means "to struggle and toil; hard work and self-effort." Vince Lombardi, the famous Green Bay Packers coach, said, "Fatigue makes cowards of us all." Think for a moment about how hard you've been pushing yourselves. Are you weary physically, emotionally, or spiritually? Jesus invites you to find rest by coming first to Him and breathing that simple prayer, *"Jesus, help us."*

Jesus then said, *"Take my yoke upon you."* The imagery would have made sense to Jesus' listeners. A yoke is a wooden harness that goes over the shoulders of one or two oxen as they pull. The religious leaders of the day laid heavy legalistic burdens on the people — hundreds of requirements.

But Jesus boiled the laws down to two: love God and love others. Taking His yoke means following His leadership. So the simple prayer is, "*Jesus, lead us.*"

Next Jesus said, "Let me teach you, because I am humble and gentle at heart." This is the only place in the Bible where Jesus describes His character. If you are weary and in need of rest, perhaps the two of you join together and pray, "*Jesus, teach us.*" He will show you where you're stressed and how to find the rest you desperately need.

Finally Jesus said, "... and you will find rest for your souls." From these words, your simple prayer together can be, "*Jesus, refresh us.*" It's totally legal to ask Jesus to do for you what He promised.

As you find your rest in Jesus, you'll be better positioned spiritually, relationally, and mentally to find rest in other areas of your lives as well.

Prayer (Both pray)

Dear God,

Finding rest is a difficult thing for us, yet we know you want us to live a well-ordered life. With that in mind, we bring before you these four requests:

Jesus help us _____
(include anything where you want His help finding rest).
Jesus lead us _____
(include anything where you need His leadership in finding rest).
Jesus teach us _____
(include anything where you know you need to learn about finding rest).
Jesus refresh us _____
(include any area of your life where you need His refreshing touch).

In Jesus' name, Amen.

Questions

1. What can be trimmed out of our current or upcoming schedule that will give us greater rest?

2. How can we get a weekend or vacation that is restful physically, mentally, and spiritually?

TEMPTATION

"And remember, when you are being tempted, do not say, 'God is tempting me.' God is never tempted to do wrong, and he never tempts anyone else. Temptation comes from our own desires, which entice us and drag us away."
— *James 1:13-14*

When we were first married, Brad worked in sales for a Christian publishing company. Every month, the company had a Salesperson of the Month. Somehow, on the last day of most months, "Bob" would end up with a humongous sale that made him the Salesperson of the Month! It seemed impossible ... and actually, it was.

After the company decided to launch an investigation, it was discovered that Bob and his wife, "Julie," had been stealing from the company. Bob would create a fake order and then submit it for processing. Since Julie worked in the computer room, she would see his falsified order and pull it. That way, Bob received his commission, but the order was removed before it ever went to the warehouse for shipping.

Over the years, we have often reflected on this incident. How does a couple get to that point? How do you even initiate a conversation with your spouse about such a topic? "Hey, honey. I've been thinking it would be a good idea to steal from my company. Want to help?"

Seriously, none of us are immune to temptation. You can be tempted in your areas of weakness or areas where you are strong. Temptation has no boundaries because Satan has no boundaries.

Author John Ortberg states:

> "Temptation rarely begins by trying to get us to do something that is 180 degrees in the opposite direction of our values. It starts close to home with the passions and desires that God wired into us and tries to pull them a few degrees off course. That subtle deviation is enough to disrupt the flow of the Spirit in our life, so coming to recognize the pattern of sins most tempting to us is one of the most important steps in our spiritual life."[5]

---

5 www.goodreads.com/quotes/11096157-we-do-not-get-tempted-by-that-which-repulses-us

As a couple, discuss areas where you each may be tempted. This takes vulnerability and honesty. If you have this conversation, you can help your spouse stay strong. Encourage each other to stop and consider the implications of giving in to the temptation. Many people who succumbed to temptation would have made a different choice if they had paused and considered the consequences.

Evaluate together whether or not the action or thought even is a temptation. Ask each other, "Will this draw us closer to God?" "Does it contradict the Bible?" "Are we rationalizing to get our way?" "Are we compromising where we shouldn't?" If, after asking these questions, you're still at an impasse, it's always wise to seek the advice of a godly friend, pastor, or counselor.

On the other hand, if you know this is a temptation, then run from it and don't continue thinking about it. Proverbs 4:14-15 says, "Don't do as the wicked do, and don't follow the path of evildoers. Don't even think about it; don't go that way. Turn away and keep moving."

Meditate on the sovereignty of God and His power to help you defeat temptation. Pray together as a couple. God's desire is for you to endure. He will show you a way out of any temptation as you submit yourself to Him (1 Corinthians 10:13).

Prayer (Both pray)

(Recite The Lord's Prayer from Matthew 6:9-13 (NIV) together as a couple.)

Our Father in heaven,

Hallowed be your name, your kingdom come, your will be done, on earth as it is in heaven.

Give us today our daily bread. And forgive us our debts, as we also have forgiven our debtors. And lead us not into temptation, but deliver us from the evil one.

For yours is the kingdom, and the power, and the glory, forever. Amen.

Questions

1. What are some areas where we face temptation (or could experience temptation)?

2. What truth impacted us from this reading that we can put into practice?

FASTING

"For forty days and forty nights he fasted and became very hungry."
— *Matthew 4:2*

rad was talking to a godly friend a number of years ago. He was an influential leader in the church we were serving.

As this friend talked about a difficult situation in his marriage, Brad asked him if he had fasted and prayed about it. He gave a shocked look, and then humbly said, "You know, Brad, I've been a Christian for 17 years and I have *never* fasted. Frankly, I don't know much about it."

Maybe the same is true for you. You may have been Christians for years, but you've never heard teaching about fasting. Perhaps the thought of denying yourselves for any length of time has been daunting, so you have never done it.

Richard Foster's classic, *Celebration of Discipline*, defines fasting as "the voluntary denial of an otherwise normal function for the sake of intense spiritual activity." Biblical fasting always involves going without some form of food. It's all about aligning ourselves with God and what He wants to do. It's not about convincing God to do what *we* want him to do.

Jesus modeled fasting. Throughout the pages of the Bible, you'll find examples of people doing a full fast (no food, see Ezra 10:6) or a partial fast (going without certain foods, see Daniel 10:2-3).

When you fast, you set your mind ahead of time to what you're fasting about. It's to pray and draw near to God. Fasting without prayer is simply a diet. That's not fasting. Fasting is a voluntary humbling of yourself before God.

THEN...

- Ask God to reveal Himself to you.
- Ask God to align your heart with His.
- Ask God to keep your motives pure, focused, and open to what He desires.

This brings you to a place of total surrender and trust in Him.

When facing something heavy or consequential in your lives (illness, major decision, concern for a family member, struggles in your relationships, etc.), consider partnering together in prayer *and* fasting. Perhaps you'll agree to fast every week until you have an answer, or maybe you'll only fast once. Either way, it will open a new dimension to your spiritual growth and your shared prayer experience.

Prayer (Wife prays)

Dear God,

We want to grow in praying biblically and following Jesus' example of fasting. Help us to be wise and faithful as we fast. As we pray, may your Spirit keep us focused on you, and the reason for our fasting, and not on the absence of food. We want to honor you completely as we submit our burdens and requests to you.

In Jesus' name, Amen.

Questions

1. What concerns or questions do we have about the practice of fasting and bringing it into our marriage?

2. Is there anything happening in our lives right now where we need to include fasting in our prayers?

DAY 16
SEXUAL INTIMACY

"The husband should fulfill his wife's sexual needs, and the wife should fulfill her husband's needs. The wife gives authority over her body to her husband, and the husband gives authority over his body to his wife."
— *1 Corinthians 7:3-4*

The intimacy that you share was designed by God for pleasure, protection, pronouncement, and possibly procreation. We read of one person who said that sexual intimacy just shows what a creative God we serve to have created that for us!

Although sex was designed by God to be like the dessert following a fine meal of connecting, for many couples, the subject is more like food poisoning. In fact, sex is one of the most intimate, emotionally charged, and painful issues many couples deal with in their marriage.

Michele Weiner-Davis writes in her book, *The Sex Starved Marriage*, that from her research, only 40% of married couples say they are very satisfied with their sex lives. Experts say that 20% of married couples are in "sexless marriages" and have sex less than 10 times a year. We've worked with couples who have gone months or years without physical intimacy.

And some couples *can't* actually have sex due to PTSD or physical limitations. Even so, there still is opportunity for intimacy without intercourse. To whatever degree you can practice intimacy, it will strengthen your connection and marriage.

We don't presume to answer all the issues here, but we do offer some key things to consider, pray through, and talk about with your spouse. Some issues may need to be worked through with a professional Christian counselor. Your marriage is worth the investment of time and resources to get all the wisdom and counsel to bring healing into this part of your marriage.

God's plan is for sex to draw couples together, to be the glue of the relationship. God designed sex to be enjoyed and to connect a husband and wife intimately, "and they become one flesh." When it is an act of self-sacrificing love, the focus of each is on the pleasure of their spouse first and foremost. Too many spouses become self-centered when it comes to sex. For the spouse who is uninterested in sex, they refuse to make themselves available to meet their spouse's needs. For those who desire sex, they may press, accuse, or manipulate to try to achieve sexual satisfaction, or turn to porn or other outlets — none of which honors Christ.

The Apostle Paul wrote to the church in Corinth:

"The husband should fulfill his marital duty to his wife, and likewise the wife to her husband. The wife does not have authority over her own body but yields it to her husband. In the same way, the husband does not have authority over his own body but yields it to his wife. Do not deprive each other except perhaps by mutual consent and for a time, so that you may devote yourselves to prayer. Then come together again so that Satan will not tempt you because of your lack of self-control." (1 Corinthians 7:3-5 NIV)

Bottom line: It's wrong to withhold sex from your spouse, and it's wrong to demand sex from your spouse.

In the context of your marriage, this may actually be an opportunity for you to honor your relationship with Jesus in how you serve your spouse. True love is self-sacrificing and may mean having sex when you may not "feel" like it. Ask God to help you have a positive attitude toward your spouse. Don't complain or make them feel guilty for their desires (or lack thereof) — but engage out of a love for Jesus and your spouse.

Be sure your spouse knows that you love them regardless of their sexual interest. Stay consistent in your romantic overtures, expecting nothing in return. Let them know that they are attractive to you. Provide plenty of non-sexual touches daily so they know your touch doesn't have to always "lead to something."

When sexual desires aren't fulfilled, you can become vulnerable to resentment toward your spouse. Perhaps you distance yourself emotionally. While you cannot control or manipulate their obedience to Christ, you can control your response. Adding guilt, blame, or shame does not honor Christ or your spouse. It will never lead to the lasting intimacy you desire. You have been called to love your spouse as Jesus has loved you: with grace, forgiveness, and unconditionally. As you walk this journey, be open and honest about your desires, both to your spouse *and* to God, through prayer. Prayerfully make the choice to be holy, pure, and committed in your marriage.

We know that the issues surrounding sex in marriage can be varied and painful, but we trust these words can be helpful guides for you as you honor God with your intimacy.

Prayer (Husband prays)

Dear God,

Thank you for the gift of sexual intimacy in marriage. We are grateful you brought us together as husband and wife to express our unity through the enjoyment of intimacy. We are committed to sexual purity and serving each other in a loving and sacrificial way. Please continue to guide us as we enjoy the fullness of who you've made us to be within the bonds of marriage.

In Jesus' name, Amen.

Questions

1. What are our perspectives about why God created sexual intimacy and how should that be expressed in our marriage?

2. What is one thing we can pray about for each other regarding our sexual relationship?

DAY 17
ENCOURAGEMENT

"So encourage each other and build each other up,
just as you are already doing."
— 1 Thessalonians 5:11

When our children were young, we started the tradition of the Red Plate. When either Robert, Tovey, or Rachael demonstrated a great attitude, or accomplished something important, we would place the Red Plate at their spot for dinner. The Red Plate in itself is encouraging, because around the plate's rim it has the words, "You Are Special Today."

Then, as a family, we told the recipient what we appreciated about them. The comments couldn't center on our children's clothing or physical features. Instead, the words of encouragement had to focus on their character, attitude, or accomplishment. Next, we asked the person with the Red Plate for their prayer requests. Then we would pray for the person of honor.

Our kids enjoyed this tradition. We still practice it today as our family has multiplied.

Encouragement matters. In marriage, encouragement from your spouse is essential. It breeds confidence, security, trust, and love. What are some ways you can encourage each other?

1. Use words. Thank your spouse when they do something thoughtful or kind. Tell them how important they are to you or what you love about them. Don't limit yourself to the spoken word; you can also give them a card or text them a word of encouragement.

2. Be positive. Ephesians 4:29 reminds us, "... Let everything you say be good and helpful, so that your words will be an encouragement to those who hear them." That means don't dwell on your spouse's weaknesses. Instead, focus on what they do well and train your mind to think the best about your spouse.

3. Give your spouse a gift "just because." This lets your spouse know you are thinking of them and care about them. They matter. The gift doesn't have to be big. It can be your spouse's favorite candy bar, flowers, a cup of coffee, or a ticket to a concert or sporting event.

4. Use actions. Reach over and take your spouse's hand. Rub

their back. Wink at them from across the room. Do a chore for them that you know they don't enjoy. These gestures let your spouse know you support them and are proud of them.

5. Spend time together. Let your spouse know they are your priority. Schedule dates and time together. When you're with your spouse, refrain from taking calls or glancing at your phone. Give your spouse your full attention.

Prayer (Wife prays first paragraph, both pray second)

Dear God,

May we grow in our marriage as we encourage each other on a daily basis. Help our words to uplift and strengthen each other. Keep our thoughts towards each other pure and positive. Show us ways we can demonstrate our love to each other through gifts and actions. We want to be intentional with our time as we make our marriage a priority.

Individually, say the following prayer of encouragement:

Thank you for _____(name of your spouse). I really appreciate him/her because he/she is_____ and _____. Help me to cherish _____.

In Jesus' name, Amen.

Questions

1. Where are each of us prone to discouragement right now and in need of encouragement? (This helps you see where your spouse needs encouragement.)

2. How do we each like to be encouraged? Is it through words, actions, gifts, or time?

DAY 18
PURITY

"Teach me your ways, O Lord, that I may live according to your truth! Grant me purity of heart, so that I may honor you."
— Psalm 86:11

"O h, by the way, you might want to bring in bottled water to drink. We have a hand-dug well, and the chicken manure from the fields runs into the well when it rains."

We were shocked! Brad was holding one end of our couch and was halfway through the front door when our new landlord gave us that warning about the water flowing into our kitchen and bathroom faucets. This was our new home for the next year as Brad completed his pastoral internship in eastern Pennsylvania.

You could smell the manure when the water ran in the kitchen and bathroom. We had a four-month-old son. Can you imagine what that would be like?

Every day, Brad carried jugs of water home from our church. We looked for other places to live, but nothing was available.

Clean water matters, doesn't it?

Just as pure water is important for our physical health, your marriage is impacted by your personal purity as well. What's flowing through your mind and in front of your eyes? Are you allowing anything into your home or relationships that may be destructive to your marriage?

If you were to look at the water in our Pennsylvania home, you would think it was pure. It was only by testing (and smelling) the water that we knew its true purity. There are five tests you can apply to your own life to know if something is pure and good for you, or impure and harmful.

1. Is this dishonoring to my/our relationship with Jesus?
2. Is this dishonoring to our marriage?
3. What does the Bible say about the issue?
4. What does your conscience say about it? James 4:17 says, "Remember, it is a sin to know what you ought to do and then not do it."
5. What does my spouse think about it?

Purity begins in your heart and mind. If you get angry with someone, it's easy to mull the offense over in your mind. You rehearse what happened and how hurt you are. Don't fool yourself. The anger you hold onto has an impact on your marriage. Anger leaks out.

Choosing unforgiveness begins in the heart. The wound was "too great" or "too recent" to forgive, and so you choose not to forgive. Perhaps there's a sexual attraction to someone else, and your mind begins to fantasize about being with that person. Or feelings of contempt start welling up toward your spouse, and instead of rejecting those thoughts, you let them simmer.

Proverbs 4:23 instructs us to "Guard your heart above all else, for it determines the course of your life." And your purity determines the course of your marriage.

Just as you wouldn't let poison remain in your drinking water for a moment, don't tolerate anything that would contaminate you and your marriage. If you struggle with watching impure movies, videos, or TV shows, memorize and claim this verse: "I will lead a life of integrity in my own home. I will refuse to look at anything vile and vulgar" (Ps. 101:2b-3a). Print this verse. Put it on your remote control and at the top of your computer monitor.

Do you struggle with impure thoughts? Immediately capture that thought. Reject it as not God honoring, and breathe a prayer asking God what He would have you think about. If you're holding a grudge or hurt, do the difficult thing and, "Bless those who persecute you. Don't curse them; pray that God will bless them" (Romans 12:14).

The choices you make, individually and as a couple, to guard your hearts from impurity, protect your marriage. Your relationship flows closer to each other and to Jesus.

Prayer (Wife prays)

Dear God,

Today, we are choosing purity. We need your help to clearly recognize where we've allowed anything impure to influence us. Our desire is to honor you and protect our marriage. Grant us the strength and courage to reject anything that is not pure and replace it with what pleases you.

In Jesus' name, Amen.

Questions

1. What are the benefits of choosing purity in all things?

2. What can we immediately recognize in our lives or marriage that is not pure and has to be addressed?

GRIEF

"The Lord is close to the brokenhearted; he rescues those whose spirits are crushed."
— Psalm 34:18

Grief is inescapable. It's universal, and every marriage encounters it at some point.

Perhaps you and your spouse are struggling with grief right now. Have you recently lost a parent? Is one of your children or grandchildren struggling with a health issue? Did one of your children pass away? Has an unforeseen tragedy hit your family?

Author Jerry Sittser knows about grief. One evening, his wife, four-year-old daughter, and mother were all killed in a car accident by a drunk driver. Describing the hours after the accident, Sittser wrote, "In one moment my family as I had known and cherished it was obliterated ... three generations gone in an instant."[6]

He continued, "I realized that I would have to suffer and adjust; I could not avoid or escape it ... The loss brought about by the accident had changed my life. One phase of my life had ended; another, the most difficult, was about to begin ... "

Many years after the accident, Sittser reflected on his experience with grief: "I discovered soon after the accident that I still had the power to determine the course my life would take, however limited that power seemed at the time. I had the power to choose how I would respond and whether or not I would trust in God. As it turned out, this power was greater than I expected. I have found a new life that is truly good." Despite his unimaginable grief, Jerry Sittser once again experienced the goodness of God. And you will, too.

As a couple, recognize that your grief response may differ from your spouse's. One of you may retreat into solitude and silence. Jesus pulled away to a remote place when John the Baptist was killed (Matthew 14:13). One spouse may express strong emotions, like anger or sadness. Agree today to respect how each processes grief. Support and comfort each other as you grieve.

We love the reminder from Psalm 23 of our Shepherd's presence tending to the wounds of our souls:

---

6. *A Grief Disguised*, Jerry Sittser, 2004

"Even though I walk through the valley of the shadow of death, I will fear no evil, for you are with me ... " (Psalm 23:4a, ESV).

Prayer (Husband prays)

Dear God,

Thank you for your presence when we grieve. We are thankful that you are a God who comforts and strengthens us in our deepest pain. Help us as a couple to be sensitive and supportive of each other in our grief.

We know that you are a God of hope and healing. We will depend on you as our rock and strength.

In Jesus' name, Amen.

Questions

1. How does each of us tend to process grief? How can we support each other?

2. How could we care for others who are grieving?

DAY 20
UNSAVED

"For the Son of Man came to seek and to save those who are lost."
— Luke 19:10

Our daughter, Tovey, has always had a passion for ice skating. When she was young, we enrolled her in skating lessons and, when we moved, we found a new rink and a new teacher for her to continue skating.

One day, while standing with the parents along the rink, Brad struck up a conversation with a mom whose daughter was in the same group. They had moved from Minnesota just like us. They had the same number of children, the same birth order, and the same genders as we did.

In the weeks that followed, we took turns taking Tovey to her lessons. The conversations continued with either the wife or the husband of our new skating friends. Early in the relationship, we mentioned our church so they would know there was a spiritual part of our lives. Eventually, we invited them to a couple of events at our church, and they invited us to their cabin.

From the very beginning, we were focused together in prayer for this family. We loved them and couldn't imagine spending eternity without them. The thought of each family member spending an eternity apart from Jesus was unbearable.

Our friendship with this family was part of what God used to catalyze their spiritual hunger and pursuit of Jesus. Scroll ahead several years. The wife eventually worked in the youth department of their church, the husband led worship at a men's retreat, and there were missions trips. To this day, the family loves Jesus.

Who is in your life that, as far as you know, would be considered "lost" and without a personal relationship with Jesus? It could be a child, parent, or sibling. Maybe it's a good friend or coworker. Perhaps it is one of your neighbors. Who is close to you, but far from God?

Perhaps your initial prayer together is to ask God to unite the two of you around one person or couple so that you can begin to pray together for their salvation. Once you determine who you are going to pray for as a couple, here are some of the things you can pray about:

- That they will be spiritually open and desire to know about Jesus
- That Satan will not have a grip on their soul
- That God will give you discernment in seeing opportunities to build the relationship
- That you will be faithful and ready to talk about spiritual matters
- That others will be brought into their life to share Jesus
- That they will place their faith and trust in Jesus

In his book, *Looking for the One*, David McIver shares a simple salvation poem written by a family friend. When God leads you to invite your friend to ask Jesus into their life, you might have them read this as a prayer:

Jesus, you died upon a cross
And rose again to save the lost
Forgive me now of all my sin
Come be my Savior, Lord, and Friend.
Change my life and make it new
And help me, Lord, to live for you. Amen.

Your shared spiritual adventure as a couple to reach unsaved people begins and ends with prayer. Here's your prayer for today:

Prayer (Husband prays)

Dear God,

Thank you for our salvation. We are so grateful for Jesus' sacrifice on the cross for our sins. We want to reach others, one or two at a time, with the hope and forgiveness that we have found through Jesus. Open our eyes and put a person or couple on our heart that you want us to regularly bring before you in prayer. Give us wisdom and insight on how to build a friendship with them that you can use for your glory.

In Jesus' name, Amen.

Questions

1. As we think about reaching someone who is "lost," what concerns or fears do we have?

2. What might the future be like for the person(s) God reveals to us once they become a follower of Jesus?

PUTTING PRAYER INTO PRACTICE

Learning to Pray for Others

In his letter to the Colossians, the Apostle Paul wrote, "So we have not stopped praying for you since we first heard about you. We ask God to give you complete knowledge of his will and to give you spiritual wisdom and understanding. Then the way you live will always honor and please the Lord, and your lives will produce every kind of good fruit. All the while, you will grow as you learn to know God better and better. We also pray that you will be strengthened with all his glorious power so you will have the endurance and patience you need. May you be filled with joy ... " — Colossians 1:9-11

Read Paul's prayer to the church in Colossae out loud. What did he request for the believers? What benefits would they receive?

Scripture is clear that we are to pray for others. In the Bible, Daniel asked his friends to pray that God would show him King Nebuchadnezzar's dream. His friends prayed, and that very night God revealed the king's dream to Daniel (Daniel 2:17-19).

Your prayers shouldn't be limited to your marriage, but should expand to include your family, friends, church leaders, government authorities, and those who don't know Jesus. In other words, you, as a couple, can pray for anyone. Pray for those who are doing well and know Jesus as their Lord and Savior. Pray for them to grow in spiritual maturity. Pray for their protection. Pray for unity.

Pray for those who are challenged with their finances, health, job, family, or their marriage. Pray for those who are grieving or sick. Pray for couples who need God's direction. Pray for believers who are persecuted for their faith.

As a husband and wife, talk about individuals or couples who could benefit from your prayers. Commit to praying for them over the next ten days.

WORK

"You shall remember the Lord your God, for it is he
who gives you power to get wealth ... "
— Deuteronomy 8:18 (ESV)

What was the first job you ever had? Who taught you the value of a good work ethic? How have the two of you navigated the schedules and pressures from one or both of you working? Do you enjoy your job(s)?

Some people mistakenly believe that the reason we have to work is because Adam and Eve sinned in the garden. If they hadn't sinned, then we would just all hang out and not have to work. The belief is that the curse on man for eating the fruit was that he would have to work for the rest of his life.

But that's not biblically accurate. The truth is, God worked first by creating the world (Genesis 2:2) before Adam even began to work. Jesus himself said, "My Father is always working, and so am I" (John 5:17).

So, work isn't bad. If God worked, and continues to work, then work is good. In fact, *before* Adam and Eve sinned, God put Adam to work. "The Lord God took the man and put him in the Garden of Eden to work it and keep it (Genesis 2:15 ESV).

Isn't that interesting? The difficulty of work came as a result of sin, but Adam still had to work. He was taking care of the garden, tending the plants, and naming the animals — he had duties to perform. Anything he wanted to eat was low-hanging fruit — literally. He didn't have to labor for it. It was after his sin that God told him work would be hard, and that it would be difficult for him to raise a harvest. Interestingly, the same Hebrew word used for Adam's consequence of toil is used for Eve's pain in childbirth.

So, if work is *from* God and it is *for* us, then how does that change the way you view your work? In part, it should instill a deep level of gratitude. God gave you your physical ability and intellect. He provided your job. It's not only a place to make money, but a place to do ministry.

Work is hard. Employers, managers, bosses, or boards can be demanding. Your ultimate "boss" is the Lord. The Apostle Paul wrote, "Work willingly at whatever you do, as though you were working for the Lord rather than for people" (Colossians 3:23). That's a whole different perspective for how you approach your work, isn't it? In fact, it drives a desire to do one's absolute best when it's for Jesus. Booker T. Washington said, "Excellence is to do a common thing in an uncommon way." And working for Jesus is anything but common!

Prayer (Husband prays)

Dear God,

Thank you for giving us the ability to work and have an income. We recognize that all we are and have is from your generous hand. When work is hard, give us insight into how we can encourage and build up each other. We want you to shine through our lives as we do our work for you above all others. Help us to see and be obedient to opportunities to represent you by word or deed in the workplace.

In Jesus' name, Amen.

Questions

1. When we think of our job(s), what are we thankful for?

2. Consider the verse in Colossians 3:23. What difference does that make in how we approach our work? Is there an area we could improve?

DECISIONS

"Show me the right path, O Lord; point out the road for me to follow. Lead me by your truth and teach me ... "
— *Psalm 25:4-5a*

*M*arriage is filled with decisions, isn't it? Some are small decisions like, "Where do you want to eat?" Other decisions are more consequential like, "Are we going to take the job?" or, "Are we going to move?" How you make decisions about significant issues matters when your goal is to build your marriage.

King Solomon wrote in Proverbs 3:5-6, "Trust in the Lord with all your heart; do not depend on your own understanding. Seek his will in all you do, and he will show you which path to take." When making a decision as a couple, the first step is to agree that you will fully submit to trusting God's direction.

The second step is to lean on God's wisdom. There are all kinds of subtle lures to draw you away from trusting God: the security of money, power, or prestige; trusting your emotions and feelings; or relying on your knowledge or intelligence. None of them are bad, in and of themselves, but it doesn't take much for one or more of them to usurp the position of God being the ONE in whom you place your trust.

Wise decision-making requires that you first lean on God's insights versus your own understanding. How often, when you are making a major life decision, do you go on the basis of what you are thinking or feeling at the time?

There may be aspects of a decision that you haven't thought about and won't be aware of until you take time to get God's perspective. We have friends who made a huge decision to trust God. They decided the husband would take a step *down* on the organizational chart so that he could spend more time with his family. It meant a decrease in pay and possibly no future promotions. As he reflected on their decision, he said, "I have less … but I have more. Not more money … just more." Their decision took trust, and it was contrary to the world's wisdom.

Third, "In all your ways acknowledge him." The word "acknowledge" means to be aware of His presence and allow Him to be your advisor in all that you do.

The outcome of following the three rules of submitting your will to the Lord is this: He will make your paths straight. In other words, He will take you where He wants you to go.

You don't need to even worry about it. In fact, as you make the decision in a godly, Christ-acknowledging way, there will be peace — not confusion. There will be calm — not anxiety — in your steps.

Finally, remember: "Larger issue equals greater prayer." In his book, *Affirming the Will of God*, Paul Little wrote of being in college and trying to determine what was next after graduation. "I was running around campus—going to this meeting, reading that book, trying to find somebody's little formula — 1, 2, 3, 4, and a bell rings — I was frustrated out of my mind trying to figure out the will of God. I was doing everything but getting into the presence of God and asking him to show me."

Pray together and ask God for wisdom. James 1:5-6 promises that, "If you need wisdom, ask our generous God, and he will give it to you. He will not rebuke you for asking. But when you ask him, be sure that your faith is in God alone. Do not waver, for a person with divided loyalty is as unsettled as a wave of the sea that is blown and tossed by the wind." And when you ask for wisdom, keep in mind the steps from Proverbs 3:5-6 and fully trust God.

As you follow God's direction through prayer and careful consideration, you can be assured that your decisions will be led by Him.

Prayer (Husband prays)

Dear God,

When we have decisions as a couple, we want them to be fully direct-ed by you. Right now, our biggest decision is _____
(name the situation). We are leaning on the promise in James 1:5-6 and humbly ask you for wisdom. We know, too, that the Enemy can try to divide us, so we not only ask for your protection, but we declare that we will honor each other and strive for unity (Ephesians 4:3). Thank you for directing our paths as we trust in you.

In Jesus' name, Amen.

Questions

1. Where do we need to grow in our decision-making process?

2. What are some significant decisions we see in the not-too-distant future?

PROTECTION

"But let all who take refuge in you rejoice; let them sing joyful praises forever. Spread your protection over them, that all who love your name may be filled with joy."
— *Psalm 5:11*

Stephanie Decker had just returned home with her young son and daughter. The wind started to howl, so the three of them ran to the basement. What Stephanie didn't know at the time was that an F4 tornado with 175 mph winds was about to hit their home.

The house began to shake. Terrified, Stephanie took a blanket, threw it over her children, and laid down on top of them.

Looking up, she saw a 20-foot steel beam falling towards her.

Stephanie knew she had a choice to make. She could save herself if she moved away from her kids. Or, she could protect her son and daughter by letting the beam land on her. She chose to protect her kids.[7]

Stephanie lost both her legs in the tornado, but her son and daughter survived, unharmed. Stephanie did what many of us would do — she protected the ones she loved.

In your marriage, you'll face challenges where your spouse needs protection. You can protect your spouse physically — perhaps from a natural disaster, animal, or other kind of physical threat.

You may have to protect your spouse from individuals who criticize and berate them. Unfortunately, sometimes this can even be family members or friends. Establish appropriate boundaries and encourage your spouse to remember who they are in Christ. Then, let them know you love and support them.

Protection also means guarding your own words and thoughts about your spouse. When you're with friends, do you complain about your spouse? James 5:9 tells us not to "grumble about each other." Don't allow your mind to imagine the worst possible scenario. Instead, talk about your spouse's positive qualities and make a conscious effort to think the best of your spouse. Refuse to see your marriage as a 50/50 partnership.

---

7 Nicole Weisensee Eagan, "Mom Who Saved Her Children from Tornado Has No Regrets About Losing Her Legs: 'It Was My Time to Step Up,'" People.com, March 9, 2017, people.com/human-interest/stephanie-decker-mom-saved-children-tornado-lost-legs

Instead, each of you should give 100% to your marriage. Be all-in. When you both invest 100%, you'll have a stronger desire to protect your marriage.

Stephanie Decker gave 100% to protecting her kids. As a husband or wife, your role is to do whatever is necessary to protect your spouse from spiritual, emotional, and physical harm. Stay alert and vigilant as you depend on the Lord to protect your marriage.

Prayer (Husband prays)

Dear God,

Protect our marriage from people, circumstances, and thoughts that bring division. Help us to recognize areas that are harmful to our marriage and give us the strength to avoid those.

God, we know that you alone are our true protector. You see everything and are almighty. You have the ability to defend us in all situations. Help us to depend on you and your power as we aim to protect each other.

In Jesus' name, Amen.

Questions

1. Do we do a good job of protecting each other? Why or why not?

2. Is there any friendship or relationship from which we need to be protected?

FINANCES

"He did all this so you would never say to yourself, 'I have achieved this wealth with my own strength and energy.' Remember the Lord your God. He is the one who gives you power to be successful..."
— *Deuteronomy 8:17-18*

Finances bring one of the greatest stresses and points of division in a marriage. What's fascinating is that Jesus, and the Bible overall, placed a disproportionate emphasis on our finances and possessions. Ramsey Solutions has this to say about it:

- Jesus talked about money more often than heaven and hell — combined!
- The Bible has more than 2,350 references to money and the management of money and possessions.

- Almost half of Jesus' parables relate to money.[8]
- In the gospels — Matthew, Mark, Luke, and John — one of every 10 verses has to do with money or possessions — a total of 288 verses![9]

But *why* is there such an emphasis on money? Because Jesus knew that at its root, it is a reflection of where our heart is. He said, "Where your treasure is, that's where your heart will be also."

As a couple, how do you handle your resources? What you spend, save, and give is a reflection of your mutual relationship with Jesus. It is a gauge of your intimacy with Jesus. Is that intimacy growing deeper or cooling off? Are you experiencing His blessings or trouble? Do you feel like your money is disappearing about as fast as you make it?

When you prayerfully submit your resources to God, it changes your mutual perspective. You recognize that He gave you the ability to acquire what you have. You live as stewards of resources that are God's and are entrusted to you.

As a couple, it takes faith to trust God with your finances. That begins with your generosity toward God as you give back a portion of what He has entrusted to you. We believe the Bible is clear that we

---

8   Rachel Cruze, "7 Bible Verses That Will Help You Leave a Legacy," Ramseysolutions.com, November 27, 2024,
ramseysolutions.com/personal-growth/3-bible-verses-legacy
9   "Statistic: Jesus' Teachings on Money," preachingtoday.com, n.d.,
preachingtoday.com/illustrations/1996/december/410.html

are to give 10% of our income to God first before meeting our other obligations. The Bible calls that a tithe (it means a tenth).

For example, did you know that only 3% of all Christians give a tithe of their income to God? That's basically on par with how much those without a faith give to charity. Faith says, "God, we are going to be faithful and give you the first portion of our income, 10% (see Malachi 3:10 and Matthew 23:23), and trust you to bless the other 90% that you entrust to us."

We've tithed our entire marriage. Sometimes it was really hard to continue to tithe 10%. For nearly a year, we were homeless. We were living on a part-time salary in the upstairs bedrooms of an older couple's home. Without communicating our needs to a wide circle, we saw God provide time and again. Once, we were nearly out of money, and the exact amount needed was sent in a single check to our post office box! God provided for us.

The evangelist Billy Graham said, "If a person gets his attitude toward money straight, it will help straighten out almost every other area of his life." This is true for you as you build your marriage!

Prayer (Wife prays)

Dear God,

Thank you for providing for us. We recognize that all that we have comes from your gracious hand. We know that you have entrusted these resources to us and we're to be good stewards. Please guide us with wisdom

in our saving and spending. Where we lack faith, grow us in our trust in you as we tithe the first portion of our income back to you. Use it for your purposes, Lord.

In Jesus' name, Amen.

Questions

1. What financial goals (or obstacles) can we commit to praying about together?

2. When we consider tithing, how are we trusting God with our giving?

DAY 25
NEIGHBORS

"Love your neighbor as yourself."
— Romans 13:9

"It's a beautiful day in this neighborhood, a beautiful day for a neighbor. Would you be mine? Could you be mine?"

From 1968 to 2001, Fred Rogers shared his dream with kids about the importance of being a good neighbor. Neighbors matter. An insurance company even promotes itself as being "Like a good neighbor … "

Being a good neighbor mattered to Jesus, too. When challenged by the religious leaders of His day about what was the greatest commandment in the Jewish law, Jesus answered, "'You must love the

Lord your God with all your heart, all your soul, and all your mind.' This is the first and greatest commandment. A second is equally important: 'Love your neighbor as yourself.'" (Matthew 22:37-39).

We know that the New Testament picture of "neighbor" is much broader than just the people who live around us. But sometimes if our faith isn't working at home — and with those in direct proximity to us — then it just isn't working.

Some of you may be familiar with the term "Emotional Intelligence" (EI) or "Emotional Quotient" (EQ). It's the ability to recognize your own emotions and those of others. You then adapt and adjust to whatever the situation is.

We believe there's room for a new category called NI or NQ — Neighbor Intelligence or Neighbor Quotient. It's being relationally aware of one's neighbors and how to best relate to them.

How well do you know your neighbors? Do you know their names? Their kids' names? When was the last time you prayed for them? What's going on in their lives?

Being a good neighbor includes more than a wave as you pull into the garage. It can mean initiating an act of kindness. This may take some courage, and yet it can lead to great opportunities to share Jesus' love. For example, we have some neighbors who are first-generation immigrants. Though they've lived in the United States for decades, they didn't fit our neighborhood demographic.

Heidi made our neighbors chocolate chip cookies, and we took them over as a welcome gift. Several weeks later, they shared that no one else had welcomed them into the neighborhood. They invited us into their home for an ethnic dinner — it was awesome — and eventually the conversation turned to our different beliefs. At the time of this writing, we can't report their trusting in Jesus, but the relationship continues to develop and blossom as we intentionally love them with Jesus' love.

Make the decision to "love your neighbors as yourself." Pull their trash can up their driveway. Help them shovel. Offer to water the flowers if you know they'll be gone. Perhaps God has a spiritual adventure in store for you ... and them!

Prayer (Wife prays)

Dear God,

Thank you for our home and for leading us to this neighborhood with these neighbors. We acknowledge that we are here by your sovereign direction in our lives. Give us wisdom and insight on how to build relationships with our neighbors. Use those opportunities to create bridges for them to experience your love.

In Jesus' name, Amen.

Questions

1. What do we already know about the neighbors around us?

2. Thinking about our neighbors, what are some next steps we might take to build relationships with one or two families?

DAY 26
CONFLICT

"Never pay back evil with more evil. Do things in such a way that everyone can see you are honorable. Do all that you can to live in peace with everyone. Dear friends, never take revenge ..."
— *Romans 12:17-19a*

O ur friends, David and Teresa, were driving to our house for dinner when it happened. They got into a fight. David got so upset at his wife that he stopped the car and hopped out. He started walking back home. Teresa, who was equally frustrated, slid over into the driver's seat and drove away, leaving her husband on the side of the road.

When Teresa arrived at our house, we saw that David wasn't with her. Brad asked her where he was. Teresa responded, "We got in a fight, and he got out of the car. So, I moved into the driver's seat and drove to your house."

Brad asked Teresa if she would mind if he took their car and went looking for David. She was good with that. Brad drove back to the area where David had gotten out of the car. As their car approached, there was a glare on the windshield, so David couldn't see that Brad was actually the driver. Instead, David assumed his wife was behind the wheel.

All of a sudden, David jumped behind a tiny bush and tried to hide. The shrub was way too small to cover David's body. Brad pulled up to the curb, rolled down the window, and said, "Hi David! Get in the car." Chagrined, David emerged from the bush and hopped into the passenger seat. The guys talked, and Brad drove David back to our house.

We told David and Teresa that they needed to talk about their disagreement. They went into our guest room and after several minutes, emerged smiling and restored.

That was many, many years ago. David and Teresa have been happily married for almost 45 years, and we're still dear friends. They serve on the board of Build Your Marriage and have a strong, Christ-centered marriage. We share their story because, as husbands and wives, marital conflict is an issue everyone can relate to.

One of the biggest causes of conflict is selfishness. A couple has a disagreement, and they see it as "he" versus "she," instead of "we." Recognizing that you and your spouse aren't in competition with each other, but rather on the same team, is integral to conflict resolution. Focus on ways you can compromise instead of competing with each other. Philippians 2:3 reminds us, "Don't be selfish; don't try to impress others. Be humble, thinking of others as better than yourselves. Don't look out only for your own interests, but take an interest in others, too."

A tool that has helped us with conflict in our marriage is to separate the issue from our spouse. The issue then becomes the problem, not our spouse. Conflict often centers around a belief, idea, goal, or desire. When you can discuss what you like or dislike about a certain idea, your spouse doesn't feel attacked. You're not criticizing your spouse's character; rather, you are expressing disagreement with a belief, issue, or desire. This makes the disagreement less personal and, therefore, easier to resolve as you build your marriage.

Prayer (Husband prays)

Dear God,

We repent of ways in which we haven't handled conflict well in our marriage. We want to do better as we express our thoughts and ideas to each other. Help us to focus on the issue, not each other's character. Show us ways we can be a team and resolve conflicts together. Guide our words and actions so that we are honorable and respectful even when we disagree. Increase the amount of peace and unity we have in our marriage.

In Jesus' name, Amen.

Questions

1. How have we handled conflict poorly in the past? What are some ways we can grow?

2. How can we intentionally approach conflict as a team?

DAY 27
CHILDREN

"I could have no greater joy than to hear that my children are
following the truth."
— 3 John 1:4

When our children, Robert, Tovey, and Rachael, were young, we started to think about raising them with intentionality. What did we want our children to learn? What values did we want to instill in them? What did we want our son and daughters to remember about us?

Heidi took these questions to heart and thought about them — a lot. She came to the conclusion that cooking and cleaning were admirable, but they didn't carry eternal implications. One day she asked herself, "If I could be remembered for one thing by my family, what would that be?" Immediately, she knew the answer. She wanted to be remembered as a woman of prayer.

That night, she began a habit that has continued for years. Heidi would go into our children's room and pray over them. Often, they were already sleeping. She would quietly place a hand on their back or lightly touch their foot and pray for them. She would pray however the Holy Spirit led her. She prayed for their protection, future spouses, friends, tests, jobs, finances, teachers, decisions, and their choices. She also asked the Lord to bless them and give them favor. She prayed that they would love God and the Bible. She prayed for discernment, wisdom, joy, and contentment.

One winter night, Brad was traveling. Heidi had a long day and was eager to crawl into a cozy bed. After snuggling under the warm blankets, Heidi remembered that she hadn't prayed over any of our kids. Since it was so cold, she decided to pray for each child from our bed.

The next morning, Heidi was in the kitchen when Robert appeared. He asked his mom if she had prayed over him the previous night. Although she hesitated, she told him the truth. It was cold, and she had prayed for him and his sisters from our bedroom. Robert looked her straight in the eyes and said, "I know you didn't pray over me, Mom, because I waited for you."

Men and women, your prayers matter. Your children are watching you more than you realize. The best gift you can give your children is your prayers. Prayers surrendered to God can unleash His power in their lives. Continue praying for your children today.

Prayer (Wife prays)

Dear God,

Today we commit our children (name them) to you. Give us wisdom and insight into their personalities as we raise them. Please help (name your kids) to love you and desire to follow you. Protect them from the evil one. Provide them with godly friends who will draw our kids to you. May they have a strong faith that doesn't waver. Establish in them your commands and help them to continue the God-honoring legacy that was handed down to them.

In Jesus' name, Amen.

Questions

1. How can we improve our relationship with our kids? In what areas are we strong?

2. Do we regularly pray for our kids? (Share specific prayer requests for each child. Then pray for your children by name. If your children are old enough, you can even ask them for their prayer requests.)

THOUGHTS

"...Fix your thoughts on what is true, and honorable, and right, and pure, and lovely, and admirable. Think about things that are excellent and worthy of praise."
— Philippians 4:8

*I*t's easy to assume that what happens in your mind, as long as it stays there, doesn't impact your marriage. But Jesus said in Matthew 12:34b, "For whatever is in your heart determines what you say."

Your thoughts come from four sources: your mind, others, the enemy, and God. It's vital to discern quickly the origin of a particular thought instead of just dwelling on it. We think it's important to say that it's not a sin to have a particular thought. A thought becomes a sin when you let that thought percolate in your mind by agreeing with it or dwelling on it. Here are some questions we ask ourselves when we're evaluating our thoughts:

1. Does this in any way contradict the teaching of God's Word, the Bible?

2. Is my thought consistent with God's commands and His attributes?

3. Is this thought based on truth? For example, several years ago, Heidi struggled with the idea that she wasn't paid well at her job. This led her down a path of negative, destructive thinking. When we dissected the thought, we realized that her premise was faulty. She *was* paid well at her job. Actually, very well. Starting with a wrong assumption led her to a false conclusion.

4. How does this thought impact my mind and my relationship with my spouse? Does it lead to suspicion, rejection, disdain, or negative thinking? Conversely, is my thought in line with who God says my spouse is? With whom God says I am? With whom God says others are? The Bible says we are to focus on whatever is true, honorable, right, pure, lovely, admirable, excellent, and praiseworthy.

5. Is the thought drawing me closer to God and my spouse? 2 Corinthians 10:5 (NIV84) tells us to "demolish arguments and every pretension that sets itself up against the knowledge of God, and we take captive every thought to make it obedient to Christ."

If you recognize that your thoughts contradict God's standards or His Word, reject the thought immediately. Renounce the thought and ask God to remove it. Refuse to mull it over in your mind. Many people have suffered disastrous consequences because they failed to control their thoughts.

Often, when we minister to couples, we reference this quote: "Watch your thoughts for they become your words; watch your words for they become your actions; watch your actions for they become your habits; watch your habits for they become your character; watch your character for it determines your destiny."

Prayer (Wife prays)

Dear God,

We humbly confess to you areas where we have entertained ungodly thoughts. We repent of these thoughts. Help us, instead, to focus on what is true, honorable, right, pure, lovely, admirable, excellent, and praiseworthy in each other and in our marriage.

As a couple, transform our minds. Give us the ability through your Holy Spirit to think more like you do. Romans 12:2 tells us not to copy the behavior and customs of this world, but to let you transform us into new people by changing the way we think. And, God, that's exactly what we want in our marriage.

In Jesus' name, Amen.

Questions

1. As a couple, have we allowed any thoughts into our marriage that are displeasing to God? If so, which ones?

2. What can each of us do to have greater control over our thoughts?

HEALTH

"Dear friend, I hope all is well with you and that you are as healthy in body as you are strong in spirit."
— *3 John 1:2*

A few months ago, we both read a book on ultra-processed foods (UPFs). Frankly, we were both disgusted to read about the ingredients in the "foods" we were eating: artificial dyes, sweeteners, unhealthy oils, preservatives, and emulsifiers. We determined we were going to eat better. Does that mean we never have potato chips, a hot dog, or some chocolate? No, it doesn't. But we are trying to make healthier choices about food. Why? Because we want to take care of the bodies God has given us and have the longest marriage possible with the most energy.

Every person enters marriage with a family health history. Does yours have cancer, heart disease, orthopedic challenges, auto-immune issues, dementia, or something else? Although you can't change your genetics, you can choose to live a healthier lifestyle.

The Bible is very intentional as it describes people who struggled with their health. Naaman suffered from leprosy (2 Kings 5:1). Job was afflicted with boils (Job 2:4-10). There was a man who was paralyzed and couldn't walk (Mark 2:1-12). There was a blind man whom Jesus healed (John 9:1-7). Paul had a thorn in the flesh (2 Corinthians 12:7-9). Hezekiah was deathly ill and then was miraculously granted 15 more years of life (2 Kings 20:1-7). Some individuals in the Bible were healed; others were not. We don't understand the reasons for this, but we do know we must trust God's sovereignty in these situations.

1 Corinthians 3:16 tells us that our bodies are the temple of God, and His Spirit lives in us. Since our bodies are temples, we should take good care of them. How can you and your spouse improve your health?

If you haven't done so, get a physical. This reveals any health issues you may have. It's also a good baseline measurement of your health.

Eat well. Talk as a couple about how you can make better choices with your diets. You don't have to get fanatical about it, but choose one or two areas to work on.

Get enough sleep. Most adults need seven to nine hours of sleep a night.

Exercise. If one of you exercises frequently, you're going to be at a different endurance level than your spouse, so be realistic in your expectations. Make exercise fun, too. Go for a walk, swim, golf, or bike ride. Find something you both enjoy and then exercise together.

As you and your spouse discuss health issues, it's important to reflect on this verse: "So whether you eat or drink, or whatever you do, do it all for the glory of God" (1 Corinthians 10:31).

Prayer (Wife prays)

Dear God,

Thank you for the gift of health. Help us to remember that our bodies are your temple and to honor you with how we care for them. Give us wisdom in this.

We don't want our health to become a topic of conflict in our marriage, so help us to respond to each other with understanding and consideration. Show us areas where we can strengthen our bodies and make healthier lifestyle choices. Give us compassion for those who are sick and struggle with their health. Help us to be your hands and feet as we serve and care for them.

In Jesus' name, Amen.

Questions

1. What health issues are prevalent in our families of origin?

2. What one change can we each make to live a healthier lifestyle?

DAY 30
FORGIVENESS

"Instead, be kind to each other, tenderhearted, forgiving one another, just as God through Christ has forgiven you."
— *Ephesians 4:32*

One of the greatest gifts you can bring to your marriage is forgiveness. We know.

Many years ago, Brad was unfaithful in our marriage. The pain and consequences were devastating. We were overwhelmed with questions and hurt. Would our marriage survive? How would this impact our children? What would our marriage look like? How could it ever be good? Would there ever be a day that we didn't analyze Brad's affair? Could I (Heidi) forgive Brad? And would Brad forgive himself? Thankfully, we know the answers to those questions as God has redeemed our marriage. Today, our marriage is stronger than ever, and the real reason for it is that we chose forgiveness.

One of the most meaningful stories on forgiveness is found in Genesis 50:14-21. We encourage you to read this scripture passage. Perhaps you know the story of Joseph, who was sold into slavery in Egypt by his brothers. The brothers betrayed Joseph and lied to their father, telling him Joseph had been killed. In reality, Joseph did some jail time after a false accusation. Yet, miraculously, he became the second most powerful person in all of Egypt. Famine struck, and his brothers came to Egypt to find food. Thirteen years had passed since they sold him into slavery. They did not recognize Joseph, but he knew who they were. Eventually, Joseph told his brothers who he was, and they were reunited.

Later, their father, Jacob, died. After his burial in Canaan, Joseph and his brothers returned to Egypt. But the brothers were afraid that Joseph would take revenge on them for the wrong they did to him. Joseph, however, was a man who had truly forgiven.

He said to his brothers, "'Don't be afraid of me. Am I God that I can punish you? You intended to harm me, but God intended it all for good. He brought me to this position so I could save the lives of many people. No, don't be afraid. I will continue to take care of you and your children.' So he reassured them by speaking kindly to them."

Joseph's perspective on forgiveness is one we should imitate for the following reasons:

- First, he recognized that it's not our right or responsibility to punish those who sin against us. The consequences are up to God.
- Second, Joseph admitted that his brothers' intentions were to harm him, but he also acknowledged that God is sovereign. God can bring good even from the depths of despair. When things are dark, don't give up hope.
- Third, he saw God's plan for his life, and he trusted God with it. Like Joseph, God has a plan for you and your spouse. He won't abandon you.
- Fourth, Joseph told his brothers not to be afraid because he, the one who was the victim, was now going to provide for them and their children. He was going to care for them in the way his brothers should have cared for him. He reassured them with kindness.

We love that. No revenge. No accusations. No amends. No judgment. Just forgiveness.

How do you respond to your spouse when they wrong you? Colossians 3:13 gives us the answer: "Make allowance for each other's faults, and forgive anyone who offends you. Remember, the Lord forgave you, so you must forgive others." Even your spouse.

As we reflect on that trying season in our lives many years ago, we are thankful we chose forgiveness. God blessed us in ways we never imagined. He not only restored our marriage, but our family remained intact. We grew in our relationship with Jesus Christ and each other. Build Your Marriage was birthed from that season, and now, by God's grace, we are helping others build a Christ-centered marriage.

In your own strength, forgiveness is impossible. But when God is at the center of your marriage, He will give you the power and the ability to forgive your spouse.

Prayer (Husband prays)

Dear God,

You set the example of forgiveness for us. We know we are sinners and imperfect spouses. We wrong each other and we sin against you. We repent of our selfish desires and intentions. Yet, when we confess our sins, you are faithful and forgive us. You don't remind us of our past wrongs or hold them against us. We praise you for that.

Teach us to model your forgiveness in our marriage. We don't want to hold grudges or be vengeful toward each other. Please don't allow any bitterness to dwell within our hearts. Instead, help us to forgive each other quickly and completely. May we be kind to each other when we work through marital struggles. Show us how to depend on you as we grow in forgiving each other. Strengthen our marriage.

In Jesus' name, Amen.

Questions

1. Ask each other this question: "Is there anything I need to ask your forgiveness for?"

2. How does our marriage benefit when we forgive each other?

PUTTING PRAYER INTO PRACTICE

Learning About Confession in Prayer

In Psalm 32:5, David cried out to God, "Finally, I confessed all my sins to you and stopped trying to hide my guilt. I said to myself, 'I will confess my rebellion to the Lord.' And you forgave me! All my guilt is gone."

This is a poignant example of what happens when we admit and repent of our sins. God forgives us, and we are free from guilt. This biblical principle is reinforced in 1 John 1:8-9, which states, "If we claim we have no sin, we are only fooling ourselves and not living in the truth. But if we confess our sins to him, he is faithful and just to forgive us our sins and to cleanse us from all wickedness."

Other than Jesus, everyone has sinned. Nobody likes to talk about their sins. It can be humbling and at times, embarrassing. It's not enjoyable to admit your dishonest choices, corrupt actions, or un-wholesome thoughts. But God's Word speaks about the benefits of confession. When we confess our sins, God forgives us. You are no longer enslaved to your sin, although you may still experience the consequences of it. You have a renewed freedom in Christ. A second benefit is that you have a restored relationship with God and others. And finally, your awareness of the devastating impact your sin had on God, others, and yourself, is intensified so that you'll want to avoid that sin in the future. When a person is truly repentant, they desire change.

James 5:16 says, "Confess your sins to each other and pray for each other so that you may be healed." Confession brings what was done in secret into the light. It paves the way for healing and restoration.

Individually consider areas in your life where you have harbored sin. Then silently (or together if you're comfortable) admit your sin to God, ask for His forgiveness, and tell God you don't want to continue with _____ [specific sin] _____.

After you complete this, pray together that God will remove any feelings of shame, and that as husband and wife, you can move forward in freedom and joy.

(*If this time of confession reveals infidelity, a crime, or abuse, we recommend seeking the advice of a professional counselor *immediately.*)

PURPOSE

"Only let each person lead the life that the Lord has assigned to him, and to which God has called him ... "
— *1 Corinthians 7:17a (ESV)*

*B*uild Your Marriage was born out of a passion we have to help couples build Christ-centered marriages. Why? Because we experienced deep marital pain and family trauma when our own marriage wasn't centered on Christ. We were Christians, but Jesus wasn't at the center of our marriage. We are determined to do all we can to strengthen marriages and thus strengthen families for the glory of God.

That's *our shared purpose*. It unites us toward a common goal. What is *your shared purpose*? What is it that only you can accomplish through your unique personalities, experiences, and abilities? We believe every couple has a shared purpose to discover that will connect them and bring them closer to Jesus. Here's our definition of shared purpose:

"A marriage purpose is a shared picture or dream of the future that is still not achieved. It encompasses the intertwining of who you are and draws you closer as you move toward accomplishing it."

Using the word "Purpose," here are seven important keys to finding your shared purpose:

P - Pray

Pray together and ask God to direct your steps in discovering your purpose. Make this an ongoing prayer. You can ask Him to do the following:

- Reveal the unique strengths each of you has
- Show you areas of passion and interests you share
- Unveil any past hurts in life that you both can work to alleviate in others
- Point out injustices you may be called to address
- Direct you to needs you would enjoy meeting

Over time, as you pray for His direction, you will experience increasing clarity about the direction you're to head as a couple.

U - Unite

You will probably experience times of friction as you pursue your purpose. You'll bring different ideas, applications, timetables, and expectations. Lean into those differences because the conversations you have can strengthen your outcome. You will sharpen each other through the conversations.

The challenge is to stay unified and not let your differences divide you. Satan would love to neutralize your shared purpose by bringing division between you. Ephesians 4:3 reminds us to "Make every effort to keep yourselves united in the Spirit, binding yourselves together with peace." If you lose your unity and your peace, then you lose your purpose and give the enemy a victory. So fight for unity at all costs.

R - Resolve

As you live out your purpose as a couple, you'll encounter challenges. Other people may discourage you. You may experience time constraints or financial roadblocks. You and your spouse may question your abilities or even your God-given purposes. Hebrews 10:36 is an excellent verse to memorize: "Patient endurance is what you need now, so that you will continue to do God's will." When God placed His purpose on your hearts, He also empowered you to fulfill your calling.

P - Pursue

What do the two of you like to do? What inspires and motivates you? This is your passion. Your purpose centers around something you enjoy and are gifted at. Your purpose should excite and energize you both. You want to pursue it. Romans 12:11 states, "Never be lazy, but work hard and serve the Lord enthusiastically." When you're passionate about your purpose, it will show. Your enthusiasm will be a catalyst for others.

O - Obey

It can be tempting to try to control the circumstances around your purpose. You may not want to move forward because of timing, money, fear, or some other risk. But God has equipped you, and He is the one who gave each of you your giftings, desires, and abilities. God orchestrated your marriage with a specific purpose in mind. As a couple, follow God's commands and the promptings of the Holy Spirit as you serve others. Obedience to God is essential if God is going to bless your shared purpose. Jeremiah 7:23b tells us, "...Do everything as I say, and all will be well."

S - Sacrifice

Dr. John Maxwell is a developer of leaders. He wrote, "Everything worthwhile is uphill." Whatever your shared purpose is, you will have to make sacrifices to accomplish it.

When you consider God's plan to provide a way for sinful people to experience forgiveness and be restored to an intimate and eternal relationship with Him, there had to be an enormous price paid. Jesus sacrificed His very life to accomplish that purpose.

Dr. Maxwell also notably stated, "Dreams don't work unless you do" and, "Just because you're struggling doesn't mean you're failing. You're either giving up or getting up. It's your choice." Being a follower of Jesus requires sacrifice. Jesus said, "And if you do not carry your own cross and follow me, you cannot be my disciple" (Luke 14:27).

Recognize that you'll have to make some hard choices to accomplish your shared purpose. But remember that your choices will lead to completion, and completion will bring shared satisfaction.

E - Encourage

Finally, encourage each other every step of the way. The Apostle Paul wrote, "Therefore encourage one another and build one another up, just as you are doing" (1 Thessalonians 5:11 ESV). Accomplishing a shared purpose is hard work. It might even be discouraging at times. You will need each other's support to press ahead, and as you do, you will grow closer to one another and build your marriage.

Prayer (Husband prays)

Dear God,

We come to you asking that you would guide us in our journey to discover our shared purpose. Thank you for designing us as unique individuals and for making us a team to accomplish your purposes. We want to glorify you and build our marriage through this process.

Today, we ask that you reveal to us the strengths each of us brings. Show us how those strengths work together as we take the first steps in this new adventure.

In Jesus' name, Amen.

Questions

1. What topics or issues are we passionate about? What similar gifts or talents do we each have that could lead to our shared purpose?

2. In what areas might God be calling us to serve Him?

SPIRITUAL WARFARE

"For we are not fighting against flesh-and-blood enemies, but against evil rulers and authorities of the unseen world, against mighty powers in this dark world, and against evil spirits in the heavenly places."
— *Ephesians 6:12*

*W*e were moving and we needed a new home for our family. Our realtor took us to a nice, suburban neighborhood just outside Chicago.

As we entered the home, I (Heidi) told Brad and the realtor that I didn't like the "feeling" of the house; something was off. The realtor didn't respond to my comment and continued the tour of the home. We got to the basement of the house, and I was completely disinterested in the home. Brad walked over to a closet and opened the door. On the top shelf were a Ouija board and black melted candles! Now we understood my "feeling," which, in reality, wasn't a feeling at all but a discerning spirit.

This home was enemy territory.

Whether you're aware of it or not, Satan and his cohorts are all around you. Their goal is to destroy your marriage and sabotage your relationship with God. Your spouse is not your enemy. Satan is!

The first step in battling the enemy is recognizing who he is:

- Satan is not God; rather, he is a created being (Colossians 1:16). This means that Satan doesn't share the attributes of God. He isn't omniscient (all-knowing), omnipresent (all present), or omnipotent (all-powerful).

- Satan rebelled against God and is known as the Accuser (Job 2:1-2). He is our enemy and prowls around like a roaring lion looking to destroy you and your spouse (1 Peter 5:8).

- Satan is a liar and the father of lies. There isn't any truth in him (John 8:44).

- Satan won't win. His destiny is destruction, and he will be tormented day and night forever (Revelation 20:10).

The second step in spiritual warfare is recognizing who you as a couple are in Christ:

- You are strong in the Lord and in His mighty power (Ephesians 6:10). With God's armor described in Ephesians 6, you, as a husband and wife, can stand firm against Satan.

- You have power through prayer to defeat the enemy. Pray for each other and pray for other believers (Ephesians 6:18).

- You as a couple must remain alert, stand firm against Satan, and stay strong in your faith in Christ (1 Peter 5:8-9).

- You can resist Satan and he will flee from you (James 4:7).

As believers in Jesus Christ, God is with you, and in the end, Satan is defeated (Romans 16:20)!

Prayer (Husband prays)

Dear God,

Thank you that we are victorious over the enemy through the blood of Jesus Christ and His resurrection. We recognize it's through your power that we have authority over Satan.

Help us to discern when the enemy is attacking us so we can resist him. As we keep our eyes and hearts focused on you, increase our faith so we are strong and courageous. We pray for spiritual protection on our marriage and our family.

In Jesus' name, Amen.

Questions

1. How have we seen Satan attack our marriage?

2. What are some ways we can encourage each other to stand strong against the enemy?

DAY 33
TRANSITIONS

"For everything there is a season, a time
for every activity under heaven."
— *Ecclesiastes 3:1*

n our marriage, we've faced an abundance of transitions. You'll probably relate to some of them. We've moved 13 times; changed jobs seven times (plus numerous part-time jobs); raised three children who all went to college; navigated three weddings, incorporating three amazing people into our family; have four (to date) grandchildren; and mourned both of our now-deceased fathers. We have had transitions of choice ... and transitions of consequence. As we age, our bodies morph, and various health factors begin to arise as well. Every marriage experiences transitions. Nothing stays the same, and as a result, neither do the two of you.

Each transition is packed with decisions, emotions, prayer, conversations, and sometimes conflict. You have already faced transitions, and there are more to come. What matters is how you navigate these transitions in a way that unites you and strengthens you.

As a Christian husband and wife, you have committed yourselves to following God's leadership. He sees you, and the promise found in Romans 8:28 holds true: "And we know that God causes everything to work together for the good of those who love God and are called according to his purpose for them." If you are going through a difficult transition, keep in mind the goodness of God and that He has a greater plan at work than you can see or imagine.

Protect your marriage by working hard to keep good communication between the two of you. Agree that you will live by Paul's admonition to the church in Ephesus: "Always be humble and gentle. Be patient with each other, making allowance for each other's faults because of your love. Make every effort to keep yourselves united in the Spirit, binding yourselves together with peace" (Ephesians 4:2-3). Choosing these qualities to govern your transitions will keep you open to what the other is experiencing and unify you through whatever you face.

Make a conscious decision to stay connected with your church and Christian friends. God has given you a community of people who can pray for you, encourage you, and cheer you on. The enemy wants the two of you to be isolated from the resources God has available to you. Furthermore, when you're isolated, you become more vulnerable to his attacks on your thoughts about each other and the transition you are facing. "Stay alert! Watch out for your great enemy, the devil. He prowls around like a roaring lion, looking for someone to devour. Stand firm against him, and be strong in your faith" (1 Peter 5:8-9).

Sometimes, the strongest catalyst for praying together is times of transition. The more intense the situation or season faced, the deeper and more fervent the prayer. As author and preacher E.M. Bounds once said, "Prayer is God's plan to supply man's great and continuous need with God's great and continuous abundance."

Prayer (Wife prays)

Dear God,

We acknowledge that you are the One we follow and trust through all transitions of life, great or small, enjoyable or painful. We trust you and know that you ultimately work all things for good, as we place our trust in you. Continue to guide and grow us in living out Ephesians 4:2-3 in our marriage. We want to honor and serve you as your humble servants.

In Jesus' name, Amen.

Questions

1. What transitions have we navigated well so far in our marriage?

2. How can we be more attentive to each other as we go through transitions?

GRANDCHILDREN

"Grandchildren are the crowning glory of the aged; parents are the pride of their children."
— *Proverbs 17:6*

It was an ordinary sunny summer day; the kind of day that everyone loves. A day that comes and goes. But then ... it happened. Our first grandchild was born and changed our world for the better. An ordinary day turned extraordinary. It became a day we will always celebrate. We got in our car and drove to the hospital, filled with anticipation to meet our grandson.

As we held our grandson, we were overwhelmed with joy, and a sense of responsibility, expectation, and love. What were God's plans for this baby boy? Would he become a musician, engineer, pastor, attorney, teacher, salesman, or something else? What challenges and joys would enter his life? Who would he marry, if he indeed did marry? How many years would we share life on Earth with him? What kind of relationship would we have with him? How could we love and influence him best?

If you're a grandparent, we're sure you can relate to our thoughts and feelings. You've experienced them as well with your grandkids. Today, we are blessed with more grandchildren, and the same joy, thoughts, and concerns arise with each successive child.

In 2 Timothy 1:5, we see an example of a godly grandmother who impacted her grandson for Jesus Christ. The Apostle Paul wrote to Timothy, "I remember your genuine faith, for you share the faith that first filled your grandmother Lois and your mother, Eunice. And I know that same faith continues strong in you."

Paul continued to affirm the role of Timothy's mother and grandmother in 2 Timothy 3:14-15. He wrote, "But you must remain faithful to the things you have been taught. You know they are true, for you know you can trust those who taught you. You have been taught the holy Scriptures from childhood, and they have given you the wisdom to receive the salvation that comes by trusting in Christ Jesus."

In these passages, we learn several details of Timothy's relationship with his mother and grandmother:

Timothy's faith in Christ is real and strong.

His grandmother and mother were intentional in teaching the Scripture to Timothy.

Lois and Eunice were honorable, godly women who were reliable and trustworthy.

Timothy's mom and grandmother taught him about Jesus from childhood. They laid a foundation of wisdom so that Timothy would accept the salvation that comes through Jesus.

Lois and Eunice had a faith legacy beyond Timothy. Timothy reached others for Christ and became a leader of leaders among the first-century Christians. His mom and grandmother were an integral part of the spiritual impact he made.

As grandparents, you want to influence your grandchildren for Jesus Christ. Here are some specific ways you can pray for them:

- Protection from the enemy
- Wisdom
- Your grandchildren will love God at an early age, and like Timothy, they will grow in their faith in Jesus
- Strong faith in Christ that is unshakable
- Godly friends who influence and support them
- Discernment between good and evil
- Courage to stand for what is right and true
- Teachers who love God and are good examples
- A spiritually mature spouse who encourages their faith in God

- Love God's Word and His truth
- Obedience

We'll close today's reading with this quote from Billy Graham:

"Impacting children for Christ is the most important responsibility most of us will ever face. The greatest resource is reading and believing the Bible and teaching it to the younger generations."[10]

Prayer (Husband prays)

Dear God,

As grandparents, give us the opportunities to influence our grandchildren, _____ (list your grandkids by name). Show us how to invest wisely in each grandchild. Help us to connect with them and love them in a way that will draw them to Jesus.

We pray that _____(name your grandkids) accept Jesus as their Lord, Savior, and Friend; and that their faith matures. Help them to spread the good news of Jesus to others while having the courage to stand up for Jesus Christ.

In Jesus' name, Amen.

---

10. billygraham.org/answers/how-do-i-explain-god-to-my-grandchildren

Questions

1. How can we connect better with each of our grandchildren? What are some intentional steps we can take?

2. Do we know our grandchildren's prayer requests? (Write down each grandchild's name and a specific prayer request for each one. You can also reach out to your grandchildren and ask them for their prayer requests.)

COURAGE

"This is my command — be strong and courageous! Do not be afraid or discouraged. For the Lord your God is with you wherever you go."
— Joshua 1:9

Courage can take a lot of different forms in marriage. Have you ever had to have a tough conversation with your spouse? Perhaps one of you is comfortable with truth-telling and digging into a subject, while the other prefers to avoid conflict. In the early years of our marriage, I, Brad, struggled to have hard conversations with Heidi.

While Heidi grew up in a lineage of lawyers who were gifted in presenting a case, I grew up trying to avoid tension and worked to keep the peace. Over time, I learned to trust God — and to trust Heidi's response — and dared to engage in dialogue that wasn't naturally comfortable. Ultimately, it has led to greater intimacy, trust, honesty, and openness as we have learned to courageously talk about subjects or issues that might otherwise have been avoided.

In our ministry, we have met scores of couples who have needed courage where one of the spouses was facing a health crisis. Recently, a dear friend of ours was diagnosed with pancreatic cancer. We had a front row seat as Tom and Sara faced this devastating diagnosis. Were they afraid of the outcome and sad about the diagnosis? Of course they were. And through their five-month journey, they pressed into the fear and were strong and courageous.

They prayed in faith that if it was God's plan, Tom would be healed. They also engaged in painful conversations surrounding Sara's care should Tom succumb to the disease. They welcomed guests and family into their home. Tom gave a presentation at his church on apologetics. One week later, Tom entered Jesus' presence. Tom had personally planned his own funeral, and Brad was privileged to give his friend's eulogy. To this day, Sara presses forward in the courage she and Tom shared as they trusted Jesus.

For other couples, it's not a health crisis, but a trust crisis. Every marriage faces disappointments and relational pain in the intimacy they share. Sometimes it's a small breach that is quickly forgiven and forgotten — and yet, even some courage is needed in the dailiness of small offenses.

But the courage to stay when there is a larger breach of trust, like an affair, or pornography, or other addictions, is extremely hard. Usually, it requires the guidance of a wise, godly counselor to navigate that kind of pain. For either the offended or the offender, pressing into the pain and working through the layers of broken trust requires strength and courage in the Lord.

It has been said that, "Courage isn't the absence of fear." Instead, it's stepping up to the plate, and as we often say, "Do it scared."

Prayer (Husband prays)

Dear God,

We want to be courageous in our marriage. May our courage always be found in you, as we have seen you at work in our lives and in our marriage. Thank you for how you cared for us in these situations (list them). We commit to encouraging each other to be strong and courageous as we trust in you.

In Jesus' name, Amen.

Questions

1. Where were we strong and courageous in the past? How did God provide?

2. How can we encourage each other to be courageous in the future?

FRIENDS

"There are 'friends' who destroy each other, but a real friend sticks closer than a brother."
— *Proverbs 18:24*

W e walked into the Christian school for "Back to School Night." Heidi immediately noticed a woman about our age. She and her husband were sitting near us. After the program finished, we walked over to them and introduced ourselves. They told us their names were "Todd and Kelly." We learned that, like us, they had just moved to Cincinnati and this was their first introduction to a new school. Their daughter was in the same grade as our daughter, Rachael. We continued our conversation, and Heidi and Kelly decided to get together for lunch.

Kelly and Heidi met the next week at Panera. They talked for hours. They had lunch again and then again. Thus began a lasting friendship of over 15 years.

The Bible describes a relationship between two godly friends, David and Jonathan. The story of their friendship is found in 1 Samuel 18-20. Here are some of the characteristics of deep friendships that are found in this story:

1. Close friends love each other unselfishly (1 Samuel 18:3). The Bible tells us that Jonathan loved David as he loved himself.

2. Intimate friends defend and speak well of each other (1 Samuel 19:4-5). Even when Jonathan's father, Saul, was planning to harm David, Jonathan stood up for his friend.

3. Good friends confide in each other (1 Samuel 20:1). They seek each other out and talk about important matters. They share things they wouldn't tell others.

4. Close friends help each other (1 Samuel 20:4). Jonathan said to David, "Tell me what I can do to help you?"

5. Good friends are loyal (1 Samuel 20:8). They don't betray one another to someone who will harm them. They want the best for their friend.

6. Intimate friends warn each other of impending danger (1 Samuel 20:13). If you realize someone wants to hurt your friend, you tell your friend. Likewise, if you see your friend heading down a path toward destruction or sin, you talk to them and encourage them to change course.

7. True friends treat each other's family well (1 Samuel 20:15). David showed kindness to Jonathan's son, Mephibosheth, years after Jonathan's death (2 Samuel 9:1ff). We love our friends' children because they are a reflection of our friends and a continuation of the legacy of our friendship.

8. Good friends guard each other's reputation (1 Samuel 20:32). You may have to defend the truth about your friend and possibly risk harm to yourself or your reputation.

9. Close friends show respect to each other (1 Samuel 20:41). When David and Jonathan said their final goodbyes to each other, David bowed down to Jonathan three times as a sign of honor. The Bible tells us they embraced and cried. Neither was afraid to express his love and concern for his friend.

10. Godly friends base their relationship on God. Your best friends are always going to be individuals who have a personal relationship with Jesus Christ. When Christ is the foundation of your friendship, your values, beliefs, and desires will unite you and strengthen your friendship.

Todd and Kelly aren't our only friends. We have the gift of many friends, some from decades ago and some from recent years. Our friends know us. They pray with us. They pray for our children and grandchildren.

What's important is that as a couple, you seek out godly friends who encourage you to follow Jesus individually and as a couple. Laugh with your friends. Have fun together. Talk about God. Make memories. Share prayer requests. Pursue friends who help you build your marriage.

Prayer (Wife prays)

Dear God,

As a couple, we need friends. Our desire is to develop friendships with people who encourage us in our marriage and spiritual journey. Lead us to friends who are fun, like-minded, loyal, helpful, and godly.

Just as we desire these types of friendships, may we be good friends to others. Show us when our friends need help and how we can best serve them. Strengthen our friendships as we grow together in Christ. Give us the ability to treat our friends' children well, to love each other, guard each other, and minister together.

In Jesus' name, Amen.

Questions

1. How can we be better friends to others?

2. Are we satisfied with the kind of friends we have? Do they encourage us in our marriage? In our walk with God? If not, what do we need to change? How can we find godly friends?

WISDOM

"Get wisdom ... Getting wisdom is the
wisest thing you can do!"
— *Proverbs 4:5a, 7*

Have you as a couple ever longed for wisdom? Should we purchase the home, or not? Do we add another child to our family? Which school should we send our children to? When should we retire? Are we allocating our financial resources properly? Is this the best doctor for our health issues? When do we move? Should we continue on this career path or not?

Several years ago, we considered purchasing a used car. I, Brad, thought it was an excellent time to do so, while Heidi was reluctant. We were stuck. We agreed to pray about it and ask God for his wisdom in the situation. Within hours, Heidi changed her mind. In unity, we went ahead and purchased the car. Months later, we were able to see God's timing and provision.

2 Chronicles 20 tells the story of King Jehoshaphat of Judah. An army from Edom was coming against Judah. Verse 3 tells us, "Jehoshaphat was terrified by this news and begged the Lord for guidance." Later in verse 12, the king said, "We do not know what to do, but we are looking to you for help." This wise king sought wisdom from God.

Like King Jehoshaphat, you and your spouse need God's insight and guidance. The couples who pursue wisdom together consistently makes the right choices. They look at situations, evaluate them, and move ahead with careful confidence. This doesn't mean every decision is 100% perfect; instead, you have godly confidence in God's insight and direction.

It is extremely rare for any couple to actively pursue wisdom from God. Husbands and wives may think through problems carefully. They may periodically ask God for wisdom when they are desperate. Or they look to God for wisdom when they are up against the wall with a major decision. But to actually pursue wisdom from God as a part of their marital relationship is generally not on their radar.

There is a difference in the kind of wisdom pursued as well. The Bible describes worldly wisdom and godly wisdom. Worldly wisdom is generally self-focused, power and success-driven. As James

3:15-16 declares, "For jealousy and selfishness are not God's kind of wisdom. Such things are earthly, unspiritual, and demonic. For wherever there is jealousy and selfish ambition, there you will find disorder and evil of every kind." You certainly don't want *that* for your marriage!

Godly wisdom, on the other hand, produces great results in marriage and life. James continued, "But the wisdom from above is first of all pure. It is also peace loving, gentle at all times, and willing to yield to others. It is full of mercy and the fruit of good deeds. It shows no favoritism and is always sincere" (James 3:17). You do want *that* for your marriage!

But how do you as a couple obtain wisdom? Receiving wisdom begins by having the right relationship with God. Proverbs 9:10 states, "Fear of the Lord is the foundation of wisdom." To fear God doesn't mean to be afraid of Him. Instead, hold God in high regard with awe and respect. You acknowledge that He is the Almighty God. He is all-knowing, all-powerful, and everywhere present. When you, as a couple, have that kind of understanding, then you are making decisions that align with who He is and His desires for your marriage.

It's out of a proper fear of the Lord that you gain a better perspective of yourselves. You see your dependence on Him and your trust in Him grows exponentially. Proverbs 11:2 reminds us, "... with humility comes wisdom." And with humility comes an openness to receive counsel from other people to whom God has given wisdom and insight. "Get all the advice and instruction you can," wrote King Solomon, "so you will be wise the rest of your life" (Proverbs 19:20).

All godly wisdom comes from God. He wants you to have wisdom. If you're in a situation where you need special insight and wisdom, hold hands and ask God for it. James 1:5 promises, "If you need wisdom, ask our generous God, and he will give it to you. He will not rebuke you for asking."

Agree to pursue godly wisdom together. Fear the Lord, ask for wisdom, stay humble, listen to wise counsel, and God will direct your steps.

Prayer (Husband prays)

Dear God,

Thank you for your promise to give us wisdom when we ask for it. We commit to respecting and revering you. You are the holy and mighty God. We choose to follow you. Guide us as we pursue wisdom. Bring wise people into our lives who can instruct us as necessary, and we will seek to learn from them. Grant us wisdom in how we live with each other. Grant us wisdom in how we make decisions throughout our marriage.

In Jesus' name, Amen.

Questions

1. How can we practically cultivate a "fear of the Lord" in our marriage?

2. Who do we know right now who seems to have godly wisdom? Is there anything for which we need to seek their counsel?

DAY 38
FUN

"When he had been there a long time, Abimelech king of the Philistines looked out the window and saw Isaac laughing with Rebekah his wife."
— *Genesis 26:8 ESV*

We love this verse! Here's a married couple, Isaac and Rebekah, who are having fun together. You can almost feel their joy. What were they laughing about? Was it a private joke? Something they had just witnessed? A memory? Although we don't know the source of their laughter, it is clear they were enjoying each other.

Fun is integral to a healthy, satisfying marriage. You make memories together, share experiences, bond as you relate to each other, relax together, and learn about your spouse.

Clinical psychologist Willard Harley stated, "If you want your marriage to succeed, you must become associated with each other's best and most relaxed moments, not just the times of stress and frustration … "[11]

Research shows that couples who regularly schedule date nights have happier marriages than those who don't. Why? Because these couples are having fun together. What are some ways you can increase the amount of fun and laughter in your marriage?

Here are just a few ideas:

> Play a board or video game together
> Watch a comedy
> Exercise
> Attend a sporting event
> Hike
> Work on a project together
> Go to a concert or play
> Fish
> Play golf, tennis, pickleball, or another sport
> Participate in a March Madness or a Fantasy Football League
> Cook together
> Eat dinner at a nice restaurant
> Have a picnic at a local park
> Bike ride
> Camp
> Read together
> Visit the zoo

---

11. www.marriagebuilders.com/recreational-companionship-is-boring-part-2-1.htm

God created marriage for our enjoyment. Make fun a priority as you engage in activities that connect you and deepen your intimacy. As someone once said, "The couple that plays together, stays together."

Prayer (Wife prays)

Dear God,

Thanks for the fun we have in our marriage. We reflect on the times we have laughed hard together and how enjoyable that was. Thank you for those memories. Give us more opportunities to connect with each other through fun and laughter. Help us to find joy in each other, just like your servants, Isaac and Rebekah.

In Jesus' name, Amen.

Questions

1. What can we do on our next date night? (Schedule it now)

2. What obstacles to having fun do we face? How can we overcome these?

LEGACY

"I will teach you hidden lessons from our past — stories we have heard and known, stories our ancestors handed down to us. We will not hide these truths from our children; we will tell the next generation about the glorious deeds of the Lord, about his power and his mighty wonders."
— Psalm 78:2-4

His grandfather practiced idolatry. He sacrificed one of his sons in the fire. He killed other innocent people. This grandfather sought guidance from mediums and spiritists. He sought omens. As a political ruler, he led many people astray, encouraging them not to follow God or His commands. Eventually, this grandfather repented, but the damage had been done. Evil reigned in his country.

His father was an evil man as well, following in his grandfather's steps. His dad didn't obey God. He offered sacrifices to idols constructed by his grandfather. And his dad never repented.

This is the legacy of King Josiah. He became the King of Judah at the age of 8. Despite his evil family line, he is known as a godly king. 2 Kings 22:2 states, "He did what was pleasing in the Lord's sight and followed the example of his ancestor David. He did not turn away from doing what was right."

We all have a legacy. Perhaps you come from an evil heritage like King Josiah did. Your grandparents and parents didn't follow God. You're a believer in Jesus Christ, and you want to start a new, godly legacy. The good news is you can. Like Josiah, your legacy starts with you.

Or maybe you come from a godly lineage like we do. Our grandparents and parents were followers of Jesus Christ. God was worshipped and honored in both our homes. If you come from a godly legacy, how do you strengthen it and pass it to the next generation?

First, recognize that you determine your legacy by your commitment to Jesus Christ. Your ancestors don't define your future. When you place Jesus at the center of your marriage, you and your spouse create a godly legacy.

Second, make a commitment to pray for your children and grandchildren. Pray that your legacy is strengthened for generations to come. Pray that your children love God and serve Him.

Third, talk to your children and grandchildren about your relationship with Jesus Christ. Share stories of how God has blessed you, protected you, and been faithful to you. Tell your children and grandchildren how God has answered your prayers. Tell your family about God's power and his miracles.

And fourth, live a life of intentionality and integrity. Godly legacies don't just happen. They are the product of a God-honoring couple that seeks to serve God and put Him on the throne of their marriage.

Prayer (Husband prays)

Dear God,

We come from a _____ legacy. When we think about our legacy as husband and wife, we want to repent of_____ and we desire to continue to _____.

We pray that we establish a godly legacy in our family as we share stories of your faithfulness, power, and mighty wonders. Help these stories make a positive impression on our children and grandchildren. May they remember them and pass them on to their children. We ask, Lord, that the godly legacy we are creating would grow stronger in the generations to come. We pray that our descendants would be known for their love and devotion to you, Father.

In Jesus' name, Amen.

Questions

1. As we each think about the legacy we received, what are the negative aspects of that legacy? What are some positive aspects that we'd like to continue?

2. What stories of God's faithfulness and power can we share with our children and grandchildren?

SALVATION

"For everyone has sinned; we all fall short of God's glorious standard. Yet God, in his grace, freely makes us right in his sight. He did this through Christ Jesus when he freed us from the penalty for our sins. For God presented Jesus as the sacrifice for sin. People are made right with God when they believe that Jesus sacrificed his life, shedding his blood."
— Romans 3:23-25a

This devotional has focused on many topics that couples face. Way to go for completing your 40-day journey of praying together. We intentionally wanted to make salvation the last chapter. It's *the* most important decision you and your spouse will ever consider. A husband and wife who share the same spiritual foundation in Jesus Christ are likely to have the most fulfilling and joyful marriage. Prayer is the bond that cements your marriage.

The Bible tells us in Acts 4:12, "There is salvation in no one else! God has given no other name under heaven by which we must be saved." You may think salvation comes in many different forms. We've heard couples say, "All roads lead to heaven," or "It doesn't matter what you believe, as long as you're sincere." But that's simply not true. Good works won't save you from your sins (Titus 3:5). Allah won't save you. Buddha won't save you. Your love for others won't save you. Your giving to charity won't save you.

The only sacrifice that can save you is the one Jesus made on the cross for you. Author Charles Spurgeon wrote, "Christ is a sufficient Saviour, because his death has unexhausted power."[12] Jesus Christ, God's Son, died for you. Think of Jesus as your personal sin-bearer. Jesus suffered so that you wouldn't have to face the reality of eternal punishment in a very real place called hell (Matthew 25:46). God loves you so much that He sent His Son to die in your place — yes, Jesus Christ died *for you.*

Perhaps you're at a point where you want to surrender your life to Jesus Christ. Here are the steps you need to take:

First, believe that Jesus Christ, God's Son, died on the cross for you. Salvation is a free gift, and it is received by placing your faith and trust in Jesus as your Savior. The Apostle Paul wrote, "God saved you by his grace when you believed. And you can't take credit for this; it is a gift from God. Salvation is not a reward for the good things we have done, so none of us can boast about it" (Ephesians 2:8-9).

---

12. www.theologyquotes.com/Charles%20Sprgeon

Second, pray to God and confess your sins. This means acknowledging where you have wronged God and others. Ask for His forgiveness and tell God you want Him to be your Leader and that you will obey and follow Him.

Third, repent of any thoughts, words, values, or actions that are not consistent with the Bible. To repent means to change the direction of your thinking so you think and act in a God-honoring way.

Fourth, tell God you want to have a fresh start and that you want to invite Jesus into your life. 2 Corinthians 5:17 says that when someone belongs to Christ, they are a new person. The old life is gone; and a new one has begun.

We want to challenge you as a couple to consider your relationship with Jesus Christ and your eternal destiny. This is the most important decision of your entire life.

On a recent trip, we were walking to our gate in an airport. We noticed the word "Departed" on the monitor where the flight's status is listed. Just a few minutes earlier, a passenger could have boarded that plane, but once the plane left the gate, no one could enter. It was too late. The plane was gone. The opportunity was no longer available.

You and your spouse have the opportunity of a lifetime today. It's not too late to trust God and live for him. Surrender your life and your marriage to him. When you do, He will build your marriage in a way that only He can.

Prayer

If you would like to accept Jesus Christ as your Lord and Savior:

Dear God,

Thank you for sending your Son, Jesus Christ, to die on the cross for my sins. I am making a decision today to live the rest of my life for you. I invite Jesus into my life. I know this choice is not dependent on anything I can do to earn my salvation. Instead, it is your free gift to me. I ask you to become my Lord, my Savior, my Forgiver, and my Friend.

Lead us in our marriage and show us how to depend on you by faith. Thank you for the gift of eternal life.

In Jesus' name, Amen.

If Jesus Christ is your Lord and Savior:

Dear God,

Thank you for sending your Son, Jesus Christ, to die on the cross for our sins. We thank you for your direction and provision in our marriage. Guide us as we continue to follow you and do your will in our individual lives and our marriage. Continue the godly heritage we have in the generations to come. We look forward to spending eternity with you.

In Jesus' name, Amen.

Questions

1. When did each of us accept Jesus Christ as our Lord and Savior? How has He changed our lives? (If we haven't, what are our reservations about doing so?)

2. How has this 40-day devotional impacted our marriage? (Make a commitment to continue praying together.)

PUTTING PRAYER INTO PRACTICE

Learning to Pray with Thanksgiving

"Praise the Lord! Give thanks to the Lord, for he is good! His faithful love endures forever. Who can list the glorious miracles of the Lord? Who can ever praise him enough?" Psalms 106:1-2

As we (Brad and Heidi) read that last phrase, "Who can ever praise him enough?" we're overwhelmed with the many ways God has blessed us. We could thank Him every day, and it would never express the depth of our gratitude for God's provision, direction, protection, and gifts; the greatest of which is salvation through Jesus Christ.

Now, reflect on your marriage. How has God blessed you? Talk about the miracles you've witnessed in your marriage. When did God intervene and rewrite your story?

Do you have children who love Jesus? Were you raised by godly parents? Are you creating a godly legacy? Do you have a home? Did you receive a good education? Is your job fulfilling? Do you own a car or other material possessions? Is your health good? Can you travel? Do you and your spouse have friends? Do you have a solid church to call home? Is the area you live in beautiful? Can you see, hear, and speak? Do you own a pet who brings you joy? Are you able to enjoy good food? Do you have access to a Bible? Has God provided for you financially? Can you listen to inspiring music? Are you and your spouse in love? Do you have a growing relationship with Jesus? Did you take a breath today?

You may not be the recipient of all these gifts, but we're certain God has blessed you in some specific ways. As a couple, bow your heads and thank God for your marriage. Thank Him for the blessings you've received as you continue to build your marriage with prayer.

"For every house has a builder, but the one who built everything is God."
Hebrews 3:4

ACKNOWLEDGEMENTS

Our first acknowledgement is to God. We are grateful for the grace and mercy shown to us through Jesus. Our marriage is a testimony to His work in our lives. The Holy Spirit has guided our writing process, and we are thankful for His leadership and insight.

Each of our moms is a prayer warrior. Luann Mitchell and Marilyn Strutz are our biggest encouragers and laid the foundation of prayer in our lives at an early age.

Our three children and their spouses continue to encourage us in our work to build Christ-centered marriages. Rob & Leandra, Tovey & Andrew, Rachael & Cole — we are so glad to see you each walking in the faith and raising your children to do the same.

We are deeply indebted to Paul Braoudakis for the editing, layout, and design. It's a lot of work to get a book ready to be published, and Paul's a pro. In addition, he's one of Brad's "Guyz" along with Mark Mittelberg and Steve Perkins — all encouragers and men of prayer.

We are also grateful to Lindsey Hilty for her edits and suggestions. Your creative ideas took this book to a new level.

We are blessed with so many close friends who have prayed for us over the years. Your prayers and love have undergirded and built us up for this calling to build Christ-centered marriages.

The leadership and congregation of The River Church have graciously given us the freedom to minister at marriage conferences each year. Thank you for your continued support of Build Your Marriage as Brad serves as your pastor.

As a non-profit, Build Your Marriage is funded by the generous and sacrificial gifts of supporters. We literally could not even exist without you, and are grateful you share the dream and vision we have to help couples center their marriage on Jesus.

From the beginning of this ministry, we've known that nothing happens of spiritual value without being sustained by prayer. At each conference, we invite people to be part of our Prayer Team. We are indebted to you for your ongoing prayer, not only as we speak, but also for special projects like this devotional. Your prayers are the fuel that God uses!

ABOUT THE AUTHORS

Brad and Heidi Mitchell are the co-founders of Build Your Marriage, a ministry created to encourage and equip couples to grow closer to each other and to Christ. Drawing from nearly four decades in pastoral ministry, they share honestly, with both wisdom and biblical insight, about what it takes to build a lasting marriage.

Graduates of Wheaton College, Brad also earned his MDiv from Trinity Evangelical Divinity School. Together they've written several books, including *Build Your Marriage One Day at a Time*, *Build Your Marriage with Couples of the Bible*, and the Amazon best-seller *Ruined to Recovery*. Whether through their books, conferences, or online resources, Brad and Heidi love coming alongside couples to strengthen their marriages.

Married for more than 40 years, they enjoy life as parents to three married children and are proud grandparents.

Brad and Heidi make their home near Cincinnati, Ohio.

BOOKS BY
BRAD & HEIDI MITCHELL

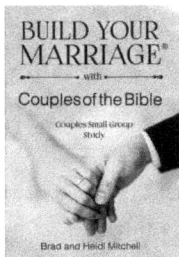

Build Your Marriage with Couples of the Bible (A couples small group Bible study)

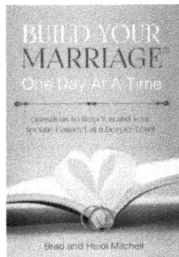

Build Your Marriage One Day at a Time

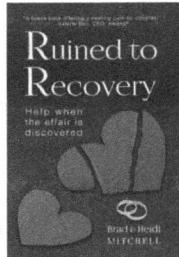

Ruined to Recovery: Help When the Affair is Discovered

De la ruina a la sanación (Spanish version of *Ruined to Recovery*)

CONNECT WITH BUILD YOUR MARRIAGE

/BuildYourMarriage   *@BuildYourMarriage*   *@BuildUrMarriage*

buildyourmarriage.org

Stories for Shorty:

A Collection of Recollections

from the Jockey Club 1982-1988

Edited by Betsy Young and Chuck Byrd

Aurore
PRESS

Publishers / Editors:	Betsy Young and Chuck Byrd
Production Editor:	Amory Huffman
Photographers (known):	Sarah Kuhl, Witt Schmitz, Amy Miller, Chuck Byrd, James Bramlage, Jan Gerber, Allegra Nicodemus, Jerry Adams, Jakki Repellent, Ric Hickey, Scott Bruno, Betsy Young, Bob Butler, Mark Kerley, Becky Baldock Powell, George DuChaine
Art Direction:	Betsy Young
Layout/Production:	Diane Allen and Jerry Dirr
PrePress:	Jerry Dirr
Cover and back photos:	Sarah Kuhl

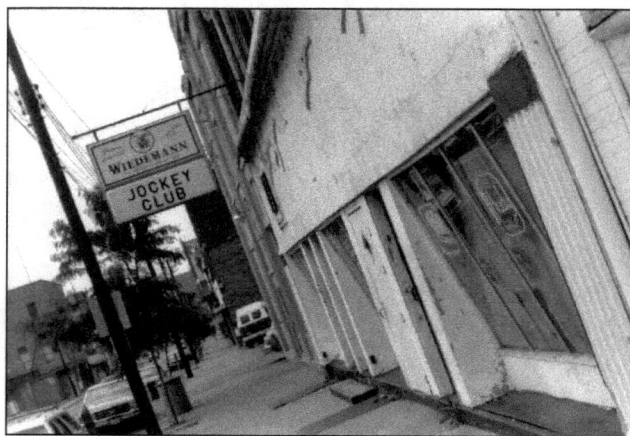

The Jockey Club, 633 York Street, Newport, KY. Photo by Jerry Adams

Stories for Shorty: A Collection of Recollections from the Jockey Club 1982-1988.
Collection copyright © 2008 Betsy Young and Chuck Byrd. All rights reserved.

Library of Congress Control Number: 2016900199

ISBN: 069221982
978-0692219829X

Second Edition © 2016

Acknowledgements

Aurore Press would like to thank everyone who contributed to *Stories for Shorty*—words, art, photos and more—and for all the enthusiastic support from beginning to end.

In particular we'd like to thank Bill Leist, Jimmy Davidson, Robert "Jughead" Sturdevant and "Handsome" Clem Carpenter for the "backyard" meetings and frequent phone calls and emails way up until we put this baby to bed. We'd also like to acknowledge our Jockey Club friends who went above and beyond to make sure the writing was well documented with pictures, Sarah Kuhl, Jakki Repellent, Greg Stout, George DuChaine, Amy Miller, James Bramlage, Max Cole and Jerry Adams. Without their help, this book wouldn't be what it is.

Thanks also goes to Kim Maurer from Sidewinder Coffee and Tea, Amory Huffman, Eric Appleby, Mike Cowgill, Mary Anne Cowgill, Mark Messerly, Tim Benz, Nolan Benz, Jerry Dirr, Diane Allen, Snare, Amy Kreitzer, Paul Schmitt, Joe Riddle, Danielle Pitzer, Ellis Edwards, everyone at Printer's Bindery, Matthew "Mud" Goodsleeve for the awesome "Shorty" t-shirts, Rick McCarty and the Southgate House, Ric Hickey, Mike Gregory and our friends at Shake It Records, especially Jim and Darren Blase. Also thanks to Bryce Rhude for keeping the JC alive and well in our memories.

Finally, thank you to all the bands who stepped up (and also reformed) to make the book for Shorty even more memorable: The Speed Hickeys, SS-20, The Thangs, BPA, The Libertines US, and The Reduced.

And as always, Aurore.

This book is dedicated to Hallman "Shorty" Mincey
and his brother, Hayne "Tiny" Mincey

and to all the JC'ers whose journeys ended far too soon.

Shorty in front of the pink door. Photo by Sarah Kuhl

Stories for Shorty is also dedicated to the memory of Billy Blank.
It was a helluva thing, Ace.

Bill "Billy Blank" Leist
January 23, 1960 – December 28, 2014

There wouldn't be a Jockey Club without Bill.
Rest in peace, my friend.

by Billy Blank

You always got your money's worth at the Jockey Club. If you didn't have enough money, you still got in the door! Plus we would have never made it if we had excluded kids.

In 1983 we were all frustrated as fuck. We had to drive 300 fucking miles for shows. Take the fucks over at Bogarts. We knew that was corporate shit which we hated to begin with. They were too cheap to pay union scale to have the construction and teardown and all that shit so they kept dragging their feet month after month after month. When you're young, a year's a long time. We got sick of it.

But once the Brew House started happening, that's when it kicked in. There were loft parties back then too but that was not a viable deal for us. We needed a fucking club for ourselves!

My dad worked with "Tiny" Hayne Mincey at Wiedemann. He worked with Tiny in the 50s, that's how that shit came up. He brought it up. He said, "Hey, there's this bar…"

Bill, Shorty, Jughead

We approached Shorty and said we'd like to have some fun and we'd like to make you some money. Can we get a date down here? Shorty said, "Can we start next week?" We were surprised about Shorty and Tiny actually going for it and giving us a chance to do it. I know for them what was happening was local bands. They were paying them money and they weren't really doing good so for them it was their chance to make a couple of bucks. They agreed that they would help us out with the sound thing because we didn't know jack shit about it. They knew that they would have to put a little money out but it wasn't as much as they were losing on these cock rock bands.

Shorty was real as hell and he packed a .38. Tiny, the trip was, he quit grooming himself as long as Reagan was in. The question is, when Shorty didn't sleep down there in the floor of the club where the fuck did he sleep? He used to put those six chairs together and sleep down there in the club.

Soon after Shorty sold the Jockey Club he called me and left a message at my mom and dad's and he wanted to open up that fucking bus station down there in the west end of Newport. I told him, "Shorty, that can't happen logistically. You'd have to put sound proofing shit in there. It's a big fucking building— empty—you had a club that people played in." It could accommodate music but a big old fucking shed for the TANK buses, it wasn't going to happen. His daughter fucked with him. That's the way I remember it. Of course I don't have perfect recall but I think his kids were pestering him to get the money. He sold it for $110,000. It wasn't much. And the cab company got it. But he lost his only joy when he sold the place and he had already reached that deal. You can't do it again.

Or can you? According to my friends over at Aurore Press, you sure as hell can try. So on November 22, 2008 we're going to raise a little hell in the name of Shorty. Goddamn, I don't need an invitation for that! Not to mention it's for charity. So check out the stories. Just like the Jockey Club, they are for everyone to enjoy. Hell, that's what made the place so special in the first place.

Bill Leist, October, 2008

Interview with "Handsome" Clem Carpenter

Clem, where and when did your interest in underground music begin?

CC: I can sum it up in just one word: disco. I hated that crap back then and I still hate it today. My roots musically have always been in the blues, R&B, and just a little pinch of Country and Western and of course like any kid that grew up in the 60s, you got exposed to progressive rock of that era, MC5, Blue Cheer, Iggy and the Stooges, the list goes on. By the time the mid-seventies rolled around, the rock scene in general had pretty much stagnated where it needed a kick in the ass. And along came punk rock to give it the well deserved and, dare I say, well needed kick in the ass. I've said this before on numerous occasions and I will say it to the very day I kick the bucket and they cremate my remains, the punk phenomenon in retrospect was the best thing to ever happen to rock-n-roll and we're still feeling the effects of that today.

What was the very first punk rock LP you bought?

CC: The very first punk rock record I bought was "Young, Loud and Snotty" from the Dead Boys. The band that made me a punk rock fan for life.

Tell us a little about how your radio show on WAIF, "Search and Destroy", got started.

CC: Well actually "Search and Destroy" was sort of a natural progression. When I originally started at WAIF, I came on as co-host of The Final Solution show with Spiv Daniels and Spiv found himself a job outside of Cincinnati and basically turned the show over to me. I decided to go with the format change and "Search and Destroy" as we know it was born. This was '79, '80 and some of the "hardcore punk" records started to show itself on the marketplace such as the first Dead Kennedys singles, first Circle Jerks album, and so on. By the time 1982 rolled around, it had become a weekly event. At the time, those bands were not getting exposed at all on any other alternative rock programming at WAIF. My show was pretty much a forum for these bands.

What are some of your favorite records?

CC: There's so, so, so many. I don't even know where to begin. As far as the San Francisco scene goes, you got to go with the Dead Kennedys right off the bat. As far as the LA scene goes, the first two that would come to mind would be Fear and the Angry Samoans. They always had that, dare I say, sense of humor as an undercurrent throughout their music. Of course we gave exposure to the DC, the straight edge scene as it was blossoming in DC, and basically throughout the country. We had a bit of a scene starting to develop up the road in Dayton and Indianapolis of note well before Cincinnati did. A little known fact is Dayton served as the US headquarters for Rock Against Racism in the late 70s and early 80s. A little trivia that you might find quite interesting.

"Handsome" Clem Carpenter hosting "Search and Destroy" on WAIF

What was your objective for "Search and Destroy"?

CC: It was basically an outlet to give exposure to some really outstanding bands that were not getting exposure not just on commercial radio but on some of the other public outlets in town at the time. As time went along we started to give exposure to a lot of the regional bands and as some of the local bands started to get going we also provided an outlet for them as well. The seed was pretty much planted and look where we are today, it speaks for itself.

Tell us your story about the Jockey Club beginnings.

CC: As far as the Jockey Club goes, we need to set the clock back to '82. At the time Bogarts was closed for renovation and originally they claimed it would only take a couple of months and the work ended up lasting pretty much most of that year. As a result, the number of shows that were coming through Cincinnati dropped down tremendously to the point to where we were having to do shows—not me, I should say other promoters—at the Brew House up in Walnut Hills. At the time we were starting to look around for a venue as an outlet for mainly local and regional bands and if some national bands happened to come along, that grabbed our interest that wanted to play the venue, that would be great. The two candidates were the Jockey Club and the second one was then known as Ma's Opra. It's now known today as the historic Southgate House. To make a long story short, we had a couple of biddings with Tiny and Shorty and the rest they say is history. The second meeting, we got a call from Tiny. I asked him if he wanted us to come and do shows and we met with him the following day at the Club and he said guys, if you want to come and do it, have at it. I was walking out and I was looking over at Bill (Bill Leist, aka Billy Blank), I said, "Bill, can you believe what we got ourselves into?" I said, "Yeah, can you believe what kind of bands we could bring in?" And we both said, BLACK FLAG! Because they were touring at the time and I had managed to get contact information for the band through, I think it might have been, Bill Levine who was a promoter up in the Indianapolis area who had done a series of shows up there.

What were the first bands to play the Jockey Club?
CC: Well, the first show was one of the Dave Lewis Hospital Records bands, Lopez Sophisticates and what would later become SS-20 (AK-47), played that date there as well. Our first national show was a couple of weeks later when the Effigies played from Chicago. And as a last bit of add on, MDC showed up and we let them play a set there. It was slow beginnings but as time went on we kind of began to up a little bit of a rep. In the early days since we didn't have the kind of financial backing we would need to go after certain bands, we had to let a bunch of shows go. We had to let Bad Brains go, we had to let the Misfits go, and a couple of other bands whose names escape me had to go because we couldn't do the guarantee at that particular point in time. As I said, as time went on, the reputation of the Club starts spreading across the country and the venue just started to develop that special vibe. It was also during that time that D.O.A. made its first of, shall we say, numerous appearances. Matter of fact it would be the band that would hold the record for the most number of headline appearances by a national band for the venue.

Tell us about your favorite shows at the Jockey Club.
CC: At the very top are the two Dead Kennedys shows, far and away. Mainly because of my little conversation I had with Jello the first time I went to San Francisco in 1984. I ran into him at a show at the old Mabuhay Gardens in San Francisco, had a chance to talk with him and mentioned about the Jockey Club, my show on WAIF radio. Apparently the conversation remained in his head because shortly thereafter on what turned out to be their final tour under their "classic lineup", they ended up doing the two night stand at the Jockey Club. And I will always be proud of that show because of some of the stuff that went

Dead Kennedys at the JC, 1985

on behind the scenes and how we were able to pull it off. I will also have to mention the Ramones, the first time around, we were able to pull that off. The D.O.A. shows, what can you say? Those guys are friends of mine to this very day but there's just so many and not enough time!

What do you remember about Shorty?

CC: What can I say about Shorty? He's sort of like the uncle/surrogate father figure, whatever you want to call it. Somebody that you want to have corrupt your morals and then did a very good job doing it. On the nights where I worked the front door with him, he was such a blast recalling some of his tales of the good old days back when Newport was REALLY the original sin city and just even to think about it is mind boggling, going back to those times. He was a class individual through and through. Nothing more else you can really say about the man. Still miss him to this very day.

If you were still doing "Search and Destroy" what do you think you'd be playing now?

CC: "Search and Destroy" died when I had my divorce from the then leadership at WAIF radio. As far as that station goes, the divorce was quite bitter. Because of that, "Search and Destroy" as we remembered it would probably no longer exist. These days it would be more along the lines as the "Final Solution" show where I would try to delve into more musical genres. Some of the stuff I've been listening to lately, it can vary from ska from the 60s, to old hillbilly music from the likes of Johnny Horton, Buck Owens, you know going back to my hillbilly roots a little bit. There's this really great hillbilly band out of Springfield, MO that I would love to bring to Cincinnati, a band called Big Smith. If they're within 600 miles of Cincinnati and those of you who are reading this book have a chance to go see them, see them! It's worth the trip. Their web site is bigsmithband.com if you want to check it out, find out the details of where they're coming and their CDs they have available and so on and so forth. And also I've been getting a little bit into the Mexican Norteño music, especially a subgenre called narcocorrido. If you can imagine Norteño Tejano music with gangster rap-type lyrics then you got a rough idea what narcocorrido sound like albeit sung in Spanish, probably the leading band in the genre, another band I'd love to bring to Cincinnati. Matter of fact, Sylvia Martinez who used to own Sylvia's Restaurant around the corner from the Jockey Club had offered to put up the money for us to bring this band Los Tigres del Norte to Cincinnati. Nothing ever came of it but that's another example of stuff I've been listening to lately in addition to the usual punk stuff and a lot of the cooler alternative stuff that you hear these days.

WAIF Benefit Flyer featuring The Reduced, The Thangs, Present Tension, Blanco Nombre and "Newport Gestapo" flyer courtesy of Art D

How do you think the Jockey Club will be remembered in the next 20 years?

CC: Realistically only time will tell. I guess as long as there's people like us still around to tell the story there will always be some memories of the Jockey Club. It may never completely fade from the scene but as I said, as long as there's people still alive and here to tell the story, the memories will still live on, plain and simple.

Clem, I just want to thank you for all the memories and all the great shows and all the great music and I hope I'm around in another 20 or 30 years to talk with you about it.

CC: The pleasure's all been mine.

Clem Carpenter was interviewed on Sunday, August 31, 2008.

Stories for Shorty

Stories for Shorty

Do the Shorty

Do the Shorty
Show how brave you are and share that cigar
Do the Shorty
Not too tall, rather portly
Do the Shorty
Bust his fucking head and fill him full of lead
Fill him full of lead, and do the Shorty
Alright now watch it now, watch it now
Do the Shorty
If you wanna take a chance
Ask him where he buys his pants
Do the Shorty

The Reduced, lyrics by Bill Leist and Rick Sims

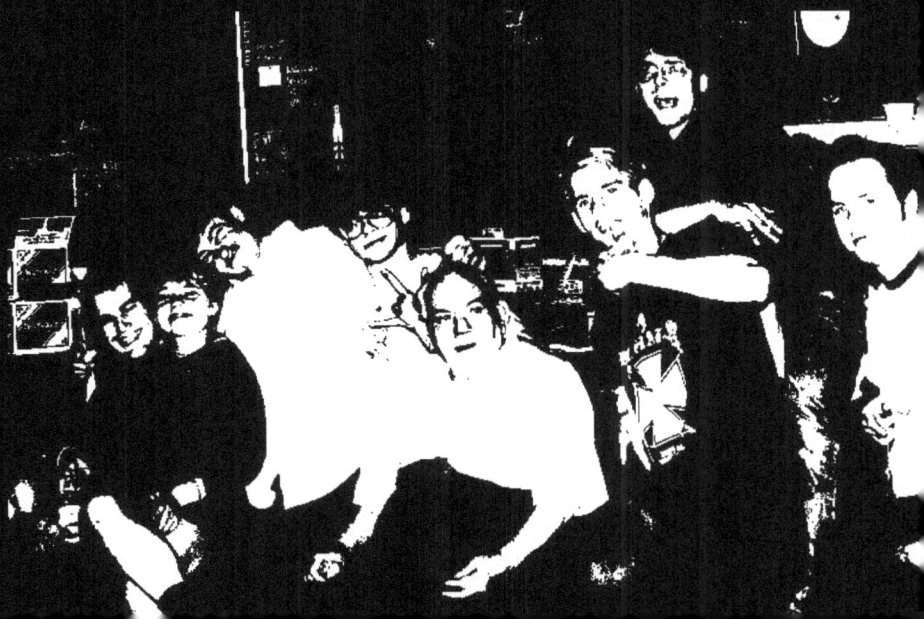

Robert "Jughead" Sturdevant

633 York Street, Newport, Kentucky, the sight of the former gaming casino, the Flamingo Club. Outside the white, nondescript store front hangs the ancient vertical fifty-foot tall Art Deco neon "Flamingo Club" marquee, hinting of the casino's former grandeur.

The Long Lamented Jockey Club
The Pantheon of Punk
The Altar of the Alternative

After WWII, the city of Newport started to make profound changes on their waterfront. The massive floodwall that exists today was constructed. In the early 1970s, Hallman "Shorty" Mincey, and his brother, Hayne "Tiny" Mincey were

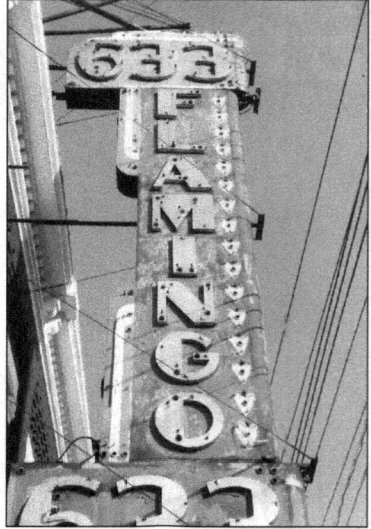

633 York Street, "The Flamingo"
photo by Sarah Kuhl

owners of a riverfront bar known as the Jockey Club. It is unclear if the name comes from the English or French club of the same moniker. The connection to the thoroughbred industry in Kentucky seems obvious. The brothers received a $10,000 relocation grant from the state of Kentucky. Those proceeds were used to purchase the Flamingo Club at 633 York Street. I am told that the structure was the longest standing building built as a gaming establishment on the North American continent.

At that time, both brothers were known as Newport nightlife figures, having lived there their entire lives. Each had a long history of involvement in the Newport gambling scene. During the Kennedy administration, Robert Kennedy's Attorney General's Office, with the help of local politicians, forced the end of legal gambling in Newport. The city was reduced to a collection of nude dancing bars and fell into a general economic slump. Nude dancing was outlawed in 1980. This is where our story begins.

From the late 1970s to the early 1980s, the Jockey Club had been a venue for classic rock bands. Today, it is not hard to imagine what a dead end scene that must have been. In 1982, the club had fallen into disrepair. These hard times in Newport compared to today's booming, glitzy plethora of shops and trendy restaurants, create quite a dichotomy.

There was a long, low ceilinged hallway that led from the street to the ballroom. This hallway was covered with the most decrepit, threadbare, dirty carpeting, whose age could be measured in decades. The walls were a dingy light brown, stained from the original white, from a million burned cigarettes.

Shorty holds court at the JC

The hallway was relatively well lit. Three quarters down, was the sight of my most memorable education to date. There sat Hallman "Shorty" Mincey at a square Formica red topped table holding court and collecting the cover charge, while scrutinizing the patronage. He was sitting with cigar in mouth and a faced roll of bills clutched in his left hand, wearing dark dress pants, service oxfords, and a white short sleeved shirt open at the collar. Like Charon at the entrance of Hades, no souls may pass without payment. Shorty always had a couple of people sitting with him, like Cerebus, to his Charon. The hallway, like the River Styx, was an entrance to another world.

The term Psychopomp relates to a person that helps the newly departed make their way to the afterlife, a saint or a bodhisattva. I think in the early days those were similar to the roles that Billy, Clem and I played. We saw the tremendous potential for good music and good fun, so we tried to open that world up to all that were ready for it. Ours was a search for authenticity in our music and in our lives. The Cincinnati live music scene mirrored the national scene. A top heavy scene dominated by rock star bullshit and narrow mindedness of all concerned. The Jockey Club was a smoke filled gritty breath of fresh air, new music and new ideas, a clean break with the past with tremendous potential in all things. Like most historic periods it had its collection of venerated relics and saints. The 633 Club, the small room in the front that had fallen into disrepair, was where Marilyn Monroe tossed dice with Frank Sinatra. The visits by the Ramones, where the band warmed up with a trap case for a drum and an unplugged electric guitar happened in that same room. The orders from Johnny Thunders' manager were to let him have coke but not heroin. An early soundcheck by the Replacements that was some of the best music I ever heard, only to watch the band sink into an alcoholic horror show where every song had to be connected with the word "Bob". The night we charged Metallica to get in. The classic performances by D.O.A. and the Dead Kennedys.

The hallway opened to an expanse of the main ballroom. The room consisted of a two story ceiling and was covered in warm wood paneling. The room's permanence was anchored by a solid Italian Terrazzo tile floor that included

The Italian Terrazzo tile floor at the JC
photo by Sarah Kuhl

small brass decorative inlays surrounding each tile. The cavernous room was the approximate size of a football field. On the far back wall hung sliding chalk tote boards for recording the latest racetrack results. In the middle of the room hung a four-sided 40s style public address system used to broadcast the actual race results. To the left, as you entered the room, there was a terrace that was built over the bathrooms. The story goes that guards armed with Thompson submachine guns were stationed there to provide security and protection.

Jughead and Billy Blank

The infamous restrooms at the Jockey Club will no doubt be well-documented in this volume, but suffice it to say, one would be hard pressed to find a more disgusting, unsanitary, sickening collection of plumbing fixtures anywhere. Both the restrooms reeked permanently of urine, including a toilet often filled with empty beer cans. The walls were covered with graffiti of all sorts that added a permanent record of the temporary musings of the clientele that were desperate enough to enter these facilities. It is written that Hercules' fifth labor entailed changing the courses of two rivers in order to clean out the Augean Stables. Such Herculean effort would have to have been deployed in this case.

Never had two more unlikely traditions collided (gambling and punk). This juxtaposition is mirrored in the physical appearances of Shorty and Tiny. Tiny, well over 6'4", had scraggly grey hair and a long beard, reminiscent of Howard Hughes toward the end of his life. In all the time that I knew Tiny, I never saw him in a pair of shoes. Wearing flip flops, his feet were swollen to an outlandish size and color. His toenails grew to a length where they began to curl under his toes. They were a very light shade of green and were the consistency of old wood. I often thought about a photo documentation to be submitted to either a medical journal or "Ripley's Believe or Not!" Shorty, on the other hand, was much better groomed and

The Flamingo in neon

well dressed. From his short sleeved, white dress shirt, to his empire waist black dress pants, those two were quite a pair. I always had the impression that it was a case of blind luck that brought Bill, Clem and I together with the Mincey brothers. But once we had made our pact, the sheer energy and inertia grew into one of the most satisfying chapters of my life. After the first year or so, there would be no turning back. We compiled a record of shows that truly stood the test of time.

Jughead

I graduated and have received degrees from four universities in the Cincinnati area. As Mark Twain famously remarked, "I have never let my schooling interfere with my education". Some of the most valuable lessons I have learned in life, I learned at the Jockey Club. While on some nights the club could be wildly popular and hold close to 1000 people, there were other nights that there were very few patrons. It is on those quiet nights that I had a chance to sit and listen to the many stories that Shorty enjoyed telling.

The most important thing Shorty taught me was how to read people, how to size a person up. How to figure out their motivation. Why is this person coming into the club? When you can figure out what the people want, the price for that commodity goes up. If you can consistently deliver on that promise you can make a lot of money on that margin.

So in the beginning what we were selling was the idea of the Jockey Club.

The money is definitely at the bar!
photo by Sarah Kuhl

Things That Shorty Taught Me

The money is at the bar. Music never pays its bill, music is a loss leader, the money in the entertainment business is at the bar, and alcohol is king. Thirst things first, what are you drinking tonight?

Read people's motivations and give them a chance to buy a little piece of a dream. People love to spend money and have a good time when they are out on the town. A good example was the Halloween costume party in the early years. This was quite an event. It gave the gays and everyone else a chance to dress up in their psychosexual personas. When you have a 6', 200 lb. guy in drag flipping twenties for drinks, that got Shorty's attention. The same goes for the really monster shows, people loved to see and be seen, to be part of a larger scene. When that sort of thing happened, Shorty realized the potential for the success of the club.

Everyone has their weakness. Find out what the people want. While Shorty was in prison in La Grange, Kentucky, the powers that be would come and get him, and drive him up to Newport to deal cards on Fridays and Saturdays and then return him to prison. Shorty used to kid me about being a college graduate. "Well, let me tell you a story about when I was in college, Jughead." By college, Shorty meant the Kentucky State Prison at LaGrange. On a number of occasions, he proudly told me of a period in his life when, while in prison, an official state car would pick him up on Friday and drive him up to Newport. Shorty would spend Friday and Saturday nights dealing cards at a high stakes poker game attended by the high-rollers. When the game closed down, early Sunday morning, the same state car would arrive to take Shorty back to LaGrange. He knew he was a good dealer and he used that to his advantage. Shorty was always very good at capitalizing on someone else's weakness. This is one of the reasons that the Jockey Club was so popular because Shorty had the vision and the wherewithal to seize all the opportunities that punk rock presented. All our favorite indulgences were milked; music, alcohol, casual sex, drugs, and the appeal of the Bohemian lifestyle, were in the mix in this wide-open scene. How I long for those days. In the Broadway musical "Brigadoon", the mythical Scottish village appears for one night. I have often dreamed that I too might sit with Shorty down at the Jockey Club, if only for one night.

Patronize your patrons. One of the things I enjoyed most was the running commentary about the collection of "sick fucks" that came through those doors. As Shorty and I were collecting the cover charge, we were never without a drink compliments right off the top of that night's take. Shorty was always nice to everyone's face, but would interject hilarious comments about each patron once they were out of earshot and into the big room. "There ain't no bitches in here fit to fuck", "The queer bait is out early tonight", "Watch out for the bitches with kickstands." The constant objectification of women mixed with that hardboiled Newport nightlife cynicism was hard to take, but Shorty lived his life by his rules. This was one of the reasons that the Jockey Club worked on some many levels, no one could tell Shorty what to do and we tried to follow his lead. There was only one rule; there are no rules.

Make your deal when you have to, but get money out of everybody. Nightly it was our job to collect as much money at the door as possible. This meant that we would never turn down underage patrons or young girls with little money. If any of the underage "end of innocence" types thought that they could use their charm and powers of persuasion to beat the admission, they were mistaken. Shorty realized that there would be many willing guys ready to buy as many drinks as these girls could consume. Those little "bitches" bring in more money. We would never turn anyone away. We would always get money out of their pockets. Shorty would always say, "If you knock the price down a buck or two, those people will always spend every cent they have. Just get 'em through the doors and we'll take the rest of their money later." See above.

Never show your cards. In the old days, Shorty had a front for a brothel and guys would come thinking they were going to see the prostitutes. While waiting, Shorty was dealing cards, and the men got suckered into playing cards while waiting for the whores who were nonexistent. The story was that the rich guy upstairs was monopolizing the attention of the girls so they had to wait. After a while, they would just get tired and go home, but not before Shorty had taken some of their money. Many a night, we would tell the patrons that the band were on its way, even if we had not heard from them. We never showed our cards.

"Your money looks like shit, Jughead." Since my father died at

Jughead with SS-20

8

an early age, Shorty was a father figure to me. Early on, when I started there, my bills would be out of order, and it was a general mess. Shorty taught me to keep the largest bills at the back and keep everything facing to the front. He only really had to tell me that once, and what he said was, "Your money looks like shit, Jughead." On other occasions, during big shows, the bar would be swamped. I was the only one that Shorty would ever let work behind the bar. I always took that as one of the highest compliments that Shorty could give me, and I was happy that Shorty put his trust in me.

The term "Old School" has become popular of late, but if that term ever fit, it surely fit for Shorty. There was never any question about who was in charge at the Club. Shorty would always carry a large flashlight. If someone got out of line, Shorty would never suffer fools gladly. He would warn you once and if you were foolish enough to continue to act like an idiot, Shorty would brandish the flashlight like a billy club and "let it fly". "I will split that motherfuckers head wide open." Shorty could be brutish and violent when the circumstances called for it. I like to think I patterned some of my stage personae after him.

Live for the clip. Shorty was a master at staying focused on making money. He taught me that the reason the Club worked was because he could maximize the chances, "Jughead, in this business you live for the clip. Take in as much money as you can when you have the chance." Shorty was never happier than at the end of a big night, and there was not one can of beer left in the coolers. When Bill and I would fail to make a guarantee for an out of town band on a slow night he would always bankroll the operation because he trusted that there would always be big shows that would bring out the crowds. I like to

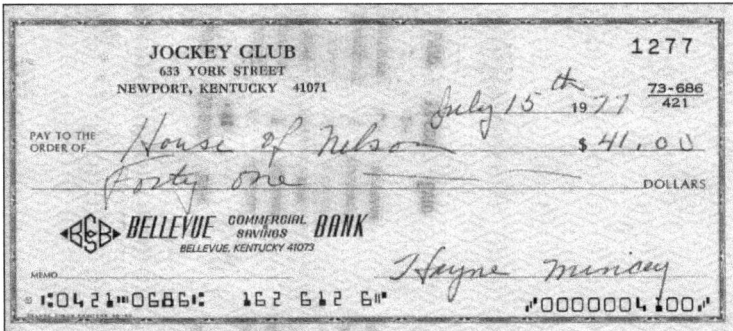

Jockey Club check signed by Tiny, 1977
check courtesy of Jerry Adams

think that we brought him some purpose and happiness to his later years. The Jockey Club was such an amazing success because of the amazing group of people who were part of the whole experience, the patrons, the bands, and the people who helped us build a truly remarkable scene. The whole deal was just preposterous enough to work, and work it did.

Here is the most important thing that Shorty taught me, "Never back down one fucking inch, take it like a man, and be a man."

Jimmy Davidson aka Jimmy D

Shorty had his summer gun. When it was shirt sleeve time he would keep a .25 caliber automatic pistol in his shirt pocket with his cigarette pack. In the winter he would carry a .38 in his jacket. Those were pea shooters compared to the "hog's leg" that Tiny kept behind the bar. A single action .44-40 Colt. That thing made Dirty Harry's .357 Magnum look downright wimpy! At first this made me a little nervous as I sat there at the table checking IDs and collecting the cover charge. A man with a gun sitting to my left was a new experience for me but hey, I figured if some crazy ass hillbilly started some shit, all I had to do was get my 6-foot, 185 lb. 23- year-old, punk rock super star hero with a bad hair cut self behind that short, fat, old man with his pants pulled up to his arm pits before I peed myself and let him protect me!! Then I came to realize fuck the guns, fear the flashlight! I never actually saw ether one of them pull a gun on anybody. My friend and band mate, Rick Sims, had told me a story about some stupid ass that had tried to rob the bar once and how Tiny had emptied a pistol into him. Starting with the first bullet in his leg, the next in his balls, then two more in his gut, the fifth in his shoulder, the sixth shot just missed his head. The police, when they arrived to sort out the mess, are supposed to have razzed Tiny about missing the last shot and offering to let him use the police target range to brush up his skills. Now I did see Shorty whack a head or two with his flashlight! The flashlight in his hand made me feel a lot safer sitting out there with a handful of money than knowing he had a gun in his pocket.

Shorty and I sat at a table just about halfway between the front door and the doorway to the ballroom, not quite across from the old front lounge known as the wet room, "the dressing room" or whatever needed to be done room. Actually we were a little closer to the bar than the front. He finally explained why we sat there and not closer to front like other clubs would set their doormen. When people came in they had to take 20 or 25 steps to get to us. They would feel stupid if they turned around and left. In that time they would pre-sell themselves on whatever we had to tell them and practice whatever line of bullshit they planned to try on us. Plus it gave us a chance to size them up. They had fully committed themselves to their role, to get into

"The Legendary Jockey Club," home of real rock and roll with a side punk attitude! So we had to play our parts. Shorty would scare the shit out of you with his casual disgusted glance that summed up the rules of the house: come in, have fun, don't be an asshole, spend your money, then leave! My job was to get your money. In the process make sure you felt like you were having an authentic experience on the wild side, becoming a real punk rocker or groupie or tourist there to look at the freaks and make sure you got your money's worth. Yeah, I know that's a fake ID from a college that doesn't exist, I know that's your big brother's driver's license (yes, because I know your brother, you idiot!), and of course I know that's a shoppers' club membership. But most of all, we played our part by listening to your crazy ass story about leaving your ID in your other jeans or your lame tale about how "I know I'm on the guest list" because the band slept on my cousins stepmom's ex-roommate's best friend's daughter's boyfriend's drummer's floor the last time they played New York!!!!??! Cut to the chase. The cover is $3 for tonight's entertainment. Yes, we only take cash! And, no, that's right, you heard me, only American money! Now stick out your hand and let me stamp it. By the way, ladies, all that flirting was appreciated, sometimes more by Shorty than me. In the end though, I really just wanted the cash. We had to pay the band. They came from far away...

Money, cigar, Bud

How many punk rock kids does it take to change a light bulb? Just one, with 326 "friends" on the guest list!

One night Shorty started telling me this story about when he ran a whore house with girls as opposed to the brothel he ran that didn't have any girls. I have no idea why he felt the need to share this with me. Out of the blue he starts talking about, "After the war, the soldiers when they got back from France, started wanting to get their peckers sucked." My reaction is, well, of course! Doesn't everyone? He goes on in detail to explain, "At that time, girls in Newport didn't do that kind of thing, just regular fuckin' was all." Ok, where is he going with this? I know he's been in prison, but huh?! He continues, "They finally figured out they was missing out on a lot of easy money. But, if the other girls found out that you would "suck-a-dick" (is that like whack-a-mole?), they would stop associating with that girl and make her keep her own plate, bowl, knife, fork, spoon, cup and saucer and drinking glass separate from everybody else's stuff. She couldn't wash them in the same dishwater as the others and they wouldn't let her eat at the table with the rest of them." My first thought was, why do whores have full table settings? We were interrupted by a group of paying customers so I never got to find out where he was heading with that particular memory. I guess Johnny Thunders said it best, "You can't put your arms around a memory." But he didn't mention anything about lips!

Brian Moore

One of my favorite memories of Shorty was when my band had already loaded in our equipment for the night and was just hanging out in the club hours before we were to play. I was wandering around the club with nothing to do when I decided to go into the front room, that was I think "off limits" to most

Active Ingredients

of the club patrons or something like that. There sat Shorty smoking his cigar, relaxing in the atmosphere we all remember. I sat next to him and struck up a conversation with him about what the Jockey Club was like "back in the good old days" when it was a full tilt gambling and dance hall. He got this far away look and twinkle in his eyes, paused a minute and told me, I remember when those big limos would pull up out front and the classy dames would get out dressed in their best outfits and jewelry, and after them would step out some important dude (gangster type I'm guessing) sporting his finest suit or tuxedo. Then another big Cadillac would pull up and another sharp dressed couple would exit, making a scene as they went into the club. Then there would be a limo with a bunch of big time gangsters walking into the club, always looking

Active Ingredients 7", "Bringing Down the Big Boys"

around for something that might happen. He also said there was always some celebrity type (I seem to remember him mentioning Marilyn Monroe) hiding out in the club, looking to lose some money or get in trouble. Shorty had this far away look that took me back to those outlaw times and I got a little glimpse into how the old club must have looked in its prime.

Celene Black

Shorty's hearing amazed me. No matter what band was playing, how loud the band played or even if it was the music played between sets, he never got a drink order wrong.

To have a conversation with someone during those times you had to scream, go out to the front lobby or into the women's restroom (which inevitably was flooded).

Order a Foster's oil can, that's what I got. Order a Bud, that's what I got. Order a 7-up (to go with the gallon of Heaven Hill that I snuck in), that's what I got. Not once did I get "what?", "huh?" or a wrong drink order. Thanks, Shorty.

Jimmy D (for Bill Craig)

My drummer friend, Bill Craig, gave this second hand Shorty story to me. I think it says a lot about Shorty's view of the world...

Just before us crazy punk rockers invaded the Jockey Club, the bands would play four sets a night and be booked for the whole week. Bill played in one of those bands. So Bill tells me about coming to play one particular evening. When he gets to the Club, there is a car on fire in the parking lot. It was fully engulfed in flames, ready to explode, smoke rolling skyward in big black plumes. Bill hurries into the club and tells Shorty, "THERE'S A CAR ON FIRE IN THE PARKING LOT!!" Shorty replied in his deadpan snarl, "I don't drive".

William Gilmore Weber

Jimmy Davidson and I were hangin' out one night, doing some bar hopping. We decided to make the trek down to the Jockey, even though we both knew there was no band billed for that evening. The bar was basically empty except for Shorty, Tiny and a few others sitting at the bar. A few minutes after we arrived, Tiny got up and went to the restroom. Jimmy and I sat and had a few and then decided

Jimmy D and Bill Weber
photo by Allegra Nicodemus

to leave. We didn't notice that Tiny never came out of the john the rest of the time we were there. The next day we found out that after we left the bar, Tiny was taken to the hospital and later that evening...died.

16

The Ghost of Tiny
by Jim Cole

I walk into the JC. 'bout 9:00 pm Friday getting ready to do a soundcheck and needin' a drink badly, having not slept since Tuesday. I heard that Tiny died a week or two ago and as I walk up to the bar, I see that the barmaid--a cross between Elvira and the ghost of Patsy Cline--is counting the

JC bar
photo by Jerry Adams

register. Not a good omen at all. I ask for a Foster's, she asks for a buck and a half, I tell her it's free at least that's the way Tiny ran the deal with me. She gets a serious look on her face, stares me in the eyes and says, "Tiny died, honey, that'll be a dollar fifty". OK, so that's what kind of night it's gonna be.

We finish our first set and I actually play pretty good. When you're that fried and sleep-deprived, it's easier to concentrate, not enough energy to become distracted. I'm walking toward the back of the Club, and Clifton's biggest coke dealer and one of his goons escort me into the men's room. After all of the gigs I've done here, it's only the second time I've ever been in the john and these two find out why. The stench, the filth, the dark corners, the graffiti, the thick green film that has covered everything...anyway they think I owe them two hundred clams on a long since forgotten eight ball and wanna shake me down for it. I make some vague promises, they're not buyin' but are so repulsed by the place they vow to catch up with me later and promptly split.

So I'm gettin' ready to do the second set but pop into the "wet room" first to freshen up with some neighborhood sharpshooters. LORDHAVEMERCY, this set takes off like a runaway freight train but by the 5th song I want more,

more than this place can ever provide. Then I see her outta the corner of my eye. She's with a couple of her friends, they're all dressed in black, got their Biba black nail polish on, the whole deal. And, they all have that pale white death pallor. I wonder, is that done cosmetically or does it come from deeper within? Do they believe this punk ethic mythology bullshit or is it just the flavor of the month? Anyway, underneath all that black and ghost-white, this one's got a lot of color, for sure. Third verse of the sixth song, do I have a solo here(?), I do now, and I'm sendin' it her direction. Tryin' to get paid from Billy and A-a-a-a-ce, never gettin' it straight, I'm bettin' she's got a visa or a master or at least an atm card. There may be hope after all...

Steve "Snare" Arnzen

No Jockey Club obituary would be complete without mention of Shorty's brother and co-JC owner, Tiny.

Bud, Jughead and Hayne "Tiny" Mincey at the bar
photo by Jakki Repellent

I never got to know him that well. Most remember him for his beard that he refused to shave until after Reagan was out of office. That seemed to fit in well with the music and clientele of the club.

I don't think he was quite as easy going as Shorty was about things. I'll never forget him tending bar at a Circle Jerks show with his Circle Jerks "Golden Shower Of Hits" t-shirt on or him giving me a dirty look for applauding Bevo and The Fastbats when they chased the 20 or so people in attendance out the door with their barrage of acid noise. He was part of what made it happen too even though he passed away about a year and a half in. He took care of the bar while Shorty handled the door in the early days.

Fastbats with the Reduced
flyer courtesy of Art D

Whenever I drink a cup of White Castle coffee I think of Tiny. He drank it all the time.

Tiny R.I.P

The Jockey Club located at 633 York St.,Newport,KY,is only 7 blocks from downtown cincinnati,ohio. Established in 1948 and first known as the 633 Club and next the Flamingo.The Jockey Club has known all types of gambling including bookmaking and horse-racing and even once a fatal shooting.The huge faded red and green remnants of a neon sign bearing the words "Flamingo-633"still have bullet holes from a 1950's shooting incedent. Behind the backdrop for the stage there are numerous art deco jockeys-and yes they're still riding their horses.

The J.C.,as it has been dubbed,was in the 1950's the largest public performance hall in the cinti area. It has known such famous greats as Jerry Lee Lewis,Ck Berry,Little Richard and his cape carrying entourage of 6,The Isley Bros. w/guitarist Jimi Hendrix and undoubtedly an up and coming starlet named Marilyn Monroe.

Today the Jockey Club is the "scene" for the alternative music crowd of cinti and northern KY. It can be truthfully stated that the J.C. is the entertainment mecca of the midwest,sporting a record of most current national act bookings in the midwest.There is always local music,too.Rumour has it that an elite few consider the Jockey Club a religious shrine...If one looks closely enough, the pink flamingos are still flying over the doorway.Just what type of freakshow lies behind the also pink door?

Usually it is worth the menial never over $5 cover to get into the door.Drinks are cheap,too.I've never seen a cooler with such a great selection of reasonably priced beer.

Most recently,Tiny,one of the two origional J.C. owners passed away. His share of the business is carried on respectively by his brother,Shorty. Shorty is found at the door smoking cigars and conversing with the local punkers.Tiny was an age 60ish man who was known for several things,the most prevolent being his long white beard which he began to grow the

moment Regan took office and vowed never to shave off until Regan was out. He also had the the ability to inter-mingle w/the freaks and punks,was a great bartender and could even tell the difference between the good bands and the bad ones. The man had been there from day one and was a valuable source of information concerning the history and events of the Jockey Club. He is sadly missed and as it was stated in SUB-CIN, "The Jockey Club has lost a valuable asset."

In closing one should note that through all the trivia and interest-ing past that the J.C. is most definitely the place for any type alternative music:hardcore,wave, artsy fartsy,blues,and upon occai-son reggae.The people of the cinti area do not realize what they have w/in their grasp as far as the bounds of entertainment reach.It is a known fact that many people(from girls to businessmen)are afraid to step foot in the door, because of a conservative fear of punks which has been blown out of proportion by the local media(propaganda pushers).

Since the begining of the new music scene the Jockey Club has known no physical violence-so Shorty assures. It is safe-get it-safe.If your band wants to play there,contact Billy Blank(an infamous character)bet-ween the hours of 4pm to 6pm e.s.t. at 606-441-5724.

Article by a.a., p.o. 3529 cinti,oh 45201 - a total punk too.freak(or so he thinks....) 4-21-84

Tribute to Tiny, Jerry Adams

Wendy Darst

I fell in love with "The Lights of Cincinnati" before I ever made it across the river. That sweep of hills on the shore as you come in had me nailed in 1981 at 16, heading down from Indiana in my Chevette for no good reason. Compared with the bucolic suburban spread of most of Indianapolis, Cincinnati was dramatic, all these Charles Dickens row houses and vertical drops, romantic in the extreme.

The Jockey was the cherry on this sundae. Holy crap, a giant club with all the bands you want to see…AND THEY WILL LET YOU IN?!?!?!? Not even looking at your fake ID, what Becky Boyd amended with a sharp pencil? As long as you have as much as a bag full of pennies? Oh, hell yes, the Jockey was the promise land, to be sure. Newport looked the part, as you came across the water from OTR or Clifton or where ever, getting progressively more excited as the motel loomed on your right at the end of the bridge, stopping at the liquor store in the boxcar for supplies…on your way to see whatever amazing thing. Whether it was local, or famous, or some poor shmoes in a van with only me and Shorty there (or so it seemed) it was always memorable. This is not to say that I remember it all. I don't, and I'm not going to look at the show list to even try. I'm going to get a beer (it should be a Foster's oil can, but something else is going to have to suffice) and spew it out, spew it out like the overrunning men's toilet at the Ramones show, with poor hapless Metallica standing in the lake in front of the bar as Kentucky's finest walk on by without a word. Because my Jockey Club memories are some of the favorite ones I have, as vague as they may be.

The Jockey was legend from the get go. We had really great things happening in Indiana, with the all ages shows at Crazy Al's and the Art Academy and all, so I was lucky enough as an adolescent to get some exposure to live punk rock. It ate my brain. I didn't want to do anything other than go to shows and listen to records, and the Jockey sounded like some kind of emerald city. We would converge from all points…I had moved to Muncie for school, people would come from New Castle, Bloomington, Lafayette to make the holy pilgrimage to the Jockey. We would go to Chicago for shows as well, but, feh. The Jockey was so much more fun…I guess it must have been the magic of Shorty. Shorty has assumed some kind of mythic Lord of the Rings style proportions in my mind, his indeterminate age belied by the strength of an ox, crazy awe inspiring rumors of gangster drama and high stakes cards in secret upstairs spaces, the ruined glory of the front bar (Brix says to Mark E Smith and everyone, "We have a clock like that…in our bedroom!"), and the stories of the place itself. Speakeasy! Hendrix! Roller Rink! Whatever, the checkerboard expanse of that giant floor is so enmeshed in my brain with music, with super powerful music, that I've tried to recreate the experience almost everywhere I've seen a show since. Shorty was the keeper of the kingdom with his toad-like countenance, there behind the bar…slow to anger but immovable in execution.

The first show I remember attending there was the Minutemen. D. Boon moving across the stage as if on wings, like his bulk was inflated from within by the amazing sounds he was making. Next one I remember was Saccharine Trust and Black Flag. I was a complete moron. I sat next to the flexing Rollins at the side of the stage and blathered inanities at him. He refused to respond, or acknowledge me, to his credit, as I moved on to throwing things at Saccharine Trust like some kind of troglodyte. They were way over my head. I was totally unable to grasp what they were doing. And I was tore. Later in the evening during Black Flag, someone picked me up and tossed me onstage like so much trash, likely to get me out of the way so I wouldn't get trampled or get in the way any more than I already had. I almost drowned in the sweat on that stage.

I'm not sure at what point it became imperative for me to close the physical distance between me and the Jockey. It was after the Battle of the Garages for sure, with the Mad Violets and Prime Movers, after Gang Green around New Years, after Lords of the New Church maybe, after a million initial band shows, after throwing a toaster at one of my roommates for not giving me a seat in her car on one of the many drives down…anyway it just had to be.
I quit school and moved to Cincinnati in 1985 with $35 in my pocket and the assumption that Aaron Graham had told his mom Diane about my imminent arrival. I was wrong. I took up residence with them across from Trivets and Big Joe's 927 as a sort of squatter, getting a job ASAP and paying her what I could, bless her for being accommodating. Granted I was out of there within a few months, living high on my salary from the Wendy's on Race Street in an apartment on Spring Street behind SCPA but that's another story.

Our spiritual home was at the Jockey, either in front of the stage or in the Women's room.

Steve "Skinhead Stevie" Hull
photo by George DuChaine

Many was the time I would be given directives by Shorty or Bud, "Keep the guys out of the bathroom." "Handle skinhead Stevie." This made me feel really important, though I'm sure they were telling Allegra or Amy the same thing, and how the hell was I going to make anyone do anything? Where the hell else were we going to smoke up besides the ladies?! The men's was gross. No matter. The ladies room of the Jockey was the clubhouse, and I had the plumbing to be in there! But most of all, and in all seriousness, it was, "Keep YOUR BOYFRIEND out of the bathroom." Aaron barely conceded to being my boyfriend, let alone went where I told him, but we all tried to tell him his days were numbered. He was being faced with banishment, banishment from the Jockey. A fate worse than… anyway, remember when it seemed like either D.O.A. or MDC was playing there every five minutes? Well, I'm pretty sure it was at a D.O.A. show that the hell broke loose.

Aaron was in full on spazz mode, all with the hair flying, the crazy face and the eyeliner, gabbing away, running in and out of the ladies', unintentionally taunting Shorty and Bud at the bar though they had told him a hundred times to stay out of there. There they sat, waiting always like crocodiles. Shorty's eyes half lidded, elbows planted, Bud facing the bar, like he's not even monitoring the ladies. And then they had had it. They'd had enough disrespecting of their dictates.

Shorty whipped either the giant flashlight or the bat out from under, and Bud right behind, they stormed into the bathroom like all hell, picked Aaron up by the belt and the back of the shirt like he was no more than a roll of old mangy carpet, hauled him all the way to the front door and tossed him out without breaking so much as a sweat. 86'ed. Done for. Banished. Quelle horreur! What scandal! Ok. I laughed so hard. It was amazing to see Shorty and Bud show what they are capable of, under those somnolent exteriors lurked…well, just don't fuck with them. Just like all the rumors said. He got back in eventually.

I'm sorry I never knew Tiny.

Entering the Jockey was often reminiscent of the Shining. This big carpeted space, formerly glorious, formerly some shade of red, manned by Bud at a card table. Past that portal, I remember seeing, in no particular order: the Cramps, the Ramones, the Fall, Johnny Thunders, Flipper, Scratch Acid,

Charlie Pickett
photo by Chuck Byrd

Killdozer, Hüsker Dü , Big Black, Green River, Legal Weapon, Tex and the Horseheads, Charlie Pickett and the Eggs, Popdefect, Agnostic Front, Angst, Agitpop, Love and Rockets, Squirrelbait, NOTA, Active Ingredients, SS-20, El Kabong, Eugene Chadbourne, and the Meatmen, as well as the bands I mentioned earlier…and still regret NOT seeing St. Vitus. I flat out can't remember everything I saw, but dammit if, like missing St. Vitus, it was always a mistake NOT to go if ANYONE was playing. I remember spinning alone in the middle of that giant checkerboard floor, not a care in the world other than maybe a little regret for the band playing that I was nearly the only one there.

I could go into detail about possibly regrettable things, about things like playing there in Manwich on Halloween or so (if you can call being propped up dressed as a mummy behind a keyboard performing), or Bud groping my flat chest at the card table (geez, Bud! Cut it out!), or doing a face plant into my broken beer bottle at Legal Weapon (and emerging completely unscathed!), or the Hüsker Dü stage dive that ended with me opening my eyes to see that floor, two inches from my face and suspended by the ankles (one of the finest caught me, flipped me to my feet, and saved me from certain death or disfigurement as if it were no more than putting out a smoke). Or I could talk about that last night when the juke box and everything else was dismembered, the bicentennial beers were long drank, and the 45s and chairs flew through the air. I still have two of the glass bricks from the demolition to this day, and remember being offered one of the toilets (uh, no, thanks). I still hear Charlette, out on the floor in the midst of the bodies on any given night, in a plain skirt, banging her hands together and shouting, "Better than Stravinsky! Better than Stravinsky!!!!!!!!"

I'll close with my all time favorite memory of Shorty. Riding there in Bill's Manwich hearse (I think), walking into a quiet place thinking there might be a show, to find Shorty dozing, straddling a chair with his upper arms and chin propped on the back, face bathed in the glow of a TV up on the cigarette machine. And there on the TV, is Sissy Spacek as the Coal Miner's Daughter. All the cavernous space around is dim, just the TV and the light from behind the bar illuminating Shorty at peace. No show tonight.

View from the Stage

This fantasy says all I have to say about the Jockey Club being as how everyone else had said everything anyway, this is my thought.
—Bevo

Uncle Dave Lewis

1982
Sometime in mid-March

Scott Lees calls me up during the day and says, "Hey do you want to come with me and have a beer at the place we're going to play in a couple of weeks?" I was surprised for a number of reasons; Scott would normally be at work, and I wasn't aware of any gig we were supposed to be playing, though we were playing a lot of them then, so in a sense that wasn't too unusual. As usual, I was unemployed and slackin' it at my parents' house, so I said "Sure, why not?"

Scott picked me up and we drove across the bridge into Newport. This was the first time I'd ever seen the Jockey, all peeling paint, warped paneling and whitewashed former pink flamingos darting across its façade in a semi-animated fashion. Tiny served us at the bar; I wouldn't meet Shorty for the first time until we played there. Scott explained that he had seen a crummy metal band play this bar and happened to ask its owner for a gig, and the owner said "ok." I was a little spooked by Newport, even during the day, but agreed it would be a good idea. Because of our musical style and notorious reputation we couldn't get any gigs in bars in Cincinnati where we might make some money, and were reduced to playing a round of art gallery openings and parties. We [11,000 Switches] played our first show there on March 31-April 1, along with Hospital Records' sister groups BPA and Cointelpro.

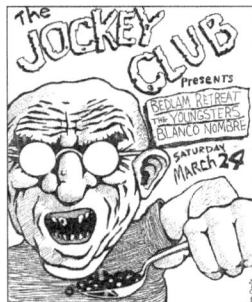

Bedlam Retreat, The Youngsters
with Blanco Nombre
flyer by Mike Davis

I agree that the "legendary" Jockey Club didn't really get underway until Bill Leist and Clem Carpenter came in September and established punk/alternative shows at the Jockey as a regular routine. However, in terms of discovering the Jockey Club as a venue for those kinds of acts, I think Scott Lees – who was in Blanco Nombre also, and moved away from Cincinnati in 1987, never to return - deserves credit. There were times during the following summer where we were having trouble finding work, and

Scott would pipe up and say, "Well, you know we can play the Jockey Club anytime we want." I was incredulous; we were being barred and bounced out of venues right and left, and that kind of colored my perspective towards booking in general – we didn't play the Jockey again until the beginning of September, just before Bill and Clem came in. What I didn't understand about the Jockey was that Shorty really didn't care what kinds of acts played there; to have any band on any night was more likely to bring people to the bar than on the many undoubtedly lonely, quiet nights that there was no entertainment.

September 5

I don't remember The Effigies, the group Lopez Sophisticates opened for on September 5. Lopez was a two-man outfit with me and Greg Fernandez (Good Cue Sign, Weird Lovemakers with Mark Gunderson) although Greg was the principal songwriter. That show was one in a million – it was the first full-length show we played, and we were struggling with the motley assortment of record players, cassette decks and rhythm machines, yet nevertheless singing along like a couple of happy idiots. We played early to the locals, and they really hated us. We did Greg's song "How to Win Girls through Hypnosis," which was performed to a tape of a Magnus chord organ and the sound of a pencil hitting a Styrofoam cup – "Honey you're beautiful, honey you're wonderful, you're getting sle-ee-ee-ee-eee-py." Meanwhile, the locals had reverted to the jukebox, "Oh Playy Meee Some Mountain Muu—sic."

November 10

It was a big deal for Clem to land D.O.A. for the Jockey the first time. D.O.A. had tried to play Cincinnati before at The Pit in July 1980, and some drunk chick fell down the stairs and pulled the fire alarm on her way down. That set off the sprinkler system and brought the fire department – end of show. I remember talking to Joey in the parking garage; although they got a token payment from the club, he was pissed about what he was out in comin' down and didn't want to play Cincinnati again.

December 23

Lunch Buddies was Chuck Cleaver's early, pre-Ass Ponys group with Walt Hodge and Dan Kleingers. They were wonderful, and I remember this show still real well; can almost hear "Shriek of the Mutilated" in my brain, forever there imprinted.

1983

Sometime in 1983 or 1984

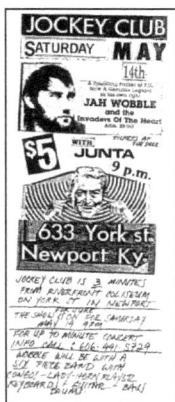

JC flyer with Jah
Wobble and more

Jah Wobble's Invaders of the Heart play the Jockey. I was on sound, and man that was a lot of inputs for our snake! Steve Shedroff was there that night, photographing as usual. Steve and I never did get along, and he and I got into some snit about something, and I told him off, big time. Jah Wobble came and actually shook my hand; he said something like "That was the best slaggin' off I ever heard anyone give anybody, mate!"

Some months later, Steve – who was often very red in the face – died suddenly of a heart attack. He was one of the most prolific photographers to work at the Jockey. Despite being complimented by my idol, Jah Wobble, I really wish I could take that all back – I still feel bad about it.

August 16-17

One of my favorite bands, Arkansaw Man from San Francisco, came to play two weekend nights at the Jockey Club. I think I'm probably the only person in Cincinnati who has any idea who they are. I plaster the town with posters and try to talk up the band; the 'Switches can't play because we are on hiatus. Hardly anyone showed up for either night, but the music was genuinely great.

Late 1983

I remember well Junta's first shows at the Jockey. Instant competition – they were different, original and good. Damn!

Bevo
photo by Witt

1984

January 1984

It's not on the list, but I played with my brother Chris in Fastbats, an ad hoc jam band led by Bevo Ruzsa before the advent of Human Zoo. I think Pedro Dux may have been on that date as well; I do recall that we had no drummer and played to a rhythm machine. Anyway, there was practically no crowd, but there was a tooth-challenged hillbilly woman, small in stature but huge as a whale, in a filthy muu-muu dancing around to our music; she seemed to take a shine to Bevo. She came up to the stage, and up went the muu-muu: she'd had a mastectomy, and there was a massive "X" shaped scar running along her chest with the pitiful remnant of a nipple sticking out of it. Then she turned to the crowd, and we got to see them turn just as white as we had.

Later she was mauling Bevo, singing into the mike – it was all very disturbing. However, that was a classic, patented Jockey Club moment. And I didn't feel so bad about it because I felt the locals were finally getting the gist of us.

Early to Mid 1984

I got a call from the Cincinnati Enquirer and they wanted to interview me for a piece they were doing on the Jockey Club. I wasn't sure why, as I hadn't been there in months at this point, but I agreed to speak to them; I knew they had my phone number. When published, the piece referred to me as "a man who wanders around Cincinnati in a black trench coat" and summarized the article by saying that the Jockey Club was best for people like "me," inferring young adults who had no purpose in life. My mother almost suffered a coronary.

April 25

The Minutemen – great show, not a great turnout though. Perhaps it was at this show that I experienced a classic, Jockey Club moment: some guy gets up to stage dive, throws himself into the crowd – which parts like the red sea before Moses. SMACK! Down goes the dude, landing on his face. And I mean he was **fucked** up; nose smashed, both eyes blacked, his face a ball of blood. By September, the Jockey officially banned stage diving, but that didn't stop some fanatics.

September 29

Seven Seconds put on a great show this night. I didn't expect anything – I wasn't down with hardcore punk at all in 1984 – but I came away really liking them.

December 13

I don't remember if it was this Circle Jerks show or one of the earlier ones – it seems like it was the last one they did at the Jockey – where the cops came in and made themselves known to the kids. It was bad – a lot of head-busting and such. I was there, but I missed all the action because I was making out with a girl in the parking lot at the Jockey – less said about that the better. But once we tried to get back into the club there were like six cruisers spinning their sirens outside the front entrance. My date was brave; she went back in, but I said, "Not for me, thanks."

This incident caused people to stay away from the Jockey for quite some time. Of course, when the big acts came – The Ramones, Cramps etc. – they'd come out, but there were many, many nights at the Jockey when good bands played and only a handful of people were there.

December 16

Flipper was definitely the worst band I ever saw at the Jockey Club. There was no attempt to play a proper song, just a lot of pounding around on instruments and drunken shouting about various things, most of which didn't make a lot of sense. It was a brain-draining drone for about 35 minutes, with added tomfoolery. I can't even certify that Will Shatter was still conscious by the end of the gig, and it pains me to write so, as I'd known Will in San Francisco a little earlier and found myself wondering what the hell was wrong with him and his band.

1985
May 2

I'm not sure why 11,000 Switches isn't listed for this date, but we definitely played, opening for the Dead Kennedys. I had known Jello in San Francisco and he wanted us on one of these two dates, and we opted for the second, less crowded bill. The Switches were definitely on fire that night, and though we played a monthly string of shows that were packed at JR's in Clifton in the months to follow, people for years afterward came up to me to comment how good we were when we opened for the Dead Kennedys. That was a three-piece, no bass, Dan Williams and I with Andrew Hamilton on drums, the so-called "Andrew Power Trio."

May 17

I think this was the Hüsker Dü show I saw; I went because I had a friend who was addicted to the album "Zen Arcade" and didn't want to go alone. I had a cold or something and spent most of the night with my head down on a table. They were loud. There was a girl with a sweet face who was dancing alone and looking at me sympathetically, and got me up to dance with her. I don't even have the dancing skills of say, Oliver Hardy, so I danced a little bit, sucked, and went back to my table. But she was certainly sweet; that was the most Fellini-esque experience I ever had at the Jockey. The turnout – considering both the popularity and importance of the band – was poor.

October 26

Big Black plays the Jockey Club for about 16 people. They still played well, but were not happy about the turnout, and vowed never again to play Cincinnati. They were lured back for a date at the Southgate House in 1987; it was like their second or third-to-last gig. The last one was a couple of days later in Chicago. The Southgate date didn't do well for them either; their equipment malfunctioned, the sound was bad and mostly Steve Albini just yelled "Fuck!" They only played about 20 minutes before giving up.

1986
March 2

Johnny Thunders' second night at the Jockey Club
photo by Witt

Johnny Thunders' second Jockey Club show was better than the first one; he was a little more together and told me he felt bad about the way the first one went. That night he played "You Can't Put Your Arms around a Memory" twice, and the second time the crowd, which had thinned out by that late hour, sang along with the choruses – he was touched by that. I was too; it was like a bunch of misfits getting together and feeling some sense of community among us all. That is one of my favorite Jockey memories.

March 18

The Fall played, and Mark E. Smith was in a really **bad** mood. I wasn't there, but I heard the story that the Jockey staffer given the job to take The Fall back to where they were staying the night got so fed up with Smith's shit that he dropped them off in the middle of the median on I-75. The Fall are often cited for their longevity, but we wouldn't be speaking of them in such terms if they hadn't figured out how to get across the interstate that night.

The Cramps—the most crowded, intense, electrifying out of town act I ever took in at the Jockey. I missed Samhain, and some say that show was more so, but the kind of frenzy that Lux Interior was able to whip up with the crowd is something I've seen nowhere else. That was the Jockey show to die for.

Manwich flyer by Uncle Dave Lewis

Manwich and Human Zoo play the Jockey; it's technically the first show for Manwich, or at least the first one under that name, and with me, on bass. Laura sings with her back to the crowd most of the gig; she's wearing a fur-lined, tiger striped coat in the dead heat of summer and high heels with soles at least a foot thick, tromping around. It's a good show and a promising maiden voyage for Manwich.

Human Zoo also plays and the thing is videotaped by Justin Gibbs; back then, getting a video made of your band is still kind of a rare and novel thing. I had bought the blank, so I wind up with the tape at the end of the night; some months later I loaned it to the Zoo as they wanted to make a cable access show out of it - never got it back, unfortunately. Bevo is performing in a bathrobe with nothing underneath, and at the very end of the show it comes undone. Beev seems just as surprised as many others were, quickly turns away and reties the robe before exiting the stage. It's hard to tell if anything – ahem – private is visible. Before I give the tape up I attach a note to the effect that, "At the very end of the show, Bevo's robe opens up. To be on the safe side, snip that out, or fade it, before you air it."

Some months later, a huge controversy breaks out in the local press about obscenity on cable access. Sure enough, the Zoo hadn't taken out the shot, and community standards-minded, censor happy Cincinnatians are all freaking out because Bevo's penis is being shown on cable. The program – which had already been running in obscurity for months – was pulled, a lot of fingers were pointed, and there were threats of jail time and other recriminations relating to this stupidity lurking in the background for a long time afterward.

October 31

Halloween night with Manwich at the Jockey; Laura finally got to wear her Jem mask for an occasion appropriate for it. We all dressed up, and I'm sure we were a riot to look at – Wendy was a bloody wraith in a diaphanous dress, and some of that blood was real, as earlier that night she tripped over a wire in the back of Playhouse 90 and landed right on her face – her knees and elbows were all scuffed up; poor Wendy was a wreck, but she still got up there and rocked.

1987
February 11

Manwich's third, last and probably worst performance at the Jockey. We lost Laura in the middle of the set, as she crawled off to some corner of the stage and passed out; the rest of the band simply filled out the set playing instrumental versions of the songs. We were incredulous though, that anyone would be able to sleep amid the din that was Manwich. In about a month from that time we would have our best show ever at Bogarts, so this mishap at the Jockey was quickly forgotten.

1988
January

The gigs were usually held on Wednesdays and weekends; not too much action through the week. But then Shorty starts booking bands on Sundays and Monday nights – these were groups like the faux-Snare Mystery Meat or some local metal bands. I would work as many of these nights as I could as I needed the 15-20 bucks I could make, but some of the metal bands that played these off nights were unbelievably atrocious. There was a group called Shocking Pink that played several Sundays and Mondays early in 1988; the best thing I can say about them is that they were funnier than Flipper.

May 5

The 11,000 Switches – proper – did not exist to play the Jockey that night as we had broken up for the final time the previous November. This was actually a date played by Tim Schwallie and I alone; an experimental jam fest that was pretty good in spots, though Tim was still a little nervous playing what was essentially for him a solo set. He's overcome that since! Eugene Chadbourne was a riot at the Jockey; I hadn't seen my friend Ted Rosenthal laughed so hard in years.

Later in the month, perhaps even the May 28 date listed below, I played solo as the Master of Horror, playing tape loops, projecting View Master images on a tiny screen and never visible myself on stage during the performance. It was early and I think three people might have seen it.

May 28

Didjits were from San Francisco and they played Cincinnati several times in the late 1980s; I never did like working for them as the singer – who wore a pink wedding suit and looked a little like Vincent D'Onofrio -- had a shtick where he would act pissed off and toss around the mike stands and things. As a soundman, that seemed personal. Pete would explain again and again, "Listen, this is part of the act." I heard one of their albums and really liked the music. But I never did get used to their show.

May 29

The last night
photo by Dee Snyder

The last night – ugh – doesn't hold any pleasant memories for me, sadly. It was a madhouse, I was running sound and it was very hard to communicate with any of the bands, who were all stressed out – it was a very loaded up slate. So I was working my ass off the whole night, and just getting to the stage to pick up a mike stand that had fallen over was a major deal, winding my way through the crowd. I got hit by a bottle at one point, but that was nothing compared to the way it was when people started tearing the wood paneling down off the walls. The air instantly filled with dust and splinters; I wound up with a splinter in my back that took three years to remove. I began shouting at them to stop it, and this worked for a short while, but then more of the paneling came down until it was all off and onto the floor. Records and slips from the jukebox were scattered everywhere. And even after this disaster, I still had to break all of the sound gear down and load it into Bob Hallas' truck. I didn't even go home first; I walked straight from the Jockey to the Greyhound bus station and took a bus to Columbus for a few days to decompress.

I have always been a firm believer that once you establish a place as your temple, you respect it and leave it as it was before you entered. However, others decided it was a kind of anarchic fun that they could not resist, and would never again have a chance to experience. In such a dense crowd, one wouldn't think that you could single out the perpetrators. Actually, I did – and do – know who instigated that whole thing, a friend of mine at the time. He just said, "C'mon Uncle Dave, they are just going to tear all of this down anyway."

About a month later, the editors of Inkwire asked me contribute a piece on the last night of the Jockey Club. I wrote about 18 pages of some of the most poisonous prose that ever came out of my pen, and submitted it, saying, "You probably won't want to publish this." And I was right; they didn't. I sorely wish I had it still; it was very detailed about the events of that night from the inside, and I'm afraid after twenty years that my memory does not serve me nearly so well. —Uncle Dave Lewis

Greg Fernandez

Friday, 9/3/82
(date confirmed by cassette tape labeled that night)

This was the second Hospital Records weekend at the Jockey Club and the second or third punk weekend. Playing were 11,000 Switches, BPA, and Lopez Sophisticates (David Lewis and I), Friday only.

The Jockey Club had yet to draw punk crowds and the show was sparsely attended. During Lopez's "How to Win Girls by Hypnosis", a song accompanied by a chord organ and Styrofoam cup, a patron played "Mountain Music" on the jukebox. The Oak Ridge Boys are not too audible on the tape but when they are they blend surprisingly well with our song.

Tim Benz

The 11,000 Switches, Cointelpro, and BPA played perhaps the first "punk show" at the JC. When we walked in, the bar was surrounded by a mixture of aged puffy guys in old guy jackets, a scattering of bikers, and a few barflies' of forever indeterminate age. It was like a glorified practice—20 of our closest friends in front of this huge empty space, and another 20

BPA
photo by Witt

people drinking beer at the bar, seemingly oblivious to our presence. Well, maybe not oblivious – They did keep turning on the jukebox to drown us out! At this point in our lives we were used to hostile crowds – indeed, we fed upon them. We'd been egged and spat upon. We once set up on 2nd street and directed improvised noise at unwitting Riverfest attendees who were forced to listen because they were stuck in traffic. We'd plug in and play at parks, and even turned a classroom at U.C. into our "practice space". If there was juice, we'd play. But there was something disconcerting about being ignored by the JC regulars. When we were about to leave we asked the owners -Tiny (a large man who refused to cut his beard until Reagan left office), and Shorty (a diminutive curmudgeon with an ever-present cigar stub in his mouth) what they thought of the show. Shorty snorted "Not loud enough" Then they proceeded to pay us several hundred dollars for playing to 40 people. Needless to say… we were hooked!

Over the years we played there frequently – almost as much as The Reduced and SS-20. Our first "big show" was opening for the Violent Femmes. We'd never heard of them, but then we saw them reviewed in People or Newsweek (who only reviewed five or six records per issue). We thought this could be pretty big. As it turned out, over 700 people were crammed into the JC on a hot Newport night. Before they ran out of beer (yes, they had to drive to a grocery to get more) we were drinking air-raid shelter beer – warm cans of old Riverfest Hudepohl from the basement…vintage 10 years ago. Yum!

Tupelo Chain Sex

We were fortunate that Bill Leist and Pete Wegele let us open for bands we loved. We played a show with Tupelo Chain Sex which featured Don "Sugarcane" Harris on violin and Stumuk on baritone sax. Don had major R&B hits as part of Don and Dewey in the 60s, and played with Harvey Mandel in the Pure Food and Drug Act in the 70s. Harvey perfected the backwards guitar sound and even played with the Rolling Stones. Stumuk was a member of Frank Zappa's touring extravaganza who resembled Tiny just a bit. I was enthralled to be sharing the stage with Sugarcane, one of the heroes from my obscure record collection. Of course, Sugarcane could barely remember Harvey Mandel… as he was a junkie. Instead, he and Stumuk argued over who should be louder all night, constantly telling the soundman to turn the other one down.

Tupelo Chain Sex flyer

Speaking of junkies, we also played with Flipper, of "Sex Bomb" fame, the most nihilistic hunk of scrap metal the west coast ever produced. On record, they were amazing. Live, they were the most tortuous, violence-inducing, claustrophobic mess I've ever experienced. If you didn't want to hurt someone (or yourself), then you weren't human. Of course when singer Bruce Loose taunted us repeatedly with "Play That Funky Music White Boy" after the show, it took considerable peace keeping efforts of guitarist Will Shatter to keep us from pounding him.

While on the subject of opiates, who could forget seeing LAMF with Johnny Thunders? Todd Witt conducted my favorite ever rock interview. Pissing next to the legend in the nasty rot of the JC restroom, Todd asked, "Hey Johnny, what are you opening with"? "Pipeline", said Johnny. Sitting right behind us at this show was a pissed-off looking Sylvain Sylvain (???). Johnny played an unannounced acoustic set the next night, which was recorded and became a perennial in-between acts JC soundtrack — "You Can't Put Your Arms Around A Memory".

We also got to open for the Minutemen. I'll always cherish drinking a Foster's with Mike Watt, and D. Boon was a crazed piston as his feet touched the ground as little as humanly possible as he skronked his way through 40 or so San Pedro haikus. I'd love to see a Muybridge photo montage of Mr. Boon in action!

In the early days my girlfriend Lisa and I went to the JC almost every weekend. Lisa was an effervescent African American with a taste for Prince, Depeche Mode, 1/2 Japanese, and designer clothes. Even though she dressed "better" than the usual JC pit dweller, there were no strangers at the JC. We made new friends every night. Lisa did not drink beer at first though. I remember she once asked Shorty "What is your wine selection"? Shorty said "We've got red… and white". He proceeded to pour her a highball glass of Ernest and Julio's finest white from a cloudy gallon jug that must have been there since the depression. Lisa soon developed a taste for beer.

BPA
photo by George DuChaine

Another famed band we shared a bill with was The Fall, who was touring the U.S. in support of their only "hit" album on this side of the pond, "This Nation's Saving Grace". My brother and I had every Fall album (at this point I think they're up to 30 studio releases), and we really wanted to meet them. But like the Violent Femmes, they closed off the JC "dressing room", (the moldy, dusty, abandoned lounge/pot smoking room, and home of the eternal jar of pickles), so no chit-chat with the acerbic Mark E. Smith! In their rider, they needed a Twin Reverb amp for the drummer, which we supplied. It turns out the drummer was a bit of an arse, saying "Fuck off" to a kid helping him and to our drummer, who took strong offense. Once again, we missed our chance to beat the fuck out of our idols. Unlike Flipper, Brix E. Smith and company rocked the JC stage with a vengeance, (and they are hands-down my favorite band to this day).

Ah, the JC. Where else could you go every weekend without a clue who was playing, and have a 75% chance of hearing a great band, a 90% chance of having fun, and a 40% chance of seeing Snare and the Idiots, hearing SS-20 play "Teenage Radiation", or throwing beer cans at The Reduced? One night we went to a very crowded JC to see the Meatmen of "Crippled Children Really Suck" fame. We'd been

Nolan Benz, BPA
photo by George DuChaine

hitting the $2 Foster's pretty heavy and in the parking lot we saw front man Tesco Vee coming out of the van with some groupies… looking coked out and resplendent in his satyr outfit. He then proceeded to play a ha-ha-aren't-we-funny set of regurgitated N.Y. Dolls-meets-Foghat riffs ad infinitum. We were camped out at the soundboard, a far-piece from the stage, and as the show went on, my friend Tim kept gripping his Foster's can tighter, and his face kept getting redder. Sure enough, during a particular audience-pandering part of the set, Tim launched his oil can in an arc worthy of an Olympian, and lo and behold scored a direct hit on Tesco Vee's devil-horned head. Shorty immediately ran out from behind the bar, pissed beyond belief. It was only by telling Shorty repeatedly, "It's like with Billy and the Reduced…They only feel the show is successful when the fans throw beers", that kept Tim from being banned from the JC forever.

My friends in the Boondocks scored a huge show at the JC opening for The Cramps. They were incredibly nervous about the magnitude of the show, but they did themselves proud, even though singer Greg Cull and bassist Matt "Thing" Becher could only complete the show from their knees, as gravity and Jack Daniel's took their toll. Of course Lux Interior of The Cramps was swilling Jack as well, and apparently destroyed part of the ceiling above the stage with the bottle, but I missed that because I was trying to get my cigarettes back from a young nymphet I barely knew who kept sticking them in her bra and writing obscenities on the back of my t shirt. Trust me; it wasn't as fun as it sounds.

One of the conveniences of the JC was that you never had to ask where the bathroom was. It is with abject horror that I remember a pre-show ritual of one of my band members (better left unnamed). He would drink many rounds of beer and eat the taco salad at the JC's illustrious neighbor…Sylvia's Mexican Restaurant. (I guess William Burroughs/Edward Hopper White Castle nearby wouldn't do?). Of course, the beer, the nerves, and the hot peppers caused a dilemma. What do you do when you have the shits and the only facilities are what to this day should probably be an EPA Superfund Cleanup Site?

We played the last show at the JC which was scheduled to be razed. Right after our set, things took on a far darker tone. Our amps and equipment were "safely" under the tables by the right wall. Gradually, the tables and chairs by that wall were sent flying, the walls were being torn apart, and we barely rescued our gear. The JC faithful started the demolition a bit early! People stole the red chairs. People rescued the black tables. People carefully saved the old horse racing betting panels behind the stage. Hell, somebody probably saved the ancient pickle jar! We were a little shell-shocked as we were crowding into our cars after the show. "I got a chair"…"I got an ashtray". My girlfriend proceeded to produce her souvenir from the greatest rock venue I've ever known: A shit-spattered toilet seat! (Note to the Centers for Disease Control – This relic still resides at the BPA practice space).

In retrospect, the JC crowd was like one big unruly family. In my JC going days, I probably had 50 friends – real friends. Of course, none of them ever had to pay a cover but me!

Vivien Vinyl

Well, everybody is adding their two cents worth about that fine old place that once existed at 633 York Street in Newport, KY. At one time it was one of the finest gambling casinos in the Midwest known as The Flamingo Club, but to those of us lucky enough to be alive and looking for originality in a stale musical scene, it was The Jockey Club.

I played the Jockey Club many times in the early days with THE DENTS, 1980 –'82, and later with ALTERIOR MOTIVES around 1982 and '83. I felt

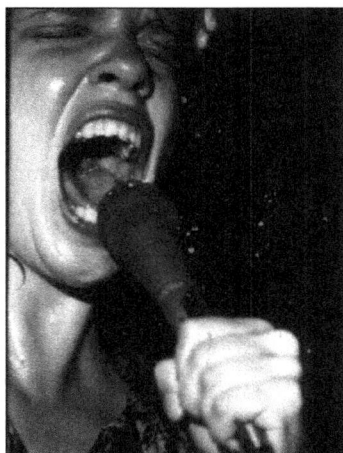

Vivien Vinyl in The Dents

so special because at the time, I seemed to be the only female in a local punk band. (I preferred that my bands be called "new wave" at the time, but that name seems to have been forgotten in the history books). I felt like I was the Queen of the Jockey Club. Two people who added to my self-delusion were Shorty and Tiny. I would walk into the club, tell them that I wanted my usual, and they would make me my gin and tonic without hesitation. How great is that?! They were great guys. I would sit at the bar and ask them what was going on that night, and they would tell me! They always had their finger on the pulse. They would somehow know who was mad at who, who hadn't

shown up, who had been seen leaving with whom, whose romances were on the skids, and all that. They had both spent lots of time in bars and were used to the daily soap operas. They clearly were enjoying it all, and always treated me like an insider and one of their gang.

The place may have been a pit, but the stage was the greatest! I think it was just a bunch of cafeteria tables put together, but it was gigantic and up high, and made me feel as a performer like I was looking down on all the subhumans below me. As the crowd

The Rituals with Alterior Motives flyer

became comfortable in these surroundings, the slam dancing began. The audience would climb onstage and jump off onto the heads and backs of the dancers below. Often they would just splat onto the hard vinyl floor.

The ladies room was not as bad as the men's room. Boy, if walls could talk! And the dressing room for the bands? A little side room that was dark and private. Bill Leist was almost always in there doing some kind of "important" business.

When Jah Wobble from PIL and his band came to play, Bill asked me to go with him that afternoon to his hotel room so Bill could record an interview with him.

Bill and Jah hit it off, and spent a couple hours laughing and carrying on. Bill later broadcast the interview on his radio show on WAIF. I told Jah that I had made chili for the band if they wanted to have a party after their gig, and they were really up for it. We had a full house for the party, but the band discovered that there were no hot peppers in the chili. Much grumbling and disappointment! I thought for a moment that the chili was going to be flying—but order was restored.

On the night that the Circle Jerks performed, I was working the night shift at the local TV station, and I was assigned the duty of shooting a nighttime weather shot to be used under the weather forecast on the 11:00 News. Well, instead, I was hanging out in front of the Jockey Club with the Jerks! When I realized it was getting close to news time, I pulled out my camera and filmed the band leaning against the building. Of course, they were all safety-pinned and spike haired. That night on the News, the anchors said something like, "Oh, I see it was a great night for our—cough, cough—area young people to get together." The only bad part was that the Circle Jerks were expecting to be profiled on our local TV!

I also remember Black Flag coming there. That night was frantic! The band was so wild! The audience acted like they were going to rip the place down! And since there was no place for the bands to ever get away from the spectators, it was a fantastic place to talk to our heroes. Henry Rollins was perfectly willing to do just that.

And going next door to Sylvia's, authentic Mexican food in the middle of the night, was the perfect ending to most unbelievable nights of wildness, as long as you didn't trip over Bill Leist pissing in the parking lot.

And my Jockey Club memories would not be complete without mentioning that, like so many others, I met my future husband there, on June 10, 1983. That means we've been together for 25 years now. If only we could say that about our dear demolished Jockey Club!

Mark Urschel

My Band ModernVending played the Jockey Club two or three times. We were based out of Muncie, Indiana and Linda Busche turned us on to much of the Cincinnati scene. Bill Weber and Pete Wegele were regular visitors to our beloved No Bar and Grill and Pete booked Modern Vending at a bunch of shows in the Cincinnati area. Modern Vending played with the Digits and at the "2nd Annual Scum of Hearts Ball". We played with Human Zoo at one of these shows. Our singer, Duncan, wore a sausage skirt at one show. We loved the JC.

MODERN VENDING

DATURA SEEDS
FROM INDIANAPOLIS, IND.

ELEVEN THOUSAND SWITCHES
FRIDAY, MARCH 27 AT 9 O'CLOCK
3 dollars admission   18 years old and up
JOCKEY CLUB
633 YORK ST.   NEWPORT, KY.

Modern Vending flyer featuring Datura Seeds and 11,000 Switches
flyer courtesy of Mike Stocks

One of my favorite memories is of the guy we fondly referred to as "party dude". He appeared at one of our shows at the JC and was really into partying with us. Not sure who he was or why he took to us but his enthusiasm for the rock and the party was pretty much unmatched by anyone else we have ever met at a show. Must have been the Schnapps.

Duncan from Modern Vending with "party dude"

Jimmy D

One of my favorite shows that I've played in my life (so far) has to be the night of the beer can barrage. I was playing the black Les Paul Custom to right side of Bill with Hap playing bass behind me to my right. Greg was in the back on drums and Rick roamed stage left with a

The Reduced: Hap, Jimmy D, Billy Blank, Rick Sims

SG. Bill was putting on quite a performance. He would spit up to ceiling then wait for it drip back down and catch it back in his mouth. Well most of it anyway, the crowd was getting a little worked up, some moshing and some slam dancing. We were playing pretty darn good that night, like a fine tuned machine. Some over achiever in the crowd decided to toss a beer can at Bill. It must have seemed like the punk rock thing to do at the time. Bill took this action to be a sign of true adoration and invited all of those in attendance that felt that love for the band to share it in a like manner. Soon beer cans began to sail at us like manna from heaven; or at least coins into a wishing well. Now for those of you that may have never been on the stage at The Jockey Club. I need to explain something, the stage lights are aimed at the band so you on the dance floor can see us. This means they shine on our faces which translates to; in our eyes, this along with the house lights being turned off leaves a circle of light around the stage you can see us from anywhere in the room. We can only see the area about 8 to 10 feet in front of the stage and the lights all the way back at the bar. This unfortunately means that a can lobbed at the stage is invisible to the performer looking out into the darkness until that moment that it comes into the light. At the point a can becomes visible you have a split second to see it, decide

The Reduced

Shorty at the bar
photo by James Bramlage

if it's coming at you, then plan your course of action. All of this while you're playing that extra hot, bad ass, melted butter, guitar lick and trying to sing the next line. An empty Bud or Miller can, will only travel so fast and hit you only so hard. Not really a big deal, they don't hurt that bad. But a half full can spinning and spewing as it wings it way toward your head, those get scary. This being the Jockey Club the beer of choice and therefore the can of opportunity was the Foster's Lager "oil can" a 25 oz. steel can with a welded seam on the side and a big lip at the top and bottom. Inertia is a law of nature. A hard, heavy object flying at your head has a lot of inertia. Yes, those things did a bit of damage when they encountered a solid surface like a guitar, or Bill's head! The Foster's can with the beer still inside was the equal of a brick. I saw Bill out of the corner of my eye, with both hands on the microphone, leaning on the stand in full rock vocal scream suddenly snap his head to the left. A mostly full Foster's can whizzed past his ear. A second slower and his face would have been smashed! Holy Shit! This is out of hand! I'm saying to myself as I watch Greg duck the same projectile and see it crash into the back wall panel. Yep, it left a mark. On the other side of the stage, Rick jumps up and scissor kicks a full can out of the air like some kind of guitar playing ninja. He knocks it to the ground, and holds it in place with his foot as that song comes to a halt. The kid that had tried to crush him with it, walks to the edge of the stage and ask for his beer back! Rick looks him in eye, picks it up, pulls open the tab spraying beer all in the kids face, then said "NO", and chugged it. The kid looked on, disappointed. I guess he didn't think that drinking the beer first was the smart way to go.

We finished our set. Then got off stage and looked around as the house lights came up. It looked like a recycling truck had lost its load. As we walked toward the bar looking to get a cold beer for ourselves. We could plow through piles of cans up to our knees like new snow on a shovel. Oh shit! Look at this mess! Shorty is gonna be mad! Shorty is gonna kill us! Never let us back in here or worst of all, make us clean it up! We got to the bar and tried to act cool. You know, like, what cans? Then we saw the coolers…They were empty…No more beer! Oh shit! Hey, wait a minute, if there is no beer in the cooler and the floor is covered with empties, that means the cash register must be full!!! Shorty and Tiny kept looking toward the dance floor covered in aluminum and steel, slick with beer and sweat. Then shake their heads in disgust. Then Bill says, "Looks like a pretty good night." After what seemed to me to be a very, very long pause, Shorty turned toward Bill and said, "Yeah, we sold a little beer."

William Gilmore Weber

According to the calendar on the website, on 1/30/87, I did double-duty... playing with both Manwich (not listed on the bill) and Human Zoo. It was Manwich's 4th or 5th show and (I believe) Dave Lewis' debut on bass. Lara Allen refused to look at the audience, and I played sitting on a chair (trying to do my Jah Wobble impersonation). It wasn't a great gig on our part, we were 1st up on a bill with BPA and a bunch of other bands. Lara kept creeping offstage when she wasn't coming over to my side to hit me on the head with her tambourine.

Bevo
photo by George DuChaine

Anyway, after a few bands, Human Zoo was up. This was at the time when the band started going downhill. We were all into our various vices, playing like shit... just not caring. We did have a rather nice crowd at the front of the stage though.

Now, if you're not familiar with the band, let me just say our singer...Bevo Ruzsa, was meant to front a band. Often compared to a blond haired Iggy, he had a stage presence and the mannerisms of your typical early seventies glam star, often dressing in ridiculous outfits - with the importance of being easily removed. Bevo's day gig you see... was a nude model. Back then he had no problem dropping trowel in front of a crowd. At some point in the show, he got a little too close to the edge of the stage. Several kids did what you would expect kids at the front of the stage would do... grab at the mic and scream along (yeah, like they knew the words). Whelp, someone didn't grab for the mic, they grabbed for Bevo's "coverings", succeeding in removing them and exposing Bevo for all the club to see.

Fast forward a year or so, a fan of the band assembled an hour's worth of video of the Zoo and handed it to Public Access to show. One of those clips was from

Bevo, Amy Miller and Jakki Repellent
photo courtesy of Jakki Repellent

the gig I just mentioned. Included in the video was the scene in which Bevo was de-pantsed.

Well, I guess Time Warner aired this collection of vid's sometime during the day, and...some mother, while doing the ironing, sat her three year old in front of the TV with this being shown. At some point, Jr. points at the TV and says "Pee-Pee". This alerted the mother and *BOING* all heck broke loose! She ran screaming that the sky was falling and blah-blah...turning it into a media event. It was written up in the Enquirer and the Post. Public access pulled it from their rotation and issued a formal apology, stating they would start screening their content more closely.

The best though, was we made it onto the WLWT Evening News which featured Jerry Springer and Norma Rashid sharing anchor duties. It was great seeing these two tell our beloved city that smut was being pumped into our living rooms for our innocent children to witness. They had a cut of Sheriff Simon Leis standing with Mayor Charlie Luken, watching the clip of Bevo being disrobed. Both men had a hand to their chins and in perfect synchronization, shook their heads in disbelief. Cut back to Jerry and Norma... snickering. I have it on video if anyone wants a good laugh...

Victor Garcia-Rivera

Victor Garcia-Rivera
photo courtesy of
Victor Garcia-Rivera

I firmly believe that finding my way to the Jockey Club had more to do with fate than with coincidence.

Being Cuban, gay, and into punk music in the early 80s, I had already been ostracized from the monoculture conservative Bible belt burg of the Queen City, so it was only appropriate that I would make my way to a club full of fellow freaks, deviants and punks.

At that time I was living in suburban Fairfield, Ohio. My family had come from Cuba with nothing but the clothes on our backs [and a few jewels that my mom smuggled in my sisters' underwear]. My father had to learn English, recertify himself as a doctor, and support a family of 7 kids. We went from renting a series of nondescript working class houses in Hamilton, Ohio, to owning the middle class suburban dream house in Fairfield, Ohio. And the suburbs bored the hell out of me.

For a couple of years I had been inspired by the punk movement of the late

Mike Gregory
photo courtesy of Victor Garcia-Rivera

Seventies, and had been trying to form a band to play songs that I had written, inspired by the bands from that era, such as Stiff Little Fingers, The Clash, Sex Pistols and Ramones. But all I could find in the Fairfield area were musicians who wanted to play Lynyrd Skynyrd and Journey covers.

It wasn't until I met Mike Gregory, who lived in Reading, through a mutual

54

friend, that I could partner with a musician bold enough to help me launch my crazy dream. With a revolving door of drummers, none of whom were exactly on the same musical page as us, Mike and I formed The Edge, making our debut at the Jockey Club on November 27, 1982.

I had first learned of the Jockey Club during my frequent forays to Subway Records and Moles Records in Clifton, where I was attending the University of Cincinnati. I decided to scout it out on my own one night in October, 1982.

If I recall right, it was a Thursday night. The show was part of a series of regular Thursday shows billed as "College Night", featuring AK-47, who later morphed into SS-20. There were maybe a dozen people in the club that night, but I dug its vibe and fell in love with the joint. The Jockey Club reminded me of the decaying old bars of my hometown of Havana, Cuba, which once were glitzy casinos and havens for the mob, but now crumbled in moldy decay. The place felt like home.

The Edge
photo courtesy of Victor Garcia-Rivera

I went to order a beer from the bar. That is where I first met Shorty and his brother Tiny. I asked Shorty who booked the place, and he mumbled something about talking to Jughead, the singer of AK-47. Shorty never took his always present cigar out of his mouth while he talked. Who was Jughead? Wasn't he the drummer for the Archies? No, he was the bass player and singer of AK-47. Well, I found Jughead and talked to him.

He gave me Bill Leist's number, so I called Bill the following day and asked him for a show. He offered us the night of Saturday, November 27, 1982 for our debut as The Edge, the first of many shows we were to play at the Jockey Club. Bill asked me if we could fill four hours worth of music. Being a total neophyte who had never booked a club before, I naively told him yes. The fact that we only had about 40 minutes of original songs didn't stop me. We had over a month to prepare for the gig, so I figured that we could just pad out the rest of the night by learning a bunch of cover tunes quickly. It had never occurred to me to ask other bands to play. In any case, I knew of no other bands, and there were few other punk bands in Cincinnati in 1982.

We learned a bunch of covers quickly and excitedly made our debut at the Jockey Club the Saturday after Thanksgiving, 1982. That our audience could be counted on with both hands mattered little to us. We were excited to play our first show, and got on well with the sound engineer, Stacey, who did an excellent job mixing us, despite continually asking me to turn down my guitar amp.

Unfortunately, among the few people who were there, were some of the "tastemakers" in the small Cincy scene, and when they walked in and heard the cover tunes, they walked out soon afterward, getting the wrong impression of our band. Although we got off to an inauspicious start, just playing at the JC was a thrill. I met Bill Leist that night, and he complimented us on some of the tunes that he liked, such as a Johnny Thunders cover. He gave me the impression that he liked us, which I later found out, was not the case.

I began to come down to the Jockey Club on a regular basis, and bugged Bill to give us more shows. The few shows that he did give us initially were horrible affairs- usually pairing us with bands that didn't fit us at all, or that were so horrible that they were horrifically interesting [such as Barking Spiders]. Our band did not get to play the coveted shows opening for popular touring bands, which were the few events that drew people to the JC. As a matter of fact, we never got to open for ANY major touring band there until 17 months later. But we made the most of the few crumbs that Bill threw at us.

Among some of the local musicians who happen to stroll in during our forlorn gigs were Musical Suicide and Snare and the Idiots, and we bonded with both bands, being as we were more or less the black sheep of the scene. I formed a friendship with Snare (Steve Arnzen), who as it turned out was a friend of Bill Leist. Through Snare, I learned that Bill was telling people that we sucked, and that he referred to me with some unkind monikers (some of the more humorous ones were "Cro-Mag", I suppose due to my large head, and "The Wop"—Bill thought

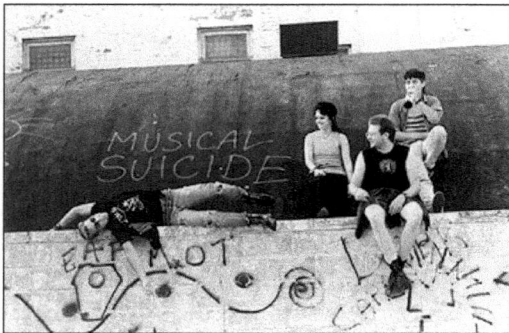

Musical Suicide
photo by Jan Gerber

from looking at me that I was Italian). Don't get me wrong, I like Bill Leist. I admire what he did with the Jockey Club. He took a chance when no one else was bothering with any consistent effort to book underground music in Cincinnati. After all, he did give us our first opportunity to play.

But Bill was like the Archie Bunker of the punk scene, as much a colorful character as Tiny and Shorty were, younger than them but equally NOT politically correct. He loved to take the piss out of anyone that was different, and you have to take into account the time frame that we are talking about. The Ramones had made a career of singing about freaks and cretins, but nowadays the term cretin would be converted into something more PC, such as "mentally challenged". I had a thick skin though. I had already been teased and bullied in school for being Cuban and for having an accent (which the good old school system got rid of by making me take Speech Therapy classes in junior high), but I tolerated Bill's animosity (while not understanding it).

However, the shit gigs that he gave us to play at the JC did give us the chance to develop our music and turn the tables on the haters. For example, I found out through some of my friends in these other bands that one of the knocks making the rounds was that The Edge had no stage presence. So when we were asked to play a benefit show for WAIF-FM at the JC, an opportunity that offered a larger than usual audience [for us], we decided to pull a prank.

We took a bunch of empty cardboard boxes from the department store that I worked at. We bought some gift wrap and bows, wrapping the boxes nicely as if they were Christmas presents. On Saturday, November 19, 1983 we went to play the WAIF benefit, lining the stage at the Jockey Club with these "gifts". During our set, I announced into the microphone: "Hi, we are The Edge, and people say we have no Stage Presents (Presence). Well they're wrong!" We then kicked the wrapped "presents" into the befuddled audience. We had made our point. The joke got people talking about us more.

At another show, one of a few where we were paired with the Barking Spiders (a band so bizarre that they cleared the room every time they played), Bill Igerent, lead singer of Musical Suicide, and I got up on stage while Barking Spiders played some long improvisational noise jam and sang a duet of the Barbara Streisand/Neil Diamond hit, "You Don't Bring Me Flowers", on top of the din.

The Edge

It got to the point where we even went to "inventing" other bands to play with! On Friday, May 6, 1983, we told Bill that we knew a rockabilly band called the Stoned City Ramblers from Kentucky that we wanted to play with. He gave us the green light to book them. The problem was that the Stoned City Ramblers did not exist- they were a figment of our imagination! Actually the Stoned City Ramblers turned out to be The Edge in disguise—Mike Gregory and I switched instruments. We played rockabilly tunes, such as "Matchbox" by Carl Perkins. One guy who got caught in the joke was the lead singer of a local rockabilly band called the Hopheads. Intrigued by our posters announcing this hot new rockabilly band, he came to the show to check out the competition. When he found out who the Stoned City Ramblers were, he left the club in disgust!

I also recall a show with a duo called Perfect Jewish Couple, which consisted of a guy and a gal, one of whom who played violin, and the other one of the duo who sang. While they played their maudlin music, we were skanking and stage diving, PFJ almost came to tears as they thought we were making fun of them.

Before he formed the legendary Human Zoo, Bevo had a band called Fastbats, whom also had a unique sound. It was the only band that I ever saw Shorty pull the plug on. I didn't know Bevo then. We got on well after he formed Human Zoo, but we started off on the wrong foot. Bevo insisted that The Edge go on first and open for Fastbats, or else "I will call my crowd and tell them not to come". We said OK—we complied, did our set and let him have his way. I wondered where his crowd went to, as there were few people in the audience that night. Their music was more, shall we say, experimental, not as melodic as Human Zoo, but Shorty couldn't tolerate it. He told me to tell the Fastbats to get off the stage. I passed his message on to the sound man, who relayed the info to Bevo. The Fastbats would not oblige. They kept playing, which pissed Shorty off. He went over to the breaker box and turned off the fuses that powered the stage. The lights went dark, but Bevo kept singing even though the PA was turned off. As I said, that was the first, and last time, I ever saw Shorty pull the plug on a band.

Probably one of the more legendary events, one that I still get asked about to this day, was the "Buck for a blowjob photo dance contest". Word got out at the Jockey Club that a short portly girl was making the rounds offering to give guys a blowjob in the men's bathroom for the bargain price of a dollar. One of our friends tipped me off that the woman who provided the blow jobs had just gone into one of the stalls with a guy to perform her oral services. I went into the restroom, took out my Kodak disc camera, raised it above the stall partition, took a quick photo and darted back out the restroom door into the bar.

When I developed the film, the picture came out perfectly framed- you could see the woman, with her top off, all mounds of flabby flesh, performing her "services" on the guy, who was sprawled out on top of the john with a blissful look on his face, with his eyes closed. At our next show, we decided to have a "Dance Contest" where the winner would get that photo as a prize. When I announced the contest and the prize, the people in the audience started shouting "a buck for a blowjob!" I heard that the guy whose picture was taken was actually in the bar that night, and that he slinked out of the club in embarrassment during the "dance contest"!

As time went on, we became more and more controversial. A little buzz started forming around us. All the while, I persisted in asking Bill to book us for more shows. He did his best to stop us from playing them.

"I'm sorry but we can't book you guys as The Edge anymore. People are talking bad about you, nobody likes you and I can't justify booking the band"

Not being able to take no for an answer I shot back at him, "OK, so we'll play under another name!"

He couldn't argue with that, so he gave us another one of the shit gigs that we were accustomed to. We went about making flyers to promote it.

The dilemma that we faced then was deciding which name we were going to play under. It had to be a name that would be interesting enough, yet still be recognizable to the few people who did follow The Edge.

Mike and I brainstormed. We decided our temporary new name would be the title of our most well known song at the time, "Newport Gestapo". It seemed the perfect choice, because the song itself was written about the Jockey Club. The lyrics were inspired by what turned out to be the first major out of town show at the JC, a Circle Jerks show in June, 1983.

As anyone who went to the JC at the time knew, the JC had an unwritten policy of illegally admitting entrance to minors. No one knew how they got away with it. There were rumors that Shorty paid off the Newport cops, but in any case, the first eight months or so the club escaped without a bust- maybe because most shows drew such small audiences that the place went under the radar.

All that changed the night of the Circle Jerks show. Not only were they one of the top draws in the country in what was then a small but growing underground scene in the USA, but just seeing the name Circle Jerks on the posters that were plastered all over town perked the attention of the local media.

The club was packed with minors that night. TV camera crews from one of the local television stations decided to check out the scene and filmed a report for the nightly news. Scenes of kids as young as 13 and 14 years old hanging out at the bar on the 11 o'clock news created too much of a public embarrassment for the Newport PD to ignore. While the crowd skanked to the music, the cops busted into the JC, menacing anyone who got in their way with their nightsticks. The music was stopped, and the hundreds of people who were in the club were forced out and made to come back in by proving they were of age with valid IDs.

When the Circle Jerks came back on the stage and resumed playing, less than half of the original audience was still left inside. Outside, dozens of angry kids, who had been kicked out, milled about. Jimmy D, who was working the door, refused to give them their money back. They lurched in wait at the back alley for the Circle Jerks to load out their gear out of the rear door after the show.

They confronted Circle Jerks singer Keith Morris as he made his way to the band's van, telling him what Jimmy D had told them—which was that the club could not refund their money because the band refused to give up their guarantee. Keith denied that was the case. He said that the decision to give refunds lay in Bill Leist's hands. The underage contingent confronted Bill, who told them, no dice—getting kicked out was their own fault because they knew going in, that the club did not officially permit entrance to minors.

These events inspired Mike and I to write the song "Newport Gestapo", one of a handful of songs inspired by the Jockey Club (another one being Snare and The Idiots' "Freak Show"). The lyrics document what happened that night:

The Edge 7" featuring "Newport Gestapo"

I was hanging around at the Jockey Club
When a cop came in, said, I'm sorry bub,
But you're gonna have to clear this place
Cause the noise here ain't to my taste

They grabbed a dancer off the floor
Said— you like to slam, well hit the door
Prove to me, your identity
Because we don't want this anarchy

Cause you're old enough to fight
In the army
But you can't go dancing tonight
Cause the media are looking for a riot

They showed who was boss but it wasn't enough
They said, move on punks, or you'll all be in cuffs
Cause the odds are against you, a thousand to one
You have the rights, but we have the guns

```
        Everyone wanted their money back
     But the man at the front said- you'll have to ask
   Because the band got the dough, and it's not up to us
       It's not our fault that there was a bust
```

The ending coda of the tune then name checks the Hockeypunk, Billy Blank (Bill Leist) and "Handsome" Clem.

We recorded a rough demo of the song, which quickly got a lot of airplay on WAIF-FM, both on Mike Riley's and on "Handsome" Clem's programs. The tune had a catchy hook, a shouted crescendo that rose on my odd phrasing of the word "Gestapo" (people thought that I was singing "gazpacho"). Also, kids in the scene could relate to it, because many of them were there that night.

"Newport Gestapo" seemed to be a perfect name for us to go under, one that would let our small group of followers know that we were playing. So off we went to put up posters in Clifton, promoting the show under our new moniker. One of my first stops was at Wizard Records. Along with Mole's Record Store, it was one of the most important places to hang flyers. This was in December of 1983

.

When I gave the flyer to Rick Roberts, manager at Wizard's, he looked it over, gave me a dirty look, returned the flyer to me, and almost spat in my face. "I am not putting this poster up. Get out of my store!"

I was puzzled, and asked him "why not?"

He replied: "Because I have a lot of Jewish customers, who would be offended by the name Newport Gestapo, and I myself am offended, so get out!"

I tried explaining to him what the name meant, letting him know that it had nothing to do with anti-Semitism. The title referred to some of the almost Gestapo-like tactics that the Newport police force used in raiding the Jockey Club at the Circle Jerks show. I told Roberts, but he wouldn't listen. "Get out!" he snarled.

On Friday, December 23, 1983, the night we played the show, I dedicated the song "Newport Gestapo" to him, stating that "this song is for Rick Roberts, what an asshole!" Someone at the club that night went back and reported

The Edge

my words to him the following week. Word got back to me that Roberts threatened to shoot me if he ever saw me walking the streets of Clifton again (I was told that he kept a gun behind the counter, because he was particularly paranoid of African-American kids who came in his store, whom he suspected of shoplifting).

When Clem Carpenter heard about these events, he played "Newport Gestapo" on his "Search and Destroy" radio program on WAIF and proceeded to denigrate the Wizard on the air. Rick Roberts heard about Clem's antics. He went to the management at WAIF demanding that "Handsome" Clem and his sidekick, the Hockeypunk (Neil Aquino) be given the boot. WAIF management forced Clem to send a written apology to Rick Roberts in order to keep his program on the air. I on the other hand, wrote something other than an apology, a song called "Rick Roberts is an Asshole" (not very subtle, I admit), that we performed at the next few gigs at the Jockey Club.

Eventually, the entire furor spawned all kinds of untrue rumors. They even reached as far north as Dayton. Soon afterward, I made one of my periodic forays to Renaissance Records in Dayton. The owner of the store made a comment to me as he was ringing me up: "I heard that Rick Roberts pulled a gun on you at Wizard Records" I told him that wasn't true, as much as Rick Roberts would have loved to have done so, but it amazed me to see the reach of the rumor mills in our small scene. The controversy had a positive effect in that it got more people to come to our shows to find out what the fuss was all about.

Among some of the people who started coming out to the shows were some of the very kids that the song, "Newport Gestapo", was dedicated to, the nascent but growing youth hardcore punk movement. They mainly sprouted from the Walnut Hills area (that scene was even known by the zip code of its residents, 45208). Most of those kids were part of the Straight Edge movement inspired by Minor Threat. They followed a new band made up of other underage musicians who formed a band called Sluggo.

While attending a show at the JC one evening, I first met Karl Meyer, the bass player and leader of Sluggo. One the excuses that Bill Leist kept giving me as to why we could not open for any of the touring bands, was that "the hardcore kids don't like your music". That explanation puzzled me, as up to that point so few of them had had a chance to hear us. Getting our music played on Clem's show had changed that, and the few kids from that scene who did trickle out to our shows seemed to like what we were doing. Karl knew who I was. He was very frank with me. "You know", he told me, "I would never come out to see you guys because Bill Leist told me not to bother, and that you guys sucked. But then I heard you for myself and I decided that wasn't true". I appreciated his honesty with me, and I told him that I was aware of the slander that was circulating. I suggested that our two bands play some shows together, even if it was somewhere other than the Jockey Club.

Karl Meyer, Victor Garcia-Rivera and Dan Sokatch
photo courtesy of Victor Garcia-Rivera

I admired Karl Meyer. At a very young age, he had started his own band, formed a record label, and had become one of the leaders of a creative and growing scene. Like me, he made some enemies for being outspoken and opinionated, but that attracted me to him even more. We became friends, and eventually he ended up playing in The Edge with me years later, after Mike Gregory had left. Karl was an important mover and shaker in the years that the Jockey Club was around, and I am proud to be his friend and band mate.

Knocking our heads against the wall in Cincinnati was taking its toll on our band, though, so we made plans to leave town. In the summer of 1983, we had decided to take a week off and play out of town, to see how we would be received outside the confines of the Jockey Club and Cincinnati. I chose Boston as our destination, because it had a lively and thriving music scene.

We booked a couple of shows, based solely on our demo of "Newport Gestapo". One of those shows was at the Rat, a now defunct bar that was one of the legendary clubs of the 70s and 80s punk circuit—a circuit that included places like the famed CBGBs as well as the Jockey Club. We received a warm reception in Boston, and Mike Gregory and I decided that we would relocate there within a year, even if our ever revolving rotation of drummers didn't follow our lead.

By June, 1984, fate intervened. I had finished school, while the store I worked at had closed its doors (providing me with unemployment benefits that I could live off of while I scouted for jobs in Boston). On top of all that, we could not get any decent gigs at the JC. So we made our plans to move east and booked our farewell show. As luck would have it, we played the finale, an all ages show with Sluggo and Musical Suicide, at PSST in downtown Cincinnati, which served as Sluggo's rehearsal space—not at the Jockey Club.

On Friday, June 15, 1984, Mike and I were at my house in Fairfield, waiting for our drummer, Tim Brookshire (who was on loan from Snare and the Idiots) to show up for a rehearsal for the farewell show that we were supposed to play the following evening, when the phone rang. It was Bill Leist. "Vic, I need a favor from you. DRI and Personality Crisis (a band from Canada) are supposed to play tonight, but they are both refusing to play because neither band will go on as the opening band. I need a band to open for them tonight because if I don't find one, both bands are threatening to back out".

What an irony—almost two years of playing at the Jockey Club, and never getting a chance to open for a major touring band, but now we had our opportunity—although it was on an hour's notice and solely as the result of two bands bickering like children! I told Bill, "Look, I would love to help you out. But right now Mike and I are sitting here waiting for our drummer to show up for practice, and we don't know if he has other plans tonight. It's almost 8:00 pm, but as soon as he gets here, I will ask him". With that, Mike and I went outside to the driveway to await our missing band mate. As soon as Tim pulled up, I told him to keep his drums in his car. "Tim, I know its short notice, but Bill Leist just called from the Jockey Club, and he has two bands from out of town playing tonight, none of whom will play unless there is some other band to open the show. Want to play the show?" Tim said something to the effect of "hell yeah!", so we called Bill back to tell him that we were on our way. We packed the amps and guitars into our cars, and drove off for the 45 minute trip to Newport.

As soon as we got to the JC, we encountered a tense situation. DRI stayed outside, fuming in their tour van (they traveled at that time with a German shepherd to protect them from theft], while Personality Crisis were off in their corner suffering their own personality crisis [pun intended). We loaded our gear directly on stage, did a quick soundcheck, and played in front of hundreds of the same kids who supposedly did not like us. The reception was amazing. Despite not having played together for several weeks, we were tight and focused, fueled by the adrenaline of having to race to make this last minute gig. The sizeable audience gave us a rousing response. But it was a bittersweet victory. In a few weeks, we would be pulling up roots and leaving town. I looked forward to playing the Jockey Club in the distant future, even if ironically, we wound up returning as an out of town touring band.

We moved to Boston in June, 1984, quickly found a drummer, got signed to an independent label, and started being a successful band, something that eluded us in Cincinnati. Our first show with the new lineup was opening up for Hüsker Dü in Syracuse, New York, a feat that we would never have accomplished at the JC.

But we never forgot the Jockey Club. We booked a return gig for Thanksgiving weekend, Friday: November 23, 1984. It would be a chance to return to our roots, as well as allowing us to spend the holidays with our families. If there is justice in this world, it seemed evident to me when we made our return to the JC. We were treated as conquering heroes. The Edge played in front of a packed house, for an audience that was there to see OUR BAND, not some other band that we were opening for. It all seemed like too little, too late. Too bad we couldn't have stayed in Cincinnati, to reap the rewards of our efforts, but those efforts weren't in vain.

While we were in Boston, we received letters from Cincinnati. One letter, that I still have to this day, came from a young guy named Darren Blase. He was in the audience the night that we got the invitation to open for DRI and Personality Crisis. The Edge happened to be the first band that he ever saw (or at least the first punk band). Darren wrote all kinds of nice things about us, and we received similar letters from other people in Cincinnati. Almost two decades later, now an adult, Darren opened a record store in Northside called Shake It Records. I have been to great record stores all over the world, but I can state that Shake It Records ranks among the best that I have ever seen. I am proud that The Edge at least had a small part in sparking his interest in music.

Jimmy D
photo by Sarah Kuhl

When we returned, I also noticed that a change had taken place in the Jockey Club. In the six months that I was away, Karl Meyer parted ways with Sluggo, and I now found him drinking and smoking- so much for the Straight Edge movement. As a matter of fact, most of the 45208 kids were now ditching Straight Edge and either becoming acid-tripping Dead Heads, or turning into metal heads. Sluggo itself veered away from their initial Minor Threat/7 Seconds hardcore influence, evolving in a more Metallica/Slayer metal orientation. More changes were to come.

New bands like Doc and the Pods and the Black Republicans (who later morphed into the Afghan Whigs) had come into the scene, less strident than the hardcore punk bands before them. Stacey got tired of doing sound at the Jockey Club and left for other gigs. Joe Hamm and Jimmy Davidson of the Libertines eventually replaced him as sound engineers. Bill Leist himself tired of the Jockey Club and eventually left for a while.

In the fall of 1985, I moved back to Cincinnati. Mike Gregory and I had a falling out in Boston. He left in June to return home. We were scheduled to do a tour of the US and Canada for our upcoming album. Our label threatened us that they would not release the record if we did not follow through with the tour. So my drummer and I had to find a bass player on a few weeks' notice. We ran an ad, did quick auditions, and hit the road. Even though we played a few memorable shows on that tour (among them: playing with D.O.A. and Conflict in San Francisco, and playing again with D.O.A. and Conflict in Los Angeles with a new and then unknown LA band called NOFX), the tour became a headache. The new bass player turned out to be a real jerk. My drummer could not stand him. The two of them fought constantly in the van. So at the end of the tour, we gave him the boot. I returned to Boston broke and homeless. A few weeks later, I moved back to Cincinnati.

Upon returning, I got together with Karl Meyer and my old drummer, Tim Brookshire, to form a new version of The Edge (eventually we added Dan

Sokatch to make it a four piece group). We made our debut opening for the Necros at the Jockey Club on Saturday, November 9, 1985, but some of the magic of the place seemed to have slipped away.

Bill had started booking bigger bands at the club, such as the Ramones, whose draw was straining its fire code capacity (I believe that the official limit was 500 people or less, but the bigger shows like The Ramones and the Damned drew almost twice that number). Bogarts, which was the club where punk and alternative bands with big draws had played in previous years, had closed for remodeling. Upon re-opening with a bigger capacity, Bogarts lost interest in booking bands that drew less than a thousand people. Their move opened the door for Bill Leist to book well known bands like the Ramones, Violent Femmes and The Damned at the Jockey Club. Before I moved to Boston, I worked with Bill in landing some of those acts. Our relationship had improved from the rocky early days. He relied on my knowledge and extensive contacts, which I had compiled from the vast network of bands and managers that I had known in my travels with The Edge.

I remember our initial attempts to land the Ramones. We had an inside contact in Greg Stout, the original bassist for Toxic Reasons, who now worked with the Ramones as a roadie. We got the phone number for their manager, Gary Kurfist. I called Gary to convince him to allow us to book The Ramones at the Jockey Club. Kurfist sent me their rider (contract demands). He did not think that the stage or equipment at the JC would be sufficient for their requirements. He also preferred that his band play at a place with a bigger capacity. For a while, we kicked around the idea of booking the Ramones at the National Guard Armory in Fairfield instead of at the JC, but that didn't pan out. Eventually the Jockey Club expanded their stage and beefed up their PA, so The Ramones finally played there. I couldn't enjoy the fruits of my labor, as I was living in Boston at the time that the Ramones show came to fruition.

The stakes had now changed for Bill Leist. Bigger shows meant more work for him. I think that the pressures and the hassles of dealing with bigger shows and higher guarantees got to him. He later decided to take a break from booking.

In the spring of 1986, with the new revamped version of The Edge now running on all cylinders, I strolled into the Jockey Club to talk to Shorty. I asked him who was now going to book the place in Bill's absence. He replied "Hell, you can do it if you want to!" I told him I had no interest in being a booking agent. I just wanted to book my own band. He told me that Joe Hamm [of the Libertines], as well as Dave Dunkum [of Snare and The Idiots] and Jerry Adams [of Peppermint Subway] had come in and had booked a couple shows for the future, but that if I wanted a date and it was open, I could have it.

We booked some shows on our own. We made our own arrangements as to what bands we played with and even worked the door ourselves. Another benefit resulted from my conversations with Shorty. When he found out that we lost our rehearsal place [we had been practicing at Seven Hills High School, where Karl attended], he gave us carte blanche to rehearse at his club. We started rehearsals at the Jockey Club with a small 6 channel portable PA system, playing mostly in the afternoons and early evenings.

It was weird being in the club during the daylight hours, but it gave me the chance to talk in depth with Shorty. He had few customers to attend to during those hours. The old man would regale me with tales of his liquor smuggling days during Prohibition, wistfully recalling the good old days, "when steaks cost a nickel and hookers charged a quarter!"

I usually got to the club early to set up the PA. While waiting for the other band members to show up, I would buy a Foster's Lager and shoot the shit with Shorty. Those are some of the fondest memories I have to this day.

One of the other factors that affected the Jockey Club was that it now had competition in Clifton. Not only were clubs like JRs, The Plaza, Bash Riprocks and the soon to be open Sudsy Malones starting to book some of the same bands that had once regularly played the Jockey Club, but now Bogarts decided to get back in the game and give the club a run for its money.

I inadvertently had a hand in the re-emergence of Bogarts, but it was bound to happen. The whole alternative/ underground scene was becoming more commercial. Two of the most popular bands to spring from the US punk scene, The Replacements and Hüsker Dü, had just signed to major labels, and wanted to play bigger and "better" places. Of the other "name" punk bands, many, such as Dead Kennedys, Black Flag and Minor Threat, were either breaking up or about to retire.
In early 1986, I found out from Chuck Warner, who owned the record label that we were on at the time, about Hüsker Dü signing to Warner Brothers

and going on tour. Chuck was good friends with David Savoy, who managed Hüsker Dü then. During The Edge tour in 1985, Chuck had sent me to Nicollet Studios in Minneapolis to talk to Bob Mould and Grant Hart of Hüsker Dü to ask them if they would be interested in producing a record for us. So I got to know David Savoy. I called him to see if we could play with the Hüskers in Cincinnati. I assumed that they were playing the JC again, as they had done in the past.

I found out that he wanted to book the band at a bigger place, which turned out to be Bogarts. The problem was that Bogarts did not do all ages shows for rock or punk music at the time. So a lot of the kids that had been a sizable part of Hüsker Dü's audience when they played the Jockey Club could not go see them there. I told David the downside of the change in venue. He agreed to work with me in an effort to influence Bogarts to change their policy.

As fate would have it, a friend of mine had just taken over booking Bogarts. I first met Dan Reed when our second record came out. I had gone to WOXY-FM in Oxford to do an interview to promote the "Alternative Allston" EP. Dan was the Program Director at the station. He was also the lead singer in a band called Chem Dyne. When Dan found out that I was leaving Boston and moving back to Cincinnati, he asked me if I would play with Chem Dyne, who was now looking to add a second guitarist. I accepted the offer and played with them until they broke up the following year. Dan Reed then left WOXY in early 1986 to do the booking at Bogarts. Through my efforts, as well as those of Dan and David Savoy, we convinced Bogarts to allow Hüsker Dü to do an all ages show there. There was one catch, Bogarts would only do it only on the condition that the underage fans would not be allowed below the balcony (the remodeling done at the club had added a balcony to the main floor, thus doubling their capacity). We reluctantly agreed.

On Tuesday, February 18, 1986, the Edge played with Hüsker Dü and a then unknown band called Soul Asylum in front of a packed house at Bogarts. But the age apartheid made it a strange event. The older crowd sat at tables at the front of the stage, acting somewhat passively. Further up, the balcony buckled with the swaying of screaming kids. It felt weird from the stage, as all the energy was coming from the rafters up above. The floor directly in front of the stage, usually a beehive of moshers and stage divers, was sedated. The show proved to be a success and convinced Bogarts that they could pull off all ages shows (eventually, they eliminated the balcony restriction so that the underage audience could go to the floor). Al Porkolab (owner of Bogarts) stole some of the Jockey Club's thunder. The local bands also now had the other clubs in Clifton that they could play at. The JC seemed to be on the decline.

Bill Leist had seen the writing on the wall when he left, but came back to book the Jockey Club in late 1986. He eventually decided that he did not want to do the task alone. He gave me a call in 1987 and asked me if I was interested in partnering with him to do the booking. His offer was flattering. We had come a long way from the days that we had been at odds with each other. I thanked him for the offer, but I told him that I was busy with my band, and that it would be a conflict of interest on my part. But I had someone else in mind that would be perfect for him—I recommended that he call Pete Wegele.

Pete had come from Sluggo, where he replaced Karl Meyer on bass. He also did a radio show on WAIF-FM under the nom de plume Tommy Rott. I had talked to him recently, and he indicated to me that he wanted to start booking some of the bands that he was playing on his radio show. I told Bill about Pete's interest in booking. I told him that I thought that Wegele would be the perfect partner for him at the Jockey Club. Bill called him. The rest is history, as Bill and Pete served as the JC booking agents till it shut down in the spring of 1988.

The Edge finally came to a halt in 1987. Our band went out with a bang (we had a video on MTV). I went back to Boston at the end of the year. I spent the winter there, while I pondered my future.

I moved back to Cincinnati the following spring. Visiting my old haunt, I learned some heartbreaking news. Shorty had sold the club to the taxi company next door. He was going to retire to the Pepper Pod to spend his last years on earth. A farewell concert was being planned for Sunday, May 29th, 1988.

I knew that I had to be part of it. One problem: I had no band anymore. Most of my ex band mates were scattered all around the country, so there was no chance for a reunion. I begged Bill to let me play the final show. He was puzzled at first, since I had no band to back me up. I explained to him that I wanted to do a short acoustic set. Any sane person would have told me to go take a hike, but Bill, god bless him, gave me the green light. In spite of the rocky beginnings that our relationship took, I have to say that we ended up on good terms. Bill proved to have a heart after all. It was a risky move on both our parts.

Some friends of mine warned me not to do it. I would be pelted with beer cans, they said. There I was in the spotlight- just me on stage with an acoustic guitar. Those who knew me thought that I had flipped my lid. Other friends congratulated me for pulling a gutsy move.

I rarely got nervous at the hundreds of other gigs that I have played in my life, but that night did seem a bit frightening. I felt alone and naked on that stage, with no band around me. How would the audience react?

The audience seemed respectful. The timing probably had a lot to do with it. If I had gone on towards the end of the night, when everyone got drunk and boisterous, it could have turned ugly. But the acoustic set proved to be a fitting opener. I received a round of applause

.

The last song that I chose to play, appropriately enough, was "Newport Gestapo". It felt surreal. The song has a chorus that stops to pause momentarily. When I played it with The Edge, I was used to hearing the ringing of the cymbals or the feedback of electric guitar that would inevitably leak out during the stops, but this time, it was just the murmur of the crowd that I heard. "Newport Gestapo" used to inspire unrestrained moshing and stage diving when I played it with a full band. To my shock, the acoustic version also inspired the dancers. Some of the guys who used to slam to it at Edge shows started moshing in slow motion, as if in a ballet. I couldn't have ended my last gig at the Jockey Club on a higher note. I left the stage, the other bands came on after me, and the mayhem ensued.

The Jockey Club will always be a special place for me and for thousands of other people. All of us, who ever played there, worked there or saw a show there, felt that way. We share a common bond which unites us, no matter what other differences we may have had with each other.

It came as no surprise to me when Shorty died soon after the place closed. Someday we'll find him up in heaven, where the steaks cost a nickel and the hookers charge a quarter!

Eerie Von

I played the Jockey Club twice with my band Samhain. The first time was in 1984 on our "Season of the Dead" Tour. All anybody knew about us was, we were Glenn's new band, after the Misfits. We had a record out I think, but nobody knew we were coming. About 30 people showed up, and Glenn sang some songs like Eddie Murphy, doing "Buckwheat". We played like the place was full, and must have impressed those two dozen people, because when we came back the year after, there must have been 1000 people. Somewhere there's a bootleg tape of those shows floating around.

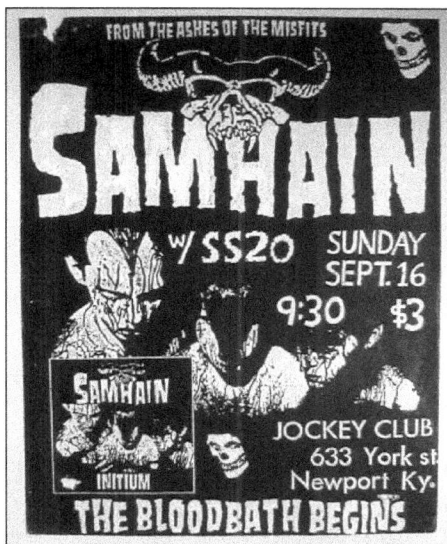

Samhain flyer
flyer courtesy of Eerie Von

The Jockey Club was a great room. I loved playing there, and it's where I met a girl, that I'm still friends with today. You don't forget a place like that, and I never will...

Jakki Repellent

When asked if I could put my thoughts on the Jockey Club on paper, I thought, "Sure, no problem". That was easier said than done as I have been disabled since 2001. I played hockey with and against men as the first female to ever do that in Cincinnati for many years. Unfortunately I was the recipient of one of those one in a million chance injuries and damaged my spinal cord. After numerous operations over the years, my health today is the worst it has ever been. Under these unfortunate circumstances, I'll try to do my best in giving you my thoughts and recollections about the Jockey Club. If I were well, I could probably write a book. So here goes!

Before there was a Jockey Club, the only place that the Repellents could play was either the Brew House or Shipley's. The Brew House consisted of playing in a bedroom size room with no stage and it was so hot in there and could only fit so many people that people we come inside and go back outside in shifts. I'm sure Jughead remembers this. Actually we played there with Jughead's band, the former AK-47, who later changed their name to SS-20. I've always wondered why they changed their name, maybe Jughead will reveal that in his writings.

My first glimpse of the Jockey Club was very unconventional, it was before the deal was finalized to use it as a Venue for Punk Rock Bands. Only a handful of us got to see it, long before it opened.

I got the chance to see it because me and my Skater Boyfriend at the time, Marty Jimenez would go down to Clem's radio show every Wednesday night, at least I think it was Wednesday. I was just tagging along while Marty was trying to hijack Clem's play list for the night and throw in some songs from his favorite Skater Bands. Clem had me talk on the radio and even let people call in to talk to me, it was a lot of fun. But it was always just the three of us, and it always kind of spooked me to be in that large place unless I was sitting right there behind Clem in a guess what you call the "Control" room.

I always took Clem home after the show and on one particular night he asked

Marty and I if we were up to see something out of our way, but potentially very special. But before I get to that, I want to say that I NEVER turned Clem down when he needed a ride. Clem rode back and forth with me to quite a few parties back in the day! I was always there to give him a ride for two reasons, number one, I liked Clem and number two, I did it out of respect. I think there were probably many younger people that did not realize how integral Clem Carpenter was in building the "scene" here in Cincinnati. Clem was definitely the grass roots for what would become one of the best "scenes" in all of North America.

Now back to that "out of the way, but well worth it" drive that Clem asked me to make. When he told me to head south for Newport Kentucky, my first thought was "Clem wants us to go to a strip bar?" I know that sounds unbelievable, but what else was there in Newport, Kentucky at the time?

Thankfully, I quickly found out I was wrong when Clem began to tell us that we were heading for a venue that Bill Leist was trying to negotiate as a great place for bands to play. I don't believe the deal had been made yet and Clem swore us to secrecy. Sorry to let the cat out of the bag, Clem. When we pulled up and I saw the "Jockey Club" sign, I already knew a bit about the history of the place. My Dad, now deceased, was born in the early 1930s and had been to the Jockey Club in its heyday and had told me several stories about it. He was a very young lawyer at the time and helped represent some very "colorful" characters in Newport. I know you've all heard a few notorious stories about the Jockey Club and according to my Dad, they were all true!

Clem had a key and when we walked in he flipped on a light and I saw that long, long corridor and I was already anticipating something great and as soon as we opened the doors and I saw the stage, I was not disappointed. I was basically speechless!

Clem even turned on the some of the stage lights and told me to get up there and check it out, which I eagerly did and the first thought that came to my mind was, "If they get this place, I'm going to get a band together so I can play on that stage"!

Once the club opened, it didn't take long for people to find out that I had left the Repellents and was back home in Cincinnati to stay. I can't even tell you how many people would ask Bill Leist about me and if I was looking to play again. Bill introduced several people to me but, but I didn't "click" with any of them until he introduced me to Tim, "Bill Igerent". He was quite the talker and so incredibly enthusiastic, that I knew I wanted to work with him. I figured since he had just spent six years in the Army that he probably had a lot of energy and a lot to get off his chest and I was right. I already knew Ben from Indiana and knew he was going to U.C. and Paul basically landed on our doorstep. I have to say, that this lineup of "Musical Suicide" meant the world to me. We were definitely a bit different than a lot of bands at the time because we become very good friends very quickly and we never argued. Yes, we did bicker, but only in jest. Over the years the vast majority of all male bands that I knew, argued on a regular basis and many had more than one, out of control, egotistical members. We never had any of that and maybe that had something to do with me being in the band and cutting through all that testosterone with what little estrogen I possessed!

Musical Suicide: Paul "Couch" Grisar, Jakki Repellent, Bill Igerent and Ben Shipman in front of the JC
photo by Jan Gerber

Jakki Repellent
photo courtesy of Jakki Repellent

As far as the demise of Musical Suicide, I know there were some very fictitious rumors as to why we broke up. My personal favorite was that I had become a Christian and I guess basically had to denounce my band and all other "works of Satan". Only a person who DIDN'T know me could make that up. Everyone that REALLY knew me found that laughable because they knew I was a very spiritual person before, during and after Musical Suicide.

To begin with, we never started the band in the hopes of being the next "Black Flag" or the next "Dead Kennedys". Because we knew they weren't making the kind of money people thought they were. Jello and Henry became far richer AFTER they stopped singing.

We started Musical Suicide for one reason – to have fun. And from the very beginning, all four of us decided that when the time came that it wasn't fun anymore, we would dissolve the band. After Tim left and we all understood why he needed to leave, it was never the same for us. I think he was one of the best front men in the business and I'm honored that I got to play behind him. For us, no one could take his place. We were on the verge of either splitting up for good or maybe trying it as a three piece band when I got sick and nearly died.

Musical Suicide LP, "Little Fish in the Big Sea"

I came down with an unidentified virus that attacked my liver with such ferocity, that it nearly took my life. Paul and I had been riding around in his little green British car, I can't remember the maker, (but it was a car you would never see on the road) doing our favorite recreational past time, smoking lots of weed and going through numerous fast food drive thru's, when I started to feel like I was getting sick with an earache and a sore throat. I mean I got in the car that afternoon felling perfectly well, but by the time he dropped me off I was feeling sicker than I had ever felt in my life. To make a long story short, I was hanging on for dear life for two months, going from 95 lbs. to 69 lbs.!

Paul and Ben stayed in touch with me the whole time and about a month into my illness we mutually came to the decision that it just wasn't fun anymore and we dissolved the band. That's the simple, honest truth. It wasn't the easiest decision to make because, as I said before we were all good friends, and Paul and Ben were like brothers to me. We didn't want to continue the charade of one singer after another, like playing "musical chairs" instead of "Musical Suicide". And it really wasn't fair to the guys who were trying to front the band. Tim was our brother and no one could take his place.

I don't think many people realize how good we had it here. I know this because I toured in the U.S. and Canada, both with the Repellents and an extensive tour with Musical Suicide. Many of those so called "famous" punk rock venues that you would read about in fanzines were mostly dives and had

NOTHING on the Jockey Club. That's why we had so many big bands play at the Jockey Club, the word spread quickly that this venue and this scene was something very special.

Now back to the Jockey Club. Only a handful of venues hosted as many "big name" bands as we did. And I do believe that Musical Suicide opened for more of those bands than any other band in town. Either Bill Leist thought we were good enough to do it or cheap enough to do it, actually make that free! Whichever it was, I thank him for giving us that opportunity, because he worked harder than anyone else and he didn't make money either.

Paul, Bill Igerent, Jakki, Nick Stavale, Ben, "Handsome" Clem
photo courtesy of Jakki Repellent

But it was never about the money. And like you've heard many others say, "I never once paid to get in the Jockey Club" was also true for me. Perhaps Shorty had a "crush" on me, because he was very nice to me and talkative, which I don't think he was with other females. And he sure put my best friend, but never my boyfriend, Jeff Stewart in his place when Jeff would try to convince him that I was his girlfriend. Shorty would never buy it and I can't say the many hysterical things he said to Jeff about it because most of it was X rated, but it was along the lines of, "She wouldn't be your girlfriend if you were the last man on earth."

And "Tiny" never charged me for a drink. He kept fresh grenadine for me to mix with diet coke. He was probably happy to have one less drunkard in the place.

For me, what really made the Jockey Club so special and something never to be duplicated again was the people. All of us who were there nearly every time the doors were open. And the core people, really didn't feel so much like friends, they felt like family. Some of us really went out of our way to look like a punk and some of us didn't and that didn't matter. Those of us with our spiky hair, torn jeans and outrageous makeup, did it because it was fun, not because we were trying to look like someone we were not. We were the real thing, no matter how we looked on the outside.

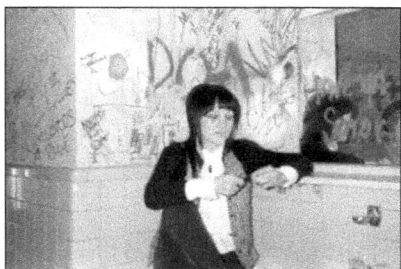

Jakki Repellent in the JC bathroom
photo by Amy Miller

And I know that you could never have the harmony that we had with today's teenagers and young people who become "Punk Rockers" by simply charging clothes at "Hot Topic" on their parent's credit cards. I know they "think" they are really scaring the heck out of me at the mall, wearing their "1983 Dead Kennedy's tour shirt", the same tour that I actually opened for the "Dead Kennedy's", but they're not, they're making me laugh to be honest.

I know that the Jockey Club touched each and every one of us and left a huge impression on our lives. For some of us, like me, it changed my entire destiny, because I met my husband, Greg Stout there, the original bass player for Toxic Reasons. We've been together for nearly 24 years and married for 21 of those years! We were blessed with a beautiful daughter, Bianca in 1989 and she made us grandparents last year! I have a wonderful nine month old grandson named Liam, who means the world to me. It's amazing when I think about the link that little Liam has with the Jockey Club. Without the Jockey Club, I would have never had the family that I do, the family that I love and cherish. And for this, I'm eternally grateful.

Who would have ever thought?

Bill Igerent

The Jockey Club—circa. July 1983—October 1984. These are the approximate begin and end dates of my "relationship" with the Jockey Club. Like many things during that time in my life the specifics are a little fuzzy. Less than a year and a half - it's not a long time by any stretch so it might seem a mystery as to why I would hold the Jockey Club so fondly in my memory.

Musical Suicide
photo by Jan Gerber

On the surface and by many accounts I should hate the Jockey Club. It's where I did a large number of things that I am not proud of in the least and I won't detail all of them here as many of them are best forgotten and I'm not really sure what the statute of limitations are on some of my transgressions.

But I will tell you it is where I broke my foot while stage diving. It's where I did a flip off the stage and the full crowd of punks parted like the Red Sea and let me land flat on my back. (I'm still not sure why I didn't break my back or crack my skull open on that little stunt.) And it is where I slammed back all those Foster's Lagers on the night that I tried to outrun the boys in blue in a VW Super Beetle on the streets of Clifton, was arrested at gun point, charged with a DUI and sentenced to a three-day over-night "program" where I was re-educated and brought to the realization that I had

Musical Suicide
photo by Jan Gerber

a bit of a problem controlling my alcohol intake. So yeah, I've got some issues associated with the Jockey Club.

But I don't hate the Jockey Club. I'm older now and realize that it was my decisions and my choices that led me to such a low place in October of 1984. I can point to a number of reasons why I ended up in the crapper at the age of twenty three but none of them are the Jockey Club. In fact, if I'm honest, the Jockey Club supported me during that year of living stupidly and I just didn't appreciate it.

Just out of the Army after a four-year stint I was looking to get a punk band together and to take on the world and blow off some steam. But when I heard about the Jockey Club in my own backyard I didn't get on my knees and thank God. No, I just took it for granted that such a place would exist. Why wouldn't there be a punk venue like the JC just waiting for me to come along?

If I wasn't so naive and had understood what it took to pull something like the JC together maybe I would have appreciated it more instead of treating it as a "given".

Maybe I would have appreciated that it was bringing together some of the best musicians in the area and giving them the opportunity to play out when nowhere else would take a chance on them.

Maybe I would have appreciated that it was bringing together some of the crappiest musicians in the area and giving them the opportunity to live out their punk rock dreams.

Bill Igerent and Chuck Byrd

Maybe I would have appreciated what it meant to be able to see all those bands that the JC hosted in such a wide open space instead of in someone's basement or a corner bar the size of a subway car.

But no. I just took the Jockey Club for granted as the natural state of things. I took it for granted that at the Jockey Club I'd find someone like Jakki Repellant to start a band with. That we'd then find someone like Ben "The Shred Rat" Shipman to join us and that we'd then find a drummer like Paul Couch (Grisar). I took it for granted that they had the talent and the patience to turn us into an honest to goodness punk rock band with a sound all our own.

I just took it as a matter of course that we'd be opening for the Circle Jerks at the Jockey Club even though we only had three weeks practice, a ten minute set, and no name for our band. That's what the Jockey Club was there for, right? To facilitate my punk rock aspirations.

I didn't even appreciate the fact that the Jockey Club gave us our band name. After the fiasco of that first gig we got off the stage and while exchanging notes with Billy Blank on how bad we sucked, one of us posited that we had just committed musical suicide, and at that moment we knew what our band name should be.

And I didn't appreciate that the Jockey Club had anything to do with everything else that came after that. The openings for big name bands like Black Flag and the Circle Jerks (again). The connections made with bands from Dayton, Columbus, Lexington and elsewhere that allowed us to play in those cities and make an underground tour of the U.S. All made possible because the Jockey Club was there. There with the opportunities. There with the people. There with the reputation.

I didn't appreciate it then. But I appreciate it now. For what that's worth.

To some it's probably too little, too late. But for me I'm going to say it's better late than never!

Thanks Jockey Club! Much appreciated!

Angst, Existentialism and Fun in an Unlikely Place

by Sean Allen

Heading south on I-71, somebody said Jello was a mime in San Francisco before hooking up with the Dead Kennedys.

Up close you could see the ghost of a former mime in Jello Biafra's animated face. He had a stage actor's ability to animate and contort his face that belied the angst of the Dead Kennedys politically and socially charged lyrics. It was spring and The Jockey Club was humid with sweat and the dankness of old man Shorty's ragged cave that felt like it had not seen the south end of a mop since the Carter Administration.

In May of '85 the scene was alive and kicking as far as we knew. This night the JC was packed. Really packed. It was, to be certain, a genuine American underground movement; to date, the last of its kind. The mainstream press in all its clueless called the JC a "New Wave" Club if it called the JC anything at all. This was not "New Wave" and it was not necessarily "punk" in the sense of British-Sex-Pistols-piss-on-your-audience punk, those things were the more famously flamboyant cousins of Hardcore. Within 36 months the scene would go the way of the buffalo nickel, but in spring of '85 it was burning bright in places like this and this place exactly.

The Jockey Club was THE Place to play between CBGB's in New York and Club Vex in East LA. Hardcore bands went around in clap-trap vans, ate powdered Donettes outside 7-11, took vitamin C ("to avoid scurvy") and crashed on the floors of incredibly rundown apartments and tenement buildings. A room at Motel 6 might as well been a suite at the Ritz Carlton, such indulgence was not an option. Unlike the typical rock music scene, sex and drugs were not compulsory and trashing a hotel room was out of the question.

In the summer of '86 I took to the road with the infamously-named Columbus band Painful Discharge. This was the East Coast tour in support of their single release Skulls and Balls. Since I owned a comfortable and running van I was specifically qualified to road manage a hardcore band. With the tacit cooperation of New York-based promoter and aptly named Johnny Stiff, another figure from the salad days, PD and I motored east from Columbus. We played the Electric Banana in Pittsburgh to an enthusiastic crowd one night and got stiffed and nearly shot in Reading, PA the next.

Reading is a thoroughly depressing place that I hate to this day. We knew we were going to get the shaft right when we got there. The part of the country was the shaft. Thus we felt fully justified in taking our payment through making several hundred dollars worth of long distance calls from the unattended bar phone. We also took our due by filling road cases with cartons of cigarettes, packets of Lance snacks and bags of Beer Nuts. We felt no obligation to observe the common load-in/load out courtesy of respecting the wood work, doors frames and walls as we hauled our alternative compensation for services rendered out the unattended front door of that hell-hole club and out of that hell-hole town. After receiving a very credible threat of high-velocity lead poisoning from the convincingly mobbed-up, Corvette-driving club owner we high tailed it in to the fog covered back roads of eastern PA, blindly snaking our way through the mountains, on to Philadelphia where guitarist Casey Rice's parents lived in chic urban luxury. Incidentally Rice went on to play guitar with Liz Phair. I think he used the stage name KC Brick during his days with PD. Not surprising, in a bio I found on the web, Rice conspicuously makes no mention of his days with PD when recalling his time at Ohio State. In retrospect it was probably a good idea to use a pseudonym when associating one's self with Painful Discharge. Mike Mancy, the band singer, didn't and I think he still regrets it although I can't say whether or not it has hurt him in his present-day role as the Toledo restaurant kingpin. A real writer would call Mancy's Steaks and ask him.

A night or so later we had a show in Richmond, VA. I slept in the van; I always slept in the van: 1) I liked sleeping in the van 2) I had the most to lose if the van got busted in to or stolen. That night we played with a short-lived group known as Unseen Force and a ripping local band called White Cross. The guitarist for White Cross gave us a video tape of this truly absurd-in-every-sense-of-the-word, project he was working on. It was a band dressed as Vikings, Norsemen, Santa Claus and other inexplicable characters. They were fast and loud as hell, put on a stage show that involved several 55-gallon drums of stage blood, scantily clad dancing girls simulating sodomy of Santa and other horrifically humorous acts of depravity. This monstrosity stage show—equal parts speed metal, comic book antics, big-time wrestling and Halloween party—was called GWAR.

As was typical we were given accommodation in Richmond on the floor of someone's apartment. I never went in because of my aforementioned love and responsibility for the security of the van and its contents. The next day we got on the road exceptionally early. Apparently the previous night's dwelling and entire contents were soaked in cat urine, but the guys of PD were too nice to look a gift horse in the mouth and just dealt with it. In retrospect that gift horse was more like a severed horse head—covered in piss.

So that was touring, ranting fanzines were everywhere and the flyers were many times painstakingly hand-produced works of street art. Sometimes they were crap. All the time they were massively reproduced by stealing late-night copies at Kinko's. Just load up the banks of Xerox machines at 15th and High and let 'em rip. Come back in about 20 minutes, collect up your documents and walk out without paying, simple as that. No one at Kinko's gave a shit, they still don't.

Sure there was political and social rage against the machine. But there was also the more immediate agenda of doing things as cheaply as possible. Also there was the underlying mischievous ethos that permeated the whole scene that was well captured in the 1984 film Repo Man when one hardcore punk says to another "let's go do some crimes; let's eat sushi and not pay." That really was about the extent of it all.

JC crowd
photo by George Duchaine

The Jockey Club was always packed, even when it wasn't. In general any hardcore show had an almost suffocating energy of struggle, angst and despair, but the JC alone had it in spades. The place was haunted with that energy way before the American Hardcore Scene arrived on York Street. It had the ghost of resistance, rebellion and death stacked to the ceiling.

At this point it is worth mentioning that romanticizing this nomadic squalor or revising history to believe that there was some united rallying point of battle against the Reagan Administration would be off base. The scene was nothing more or less than what it was at the time; an interesting, alternative and usually fun thing to do. Assuredly no one now will make the mistake that those who migrated to the corner of Haight and Ashbury in '67 did. The flocking electric sheep of the Summer of Love actually believed their own high-minded utopian bullshit. Even in 1985 we knew well that was an idea only an asshole would buy into. Reagan, the ACTOR, was President, it was clear the reactionary set won the match. I was just fun to yell "fuck you" once in a while.

As best can be recalled the May '85 DK show was exceptional; loud, raucous and ridiculous. Being pressed against the stage I found it curious that for all his preaching against tyranny, Jello had a sadistic fondness for stomping on the arms of those of us who had nowhere else to put our upper extremities than on the front lip of the stage. The entire show he manically paced the stage mashing forearms under foot. Maybe it was some sort of territory defense tactic they taught at mime school. He was a low-rent rock star so some dickishness was to be expected.

PD got back from the road at the end of the summer of '86 and we went back to our classes, our jobs and weekends playing here or there. Of course, goofing around at Crazy Mama's was always a standard activity. By '88 everyone would be listening to Metallica with a dash of Public Enemy as a klan of ignorant hill jacks dressed as skinheads managed to deftly infiltrate and wreck what little there was left of the hardcore scene. And the Jockey had its last show.

Eventually old Shorty went paws up and The Jockey Club was ground into the dirt. The ability to have one's own underground scene tenuously connected by copper wire technology, the U.S. Postal Service and sponsored by no one, disappeared into the dust just like Shorty and his club. The scene was perfectly existential, it's meaning and essence self-created it was there and gone like a St. Elmo's fire.

One can rage all they like, in the end the machine wins. Evidenced by any given history but also by the here and now; for example I hesitated to mention St. Elmo's Fire fearing that, understandably, one might think I am making reference to that dreadfully treacle film from, coincidentally, 1985. In actuality I mean to conjure an image of the electrical weather phenomenon in which balls of fire or lightning appear brightly in the sky and immediately disappear. In an alternate reality where the machine is defeated, St. Elmo's fire, the celluloid crapo brought to us by the exact same hack that ruined the Batman franchise in the mid 1990's, would not be in the memory of any sane person and bands like Sluggo and the Necros would be commonly known in the annals of rock music history.

As the 1980's began the quest for fun with angst was found in Kentucky at the edge of Appalachia, in the sticky-wood palaces of OSU's dilapidated South Campus, on the roads leading in and out of shit-box towns from South Boston to Bakersfield. As for the Jockey Club, this was a place on the wrong side of the river and everyone knew it. Juxtaposed to the gleaming Queen City, the JC was in the cradle of the damned just northwest of Fucked Estates.

Most of us that were there then are here now curiously with mortgages to manage and kids to care for. The Jockey Club at 633 York Street in Newport, Kentucky USA was the god-forsaken bassinette that held the being and nothingness of our semi-rebellious youth, if only for a moment.

Joey "Shithead" Keithley

The Jockey Club, for me that was a cool point in time, carved out of the lingering shadow of another cool point in time. You just have to think of the history of Newport Kentucky and that grand old club itself and it was almost absurd that a bunch of gangly weird looking punks would invade The Jockey and bring back some real "show biz pizzazz" to that old joint. I can't forget the look on Shorty and Tiny's faces as we strolled in and asked for a beer. It was the look that said "I've thrown better men out the back door for fun than serve bums like you" type of look. But they would eventually and suspiciously hand over a can of Stroh's.

D.O.A.
photos by Witt

I think we set the record for the most times any out of town band ever played there, 10 times between 1980 and 1985. Every time we arrived the ritual was the same, first, get the can of obligatory swill (after all it was free), next, one of us would go to take a leak in the can and then make a loud joke about the stench. Fuck! The Jockey Club bathroom had to be the worst smelling thing this side of the black hole of Calcutta. I don't think it had been cleaned since Elvis Presley pissed in it in 1958!

So I would run off to the White Castle down the street, to use the crapper there. After dropping the kids off at the pool, I would order four White Castle burgers (to refuel, I suppose). Speaking of White Castle, we would usually meet our buddy Ed Pitman (Toxic Reasons) there. Ed would usually show up with 48 Iron City Beer (which was pure shit, but again free) and then regale us with his tale of eating 73 White Castle burgers in one sitting.

The gigs were always a blast, with the crew of Bill Leist, Clem and Jughead making sure that we had more than enough sub sandwiches to stuff our faces with. We would munch them down in the old dressing room that looked like Chuck Berry, at not getting paid in full, had put his foot through every wall in the place, either that or the walls had just plain rotted away.

They had this old time stage with red carpet and these steps going up from the audience to the stage, which had been how the performers of yesteryear had walked down from the stage to croon to the audience, in the club's glory days. To us, it just seemed like an invite for the punks to come and fuck with our shit on stage. In the end it worked out, as we would do a cover of the Sinatra classic "That's Life", as the end of our encore. I would take off my guitar and make the walk down those glorious old steps and croon to the audience. Now I know some of the punks maybe felt like puking at that point, but after all it could have been the Stroh's or the Iron City. Ah, The Jockey Club, what memories...at least we never got gunned down on the sidewalk.

Dave Gregg Interview

by Jerry Adams,
Altered Statements

D.O.A. 3-17-84 /jockey club

Having the punk rock tendancies
that I do I was most surely at the J.C.
for the last D.O.A. show. I talked with guitarist Dave Gregg and we talked a lot. Here
you'll find the most interesting excerpt
of our conversation.

a-So?

DG-This is our 4th time at the J.C.
here in Newport,Ky-sin city of the
midwest.

a-How does it feel to be successful in
the respect that you have a large following?
DG-The reason is because we've been around
for 5 years.We've played Lexington,Louisville,
and Cincinnati.Success feels great because
we put the work in.If it did'nt feel good
I would'nt do it.We have straight jobs in
Vancouver when we do go home.Success for us
and I use the word not as monatary success,
is personal satisfaction.We'll have no real
arrival at success because that aspect just
does'nt suit D.O.A.

a-What are your recordings?

DG-Our most recent album is a compilation
of our 1st two which are out of print.It's
called Bloodied but Unbowed.Our single
was a benefit for the Vancouver 5 and it's
called Right to be Wild.Our EP is calles War
on 45-it's just a record record.The band
is trying to get out of the distribution
business and let other people take care of that
aspect of it-that way we can concentrate
on writing and playing music.

a-What does the term Hardcore mean to you?
DG-In 1981 D.O.A. released an album called
Hardcore 81 and we backed it with a tour.
It was all called punk rock. In our own
opinion D.O.A. was responsible for the
popularization of the term hardcore. The
term influenced a lot of people.At the time
hardcore meant hard working,unconpromising
rock and roll. Now, 3 years later,Hardcore
is a popular word come to mean a narrow
genre of music which has nothing to do with
what we meant the term to mean. It's like John
Rotten looking at some aspects termed punk
today.It's just been the popularization
of a word.

a-Closing statements?

DG-Hi mom,,.

D.O.A. RECORDS ARE AVAILABLE AT RECORD ALLEY.
ARTICLE by a.a.----Thanks Dave,see you next time!

Snare

One of my most interesting memories of the club was the way these two old guys, Tiny and Shorty, were completely unfazed by all these strange looking/acting young people and their extremely loud and angry and sometimes weird music. It was more shocking than any band or fan I came in contact with. It

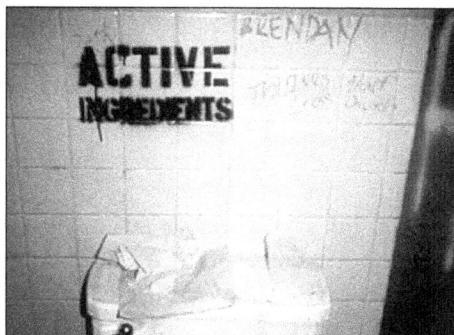

JC bathroom
photo by Sarah Kuhl

told me these two guys had seen it all.

There was definitely some kind of charm about the place that we all fell in love with the whole thing. Not just the music, but the owners, the lax set of rules, the regulars, the Foster's and yes, the wonderful smell of the restrooms.

I'll never forget Tiny at a Circle Jerks show with his Circle Jerks "Golden Shower of Hits" t-shirt. I'll never forget him getting pissed off at me for applauding Bevo and The Fastbats performance while they emptied the club of the 15 or so people that were there.

I'll always remember all 260 LBS of Ed Pittman from the Toxic Reasons on stage jumping up and down shaking the bands amps.

I'll always remember me and Bill Leist taking Jello Biafra thrift store shopping and Jello flashing us when we went to pick him up at the old Gateway Motel in Covington.

One of my earliest great memories was meeting "Handsome" Dick Manitoba when

John "99" Haynes
photo by Amy Miller

he was road manager for the
Del-Lords. Their van broke
down and I tried to set them
up with a ride to Louisville.
One time when The Dicks
played there some chick
jumped up onstage and got
on the mic and said, "What
is this bullshit? Play some
Rock n Roll!" When they
launched into the next song,
the guitarist shoved her

Snare and the Idiots
photo by Sarah Kuhl

down the stage steps (Remember the three-tiered stage in the early days?).

Who could forget John Haynes and his knack for stealing American flags?

I remember on many a night going to the club and seeing an amazing band
to a capacity audience of hardly anyone. Some of these bands were the Le Roi
Brothers, Death Angel and 63 Eyes. I would say Mission Of Burma but I left
before they started playing. Had to work the next day.

I remember the clubs first out of town show was the Effigies on a week night.
MDC were booked at Shipleys (AKA Top Cats) and were paid $50 NOT
to play, so they came to the club and played after The Effigies. That night I
realized I was seeing history unfold.

Bill and I went to Jello Biafra's motel room at the now-defunct Gateway Motel.
He was sitting at a desk with song titles written on individual slips of paper.
This was his way of arranging a set list. We took him thrift store shopping in
Newport and Covington. He would get really excited when he saw one. He
spotted a St. Vincent De Paul store in Covington and said, "Oh, goody! Let
me out right heeere!" as he excitedly jumped out of Bill's car with his Maytag
repair man's jacket on.

I remember he bought a Neil Sedaka album. Some Doo-Wop group he liked
sang back-up on it. He bought the geekiest, out-of-style clothes he could find.
He found a purple turtleneck he liked and was slightly disappointed when it
had an Izod logo on it. He still bought it though. When he first got in Bill's car,
I think he made some comment about the plastic Jesus on his dash. He later

recorded a song called "Plastic Jesus" with Mojo Nixon. I don't know if it was inspired by Bill or not.

The Del-lords got their van fixed and I didn't hang out in Louisville. Manitoba was fun to talk to. He told us stories about touring with KISS and about the time the Dictators played before a bunch of Hell's Angels in New York.

I just drove past the site of the old Jockey Club that's now a cab company. I saw all the cars in the lot and in the back of my mind I was hoping there would be a big show tonight. One thing that came to mind is how the Jockey Club really cracked open the music scene in Cincinnati. Before the club there wasn't anything but Heavy Metal cover bands and Top 40. The Jockey Club really was the catalyst of the vibrant music scene this town has had for the last two decades. Now there is great music of all genres. A band couldn't get a gig in those days if they played originals. Now bands can't get gigs at a lot of clubs if they do covers. Few local bands had an outlet for their material before the Jockey Club. The JC was our CBGB'S.

Chris Donnelly

I was 13 years old and in 1982 I saw an early D.O.A. show at the JC. Within a few months, I was doing these crude magic marker/scotch tape/cutup photo flyers for the Jockey Club shows like Hüsker Dü, Fang, and others. A few months after that, friends I had made through hanging around the Jockey (as well as Another Records, Zoo Records, and Clem's show on WAIF) decided to form a hardcore band, Sluggo.

Sluggo
photo by Amy Miller

Billy Blank possibly realized that we genuinely appreciated the Club and the access we had, so he got the entire band fake IDs from some place in Florida. So, from around 1983 on, Sluggo played the Club a lot. And when we weren't playing, we were there. The following is was I recall:

...300 pounds of PA speakers falling over at the first Replacements show, almost killing Rick Schuler from Squirrelbait...Bass player from the Dicks smashing his bass over the head of some pissed off Newport lady, who walked in the club just to use the microphone to vent her frustrations...John Brannon from Negative Approach doing their set on mushrooms, and not knowing how to get back on stage...Agnostic Front wanting to kill us because we cancelled our opening slot and Julian mildly dogged their record in his fanzine...Chris Doherty from Gang Green spinning on his head on stage during their encore, only to lose chunks of hair and skin to the seams in the JC stage...the Necros having Pete Wegele do lead vocals on "Ramblin' Rose"... Henry Rollins getting annoyed with Karl Meyer and I during their set because we demanded they play some S.O.A. songs...

Sluggo
photo by George DuChaine

People setting off entire packs of bottle rocket during Suicidal Tendencies… The guys from Metallica hanging around the pinball machines after the over-sold Ramones show…Neil Aquino throwing squid at almost every band…Jeff Ament, Stone Gossard and Mark Arm staying at Pete's parents' house when Green River played…Opening up for the Dead Kennedys on my prom night… Colin from GBH acting like a roadie for Sluggo, demanding more time for a better soundcheck for us…Joni Cline introducing me to El Duce…Covering "Minnesota Strip" with Clem on vocals…

It certainly was the best way to have fun in Cincinnati in the 1980s.

That's the way I have chosen to remember it.

J.J. Pearson

Most of my memories are clouded by oil cans of Foster's… I have one regret though. It was one of my "others I had harmed" on my fourth step (of 12) when I nailed some young girl in the parking lot and I'm pretty sure I gave her the Clapp! I felt like a scumbag about it for years and years… besides that little foot note, I always had a good time at the ole "Jockey Club" … but we could never take the right bridge across the river… every fucken time we'd fuck it up and have to wonder around forever before we found the place…

Walt Hodge

The Jockey Club was a unique forum for the Cincinnati and Northern KY underground music scene. And it was a scene. It was not just the bands that played there, but a very unusual mix of humanity. On any given night, you'd find hipsters, youngsters, bikers, rednecks, business suits, poseurs, political

The Libertines
photo courtesy of Walt Hodge

activists, punks (of course), and the occasional pasty faced nerd that might actually be a mass murderer. But rather than a clashing of cultures resulting in constant fights, it was cool and generally peaceful. Hell, after a few Foster's or Rolling Rocks you'd talk to anybody. I believe it was Bill Leist that dubbed any night there "The Freak Show". I wrote a song for the Libertines titled "Something in the Water" that was inspired by people watching at the JC.

The Libertines' "(Everybody wants to be my)
Sister" 7-inch
photo by Scott Bruno

Early on, shows were lightly attended by the art and alt music folk. The word needed to get around a bit. That meant that you played for the other band and the locals sitting in the back at the bar with Tiny. Eventually, a regular group of cool people started showing up, finally outnumbering the old barflies and uninterested factory guys.

I remember the first packed house show at the Jockey Club, with Violent Femmes, BPA, and the Libertines. It was so great to see the place filled to overflowing.

Everybody having a great time, it certainly was a euphoric moment for us. After the show, Todd Witt from BPA and me were dispatched to collect our share of the bounty. As he and I walked toward the front room to collect the loot, we were both thinking to ourselves "Let's see, tickets were $6 in advance, $7 at the door, the place was PACKED… maybe 300, 400, 500 people? WE ARE GONNA GET PAID!!!" Sure enough, Bill was counting a substantial pile of cash that night. We quickly lost our erections when we were handed $50 each. At the time, we were both really mad. It was explained that there was a guarantee promised to the Femmes, and higher than usual advertising costs to ensure a sold out show. Todd and I weren't hearing any of it that night. We felt like it was one thing to be gouged by a bar owner almost every place else. But not here, in our house, by our friends. It was a bitter pill that took a while to swallow.

By today's standards, that was tame. A number of promoters expect the bands to pay them to play a show or festival. Now that is complete bullshit.

Billy, all is forgiven. Split it wide open!

Ric Hickey

My band The Speed Hickeys also played a number of shows at the Jockey Club, proudly racking up at least a dozen or so appearances there. Usually we were on a bill with 3 or 4 other local bands that we knew nothing about going in, but eventually got to know them all from gigging together all the time. (Sadly, I have lost track of all the soundboard recordings we made there including at least three different gigs where "Handsome" Clem sang The Dictators' "Next Big Thing" with us.) SS-20 was one of my favorite acts to see at the JC and I probably went to 50 of their shows there. In truth, The Reduced was my #1 favorite JC fixture. But they didn't play out as much as SS-20 and couldn't seem to keep their shit together. I know now that that was part of their charm all along. They were shambolic Slop Rock junky kings that came closer to The Stooges' messy majesty than any other band I have ever seen. Trust fund babies and rich kids couldn't create that music if they tried. Not even in a laboratory. The Reduced were the real thing and their shows were dangerous. Bill, sometimes emerging from a glass coffin to open their set, would stalk the stage and hurl huge gobs of spit on everyone in sight. The crowd pelted the band with a shower of Foster's oil cans throughout their every performance and Bill always asked for more. "That all you got?"

On Thursday May 26, 1988, the Speed Hickeys opened for Dag Nasty. Three days later I was record shopping at Wizard's Cave in Corryville when I saw a stark and desperate flyer stapled to a telephone pole. Dashed off with a Sharpie and quickly printed at the Kinko's on Short Vine, it said "JOCKEY CLUB LAST SHOW EVER. TONIGHT SUNDAY MAY 29. THE REDUCED. SS-20. THE AUBURNAIRES. TBA. THE BUILDING HAS BEEN SOLD. THIS IS IT, FOLKS."

For a second, I was in shock. "Unholy fuck…", I thought, "I have to get down there tonight." Just three nights earlier when we played with Dag Nasty I'd seen no clue that the end was near.

In a place that was always rife with debauchery and drunken madness that last night at the Jockey Club was one of the most insane scenes I have ever beheld. During The Auburnaires' set someone reached up and set the carpet on fire on the stage. I don't remember the band looking too concerned about dousing it. While The Reduced played, I watched the walls rippling as people tore down the paneling. By the time word spread that someone had broken into Shorty's 45 collection, hundreds of the records were sailing through the air over the heads of the mangy crowd. Soon Shorty was bopping around, cracking people on the head with a giant flashlight if he saw them flinging his records around or trying to make off with a table or a chair for a souvenir. (Escaping any serious injury, I was able to score a chair for myself and even the diamond-shaped window frame off the front door went home with me after some leather-clad punk busted it out with his elbow and shook off the frame in front of me on the sidewalk outside!)

One night in 1985, after delivering the money raised by advance tickets sold at Record Bar, I saw a still-skinny and long-haired Henry Rollins perched like a rabid raven on a doorstep three doors down from the JC, frowning strenuously and seething with anger at the whole planet. Turning back after initially walking right past him, I told him I liked the piece he'd written for SPIN magazine. He gave me a terse nod and a quick wave. Even way back then his writing was smart and funny. But here on this night, on the sidewalks of

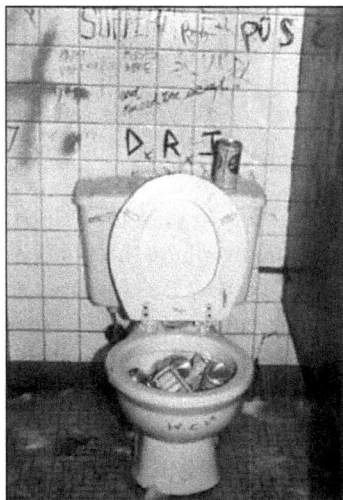

JC men's room

Newport, he clearly needed to retreat deeply within himself to conjure and save every last bit of energy for the show. During Black Flag's set that night, Henry made one of the most hilarious and accurate statements about the Jockey Club that I have ever heard. Commenting on how things changed over the years, how "candy bars just get smaller but more expensive", he said "One thing never changes. And that's the smell of the Jockey Club bathroom".

Bryce Rhude

My band gestated for a long time. Longer than most. Very insular, we just hadn't a clue and smoked away several years after high school totally oblivious as to how bands went about getting shows. All I saw of the live band scene in Cincy was some baaaaad shit. But I knew my band was different, I never lost the faith, I just didn't know what to do. I left town just as the Jockey Club was starting up (as I would learn years later). I cooked pizzas in St. Louis and saved money until I got back to town maybe a year later and the band resumed almost instantly. Not being a newspaper reader, I was still unaware of the club. All I listened to on WAIF was "Rockin' and Surfin'" (some things never change) and they weren't promoting the Jockey. Then one of us learns The Dickies are coming to The Jockey Club. Concert bands coming on at 10pm or later seemed inconceivable to me, I guess I thought things would be more like at The Coliseum where I'd seen Cheap Trick, ZZ Top, and others go on at maybe 8 or so, where I was usually back on the street by 11pm. Even at The Ramones at The She in Dayton my friend and I got there several hours too early and sat in the lot smoking joint after joint. A long day but we did get to see the guys arrive and we heard their loud soundcheck through the walls.

So, finally, in the fall of 1983 we go to The Jockey Club. We get to there about 7pm at the latest. One of the only times I ever saw that big front room bathed in semi-sunlight. The staff was already there, and was happy to take our money. The Dickies! I even held them in higher regard than the beloved Ramones. This was gonna be good, um...several hours from now. It's Bill Leist who cards me and I'm holding a Missouri driver's license. He is impressed and thinks I came all this way for this show. I hadn't but kept quiet. I'd come from Amberly...(I would have come from Missouri to see The Dickies...this was before you could just Google your fave band and learn where they are each night. If you didn't see the poster in the record store you were outta luck. WEBN wasn't helping out any with bands like Ramones or Dickies). So here we are again so early to see a punk band at a club. It's pretty ridiculous. But these errors come with advantages. The Dickies arrive for soundcheck. They look beat. Street clothes. Straight to the stage. They just destroy "Nights in White Satin", it sounded like the record, only better. They all tumble off the stage. Leonard, at my prompting joins us at our table for a few moments. I bother him for some lyrics to "Fan Mail" and kick myself for years that that's all I could think of to say to him. (We're friends now in this internet age and

I've since made up for this gaffe.) We all wanted to ask about Chuck but that would have been in bad taste. We pretty much stayed glued to our table and didn't mingle with the staff too much. But the hours are ticking off. I'm stretching my legs and Stan Lee approaches me back by the pinball machines. He has a demo cassette of "Stukas Over Disneyland" in his pocket and offers it to me to borrow if I wanted to go out to my car and have a listen. I turned him down, I think because I wasn't gonna miss one second of this wholly new and exciting face-time with rock stars!! Well, the show was great, eventually! The five-man Snare and The Idiots opened up and really impressed us too. During slam dancing I see a syringe go skittering across the floor, stopping near our table. Whoa. Hard drugs. We all look at each other. This, who knows, could be a factor in how my band resumed its seclusionary status immediately following this concert.

Doc and the Pods
photo by James Bramlage

Another year goes by. We see The Libertines at Bogarts, and that finally makes a light go off in our heads. We knew we were at least that good, and needed to get going. Still, we knew no one, remained shy and stupid. Frustrated, we threw our own show. Doc rented a hall and got some kegs. We packed it. While there at The Bechtold Park Lodge that wintry Friday eve, a smarter, bolder friend of ours, Sheldon, makes a call to Bill Leist from the pay phone on the wall. He booked us at the JC, just like that! So here we are, the band that has wasted five years doing nothing but rehearsing, playing our first (depending on your point of view) show, and then gets given the word that tomorrow night we are to appear at THE JOCKEY CLUB. We were jumping up and down in glee at this incredible news. Arriving way too early and eagerly again, we sit and wait. Eventually we meet our soundman, Jimmy Davidson. He was not there to work, he was just cruising in for a beer or something. He sticks around but there are no microphones. We were carrying one expensive ribbon microphone that naked Bevo would destroy a little more than a year later so we used that. We all three sing into that one mic, like the early Beatles or something. No amps or drums get any reinforcement. Fine by us, that's the way we'd been doing it for a looooong time. Now I don't recall much of the actual show but it was told to me that we'd gotten a standing ovation, and that it was the first one of the year (how anyone but Shorty would know this for sure I do not know) and here it was December 28th! So that debut was kinda iffy as far as the management handled us, so maybe they wanted to make it right, and hell, they didn't expect us to be good, so we were invited back for Sunday, making it a 3-nighter for us. A murder in the block kept us pinned down for awhile and we couldn't leave. This began the run of appearances that really made us fall in love with the club and the people involved and the whole scene. We met everybody, including The Thangs (kindred spirits) and saw a ton of shows. Everyone loved us, except for one dude, who I extended a hand of friendship to and he stuck his nose in the air and huffed off angrily. Some of those on the scene for some time were not keen on these hot new upstarts. I stayed unemployed all thru 1985 and hung on the phone a lot keeping the band working. Some of these marathon calls were with Billy who was also a heavyweight telephone addict, man his line was always busy, and if you could get through his Mom would say he just split. I guess he hadda get away from that damn phone! He'd just shoot the breeze with me and was a very curious guy, wanted to know the inner workings of the band; who was the de-facto leader. We went to Dee Felice and had happy hour cheap cocktail shrimps and discussed my still intact virginity,

Doc & The Pods
flyer by Bryce Rhude

drove around Newport making stops in his 1965 Fairlane with the hugest amount of pot I'd ever seen, right on the front seat. I was scared a bit, and also thrilled. There was something intoxicating about year-one of Doc and The Pods at The Jockey Club. I made flyers for the club and got free admission to a ton of shows. I loaned my PA cabinets as side-fill monitors, and was there often in the daytime either dragging them in or out. So I saw Shorty in his natural element, watching that little black and white TV at the bar with all the lights up. He was cool with me. Shorty actually liked The Pods, something I don't think he could say about a lot of the groups he hosted. We even got to record there once on a Sunday afternoon. Jimmy set it up and Shorty was there. Some big show had happened the night before and there was a smashed toilet all over the stage as we recorded. Steve rolled in late and hungover and proceeded to lay down and close his eyes amidst ceramic shards.

Since I possibly incorrectly considered myself somewhat of an insider, I made myself quite comfortable at shows and loved going to side stage, behind the mains, an area generally off limits to the public, find some privacy and smoke down. Jimmy D brought me to side stage during Hüsker Dü so that I could see stage-diving close up. At side stage I once again saw a staggeringly huge brick of hashish. I began to suspect that a bit of dealing was key to the club's ability to bring in big national and international acts. I missed a lot more shows than I saw, but I do recall being knocked out by The Auburnaires, The White Animals, The Cramps, The Prime Movers, Tupelo Chain Sex, Legal Weapon, Boys From Nowhere, and of course, The Thangs. Sluggo sure would make me laugh. I saw The Ramones four times and of course saw both JC shows. I'm sure I'm forgetting zillions of great bands. We got busy and played a lot of different places in and out of town. I fell from free-admission status after doing my Tex and the Horseheads flyer where they were barely mentioned but the Pods were in 8" tall letters, so we didn't play there again for a long time, maybe a couple of years. But we didn't even really notice it, until we walked in there one night to play a show and were overcome by a wave of nostalgia. We all wondered why, and regretted that, we'd been gone so long. We thought we were breaking up and were really happy to come back and play again at where we had gotten our semi-pro start. We considered it as our coming full-circle. We were paired with a fun band we'd played with several times in Indiana, some really nice guys named The Rosebloods, and it was a very relaxed night, kind of a golden, glowing evening. I remember feeling very happy, and proud of our meager accomplishments, of who we'd met and befriended along the way.

A week later we get word the club is closing and we got to play there yet again for the hastily assembled final show. Snare and Doug Falsetti both joined us onstage to croon numbers, Doug singing "This is Where I Belong", a song we knew but never played live, like we must have been saving it for this very night. Somebody broke open the jukebox and threw country 45s everywhere. During our set people started ripping the wood paneling off the walls. Shorty must have been pretty disturbed by the vandalism, but then again, the place had sold and it wasn't going to be a club anymore, but just a garage, so who cares? Kip, like many others, wanted a souvenir and was dragging a chair out the back door when Shorty whomped him with his billy club flashlight. Shorty could move when he wanted to and still had some fight in him. I never ever drive by there without turning my head to the left to see if I can recognize anything familiar. I still kept on going to Sylvia's Mexican Restaurant for years afterwards hoping the magic was still occupying that block. It wasn't. I'd park in the back where you could still see graffiti. I came along late, and left early, but I got to be a part of the peak. These fond memories are basically what prompted me to do an online calendar of all the Jockey Club's shows (still in progress). This grew into a huge website that brought many generous contributors out from under rocks, and remains a vital hub for long lost JC'ers to reconnect. But the thing is, and I've given this a lot of thought, I don't even remember starting up The Jockey Club Remembered web pages, at least not initially. It's like I was under some form of control by a higher power. Channeling something, or someone. And when my head cleared I was sitting on something bigger than myself. I know now from the knock-out response, that I've tapped into something very meaningful to a lot of people. I'd question it occasionally, like, hey wait, what am I doing here, this is silly, there are new clubs and new shows, and the show goes on, but the surprising reaction by the public makes me realize this place was and is important, and indeed meant everything to certain folks. I had a good time and my brief rock and roll career got kick-started there, but others truly found themselves, grew up, met the love of their life there, and so on.

Chris Smith

For many years, Chris and Jim Smith were the proud owners and operators of the Jockey Club information/concert line. From about February of 1984 until the end of the club in May of 1988, you could call 513-861-3094 to get show information. In the earlier years, you would also have the option of calling 606-441-5724 (Bill's place). By early in '84, Bill was glad to have Jim and I take over the line due to the increased number of calls. Our number was listed on many of the flyers posted during those years. We talked to and met many folks as a result of the line and of course the club itself.

I proudly hung and distributed flyers for the Jockey Club for many years as well. Bill and I would make weekly visits to Kinko's on Calhoun Street to make hundreds of copies of flyers for upcoming shows. It was always a thrill to see the new flyers for the first time. In many cases, I would help in their design along with others such as Michael Riley, Tamara Thomas and Bob Butler. These were special times in our lives, whether we realized it at the time or not. The JC was a home away from home in a sense for those years and there was so much music happening that of course made the club possible in the first place.

A shared passion for the music is what fed the success of the club. It was infectious and grew like crazy in those early days. Sex Gang Children, the Reduced, The Replacements, The Vibrators, GBH, UK Subs and Black Flag are but a few of the early shows that really made an impression on me. Life was changing, music was changing and the Jockey Club was there for the ride and how incredibly lucky were we to be a part of its long and proud history.

Dave Davis

As one of the regular sound guys during its run, I saw the Jockey Club at its best and worst. I didn't realize it then, but it was a career-building experience, introducing me to my future clients in a setting where I could shine. Before the Jockey Club, PAs for punk shows around here consisted of cast-off, half-working guitar amps, car or home stereo speakers, and a few beat up Radio Shack mics. So from the beginning the JC's PAs were a step up, thanks to Bob Hallas and Stacey Doose in the early years, and Shawn Norton later on. I learned each of their systems the hard way, and found it much easier to do the job with decent gear. The usual suspects running them included each of the aforementioned owners, plus Jim Davidson, David Lewis, and me, with many others filling in dates around our availability.

When the room was empty (often), running sound was a tough job, since the tile floor and wood panel walls made it sound like an empty garbage can. But when there was a crowd, it was one of the best sounding rooms anywhere, because it was so big and solid—with people making the hard floor less reflective, sound travelled straight and true, over the sea of heads. With a crowd the challenge turned from avoiding empty reflections to getting it loud enough for the fans in the back of the room. This wasn't easy: the PAs were better than before, but less powerful than systems in similar-sized clubs like Bogarts. We all learned to make each successive rig scream. And with the right band, that roar could be truly awesome.

Generally speaking, audiences were separate and unequal. The JC was home not just to punk bands, but at the core of the "art damage" scene that grew around the WAIF radio program of the same name. Even cover bands (The Barking Spiders!) and metal-heads, not quite ready for Annie's, took their turns on the stage. Unfortunately audiences were unevenly distributed, in predictable ways. Well known bands, local and national, drew well from their established fan bases, while more experimental (often more interesting) groups struggled to pay the soundman without digging into their pockets. History has since shown this to be a regional inferiority complex, not a failure of the Jockey or its promoters. Cincinnatians only support winners, which is defined by fame and recognition outside Cincinnati. Bands like the Whigs and Ass Ponys started selling-out shows AFTER getting their label deals, not before. Consequently national shows, with bands like The Ramones or Johnny Thunders' Heartbreakers, were always packed, sweaty affairs, while great but less-well-known bands like Green River, The Zero Boys, Toxic Reasons, and even D.O.A., struggled to fill the mosh pit.

Any history of the JC must acknowledge this reality: if it were as beloved and popular as its former patrons universally remember, it would still be with us! Truth be told, most shows were attended by wives, girlfriends and posses of the bands on stage, joined by a tiny and ever-changing group of regulars. The best show I ever saw there, hell one of the best shows I ever saw ANYWHERE, had Big Black playing basically to me, Shorty and a half dozen people I managed to contact with frantic calls after the loudest, most terrifying sound-check in the history of the club (seriously). This was before the age of cell phones and internet. News always travelled too slow. The Jockey Club was clearly a place out of time, noticed more by its absence than its existence in every guise. The Southgate House is a pale, if better-run, reflection of what the JC wanted to be.

One night early in JC history I worked a show featuring San Francisco's Million Dead Cops (aka MDC). The day before they'd pulled off a stunt that would make the Sex Pistols proud... Shipley's (later known as Top Cats) had booked them without knowing what "MDC" stood for. Since they had a contract with the club and a record to sell, the band was pretty upset, when Shipley's cancelled the show (they figured out the name from the merch). Fortunately the band's bull-dyke (using the term fondly) roadies were as scary as they were smelly (their van was unapproachable, and even in the club you gave them wide berth). Somehow they managed to shake down the management of the staid Clifton club for more than their guarantee, AND got to play to Cincinnati after all, via the Jockey. It was a much better fit (as I recall they were paired with the similarly unmentionable Fucking Cunts).

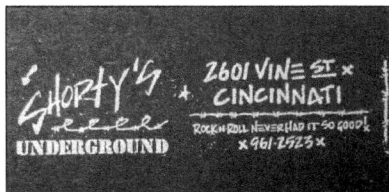

"Shorty's Underground"
Everybody's newspaper ad provided by Max Cole

The photos left today are a pale highlight reel, missing a lot of the characters and agendas that defined the place. People played there mostly because there weren't a lot of other options. When that changed, the JC died. As original music returned to Short Vine and around UC grew, the Jockey Club declined rapidly. For a short time, it's bookers worked hard to revive it, first at the Top Hat, a strip club in Newport, and later at Shorty's on Vine (or do I have it backwards?), but the business model was broken: It was never easy to book shows when all you can promise is a cut of a tiny split of the gate, after paying for the PA and crew. It was impossible to compete with other clubs offering (crappy) guarantees and willing to cover the PA. So that was that.

When the JC closed we didn't lose a place, but an institution. The best/brightest bands on the scene barely noticed it's passing, but fans saw a big difference on stages around town. Lacking a place to develop chops and learn the ropes, the development of younger bands was stunted. While groups like Shag, the Afghan Whigs, The Auburnaires and Ass Ponys thrived in new venues, younger artists simply lost opportunities. Eventually a shyster cokehead bought up and closed down the competing Clifton venues, to pit young bands against one another in a painful race to the bottom in his Laundromat. Since then, the Southgate House has emerged as a functional replacement. It's a better venue in every way but one: the JC booked anyone with a pulse, delivering diversity not seen before or since the Jockey Club, while introducing new bands to the stage.

Jim Danehy

The Jockey Club was the real deal, a legendary club, an interesting experience even on a slow night. It was a real dive, a real punk club, with real angry, drunk punks that only came out at night. It was an old abandoned night club leftover from a previous era that fell into being a punk club. It was like visiting an alternate reality, or walking into a comic book, it was surreal. This was long

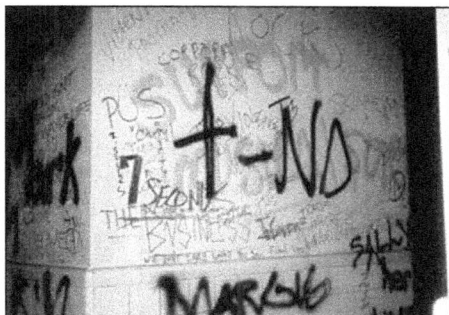

JC bathroom wall
photo by Sarah Kuhl

before "punk" went mainstream, long before punk was a fashion style sold in suburban shopping malls. If you were a punk band traveling across the country you had to stop at the Jockey Club. It was scary and inviting all at the same time it had a really weird charm about it.

When a new sound company came in with a new sound system went into the Jockey Club, there were issues. The main speakers were installed in standard fashion on either side of the stage without a second thought being given. The speakers were stacked up to a height of about 14 feet off the ground. These old school speakers were configured so that you can easily climb up the front of them, and get to the top of the stack. At that point you would of course throw yourself off the top landing on the crowd, or flat on the floor.

Heavy metal screens had to be installed on the front of the speakers to prevent this.

This club attracted dark and dreary characters looking to get drunk, stoned, high, fight, and destroy things. This is the place where people wore things that no one else wore, and had hairstyles that no one else had and smelled like no one else smelled. They only came out at night, and you wondered where they went during the day, they must have vanished somewhere into the armpit of

Newport KY. When Suicidal Tendencies played, the life squad was called, and they were carrying people out on stretchers. There was no polite mosh pit like you might see today. There were, relatively speaking, softer nights as well where there was interesting music and less mayhem. But any night you were there it was like walking into a comic book.

Jerry Adams

JC sign
photo by Jerry Adams

Well, I rolled into the Cincinnati/Northern Kentucky fresh out of EKU with a stint in France to settle in Covington, Kentucky just four blocks from The Jockey club. Since I knew practically no one I immediately got involved at WAIF FM, where at the time among others Billy Blank was doing OUT TO LUNCH, Clem Carpenter was doing SEARCH AND DESTROY, Uncle Dave Lewis was doing ART DAMAGE, Craig Kelly and Jim Phillips were doing ANOTHER MUSIC FROM A DIFFERENT KITCHEN and Al Bum was doing his program as well and they all supported punk, alt and local music. And so it began...

To try and keep to the point the first people I met at The JC were THE REDUCED: BILLY BLANK, SIR JAMES SMITH FROM OUTERSPACE, MITCH TURMOIL (RIP) AND DAVID HILTON. Then thanks to Bill and his encouragement, I began to meet anyone and everyone. I was fascinated with the history as it was the sister club to THE FLAMINGO in Las Vegas. With its rich sordid past and history, it was a mesmerizing place. You could feel the vibe of all the famous people who had been there and those yet to come. I began

Snare and the Idiots
photo by Sarah Kuhl

meeting and hanging out with a lot of people: SNARE AND THE IDIOTS, PRESENT TENSION, SS-20, PEDRO X, BEVO AND THE FASTBATS, BPA, THE FUCKING CUNTS, THE EDGE, MAJOR MORGAN

AND THE WASTEBASKETS, 9 POUND HAMMER, VAIL OF TEARS, DEMENTIA PRECOX, HUMAN ZOO, WOLVERTON BROTHERS, SUBTERANIAN FUNK, THE LIBERTINES (Joe -RIP), PERFECT JEWISH COUPLE, TUPELO CHAIN SEX, TEX AND THE HORSEHEADS and the list just goes on…

I was teaching French at CAMPBELL COUNTY HIGH SCHOOL at the time and the hierarchy there just kept digging at me to find out what I really did in my off time, which was none of their business, sooooo…

Having set the backdrop, I had gotten to be good friends with among many: Mic Edd, Jimmy Smith, Mitch Turmoil (Ricky Sims), Mike Gregory, Snare (Steve Arnzen) and Bill Weber—riding around from late night adventure to adventure in his big black Cadillac hearse. I had been going to the club for a good six months after it opened when Billy Blank pulls me aside and says, "We need a Jockey Club fanzine and I want you to use yer noggin' and do something, ace. I'll take care of you." All the while now on speaking terms, I had not gotten to know Shorty quiet well as of yet but that all was due to change and how…

So I got with Max Blitz (John WAGGLE) and we started the quarterly ALTERED STATEMENTS. By issue two, I took it over myself and I will publically say John was not to blame. It was probably Mr. Hudepohl or Mr. Fosters, perhaps Uncle Sid…anyway, PETER AARON WEGLEY (Chrome Cranks) had been doing SUBURBAN MUCKRACKER, TIMMY FITTS (Musical Suicide) was doing SUB-CIN and here we "spewed" out Altered Statements—before computers—all hand typed, xerox reduced, re-pasted and the re-copied and thrown to the wind. There were a lot mailed out and a lot given away, say MOLES, OZARKA, RECORD ALLEY (my bud: Dana-now in Key West and married…) and last but not least, THE JOCKEY CLUB. I was also doing scene reports for MAXIMUM ROCK AND ROLL to further the mission of THE JOCKEY CLUB.

ALTERED STATEMENTS published its final copy on the night the JOCKEY CLUB closed--issue four being probably the best. It was a misunderstood rag of rough looking punk rock and poetry meant to look rough and not professional--isn't that punk? I thought so. Some people got it, some didn't.

So in the midst of all this I was writing under the pseudonym ASHLEY ALLEN as not to alert my employers of what they would call subversive activity (and this was in the day before piss tests…) or anyone else for that matter. I had P.O. box 3529 from 1984 up until 2007 and due to personal shit like finances, being laid off and divorce, I finally lost it. I hope to get it back in the future…

Now there have been a lot of things said about BILLY BLANK, some true others just "vicious" rumors of urban myth and I'm sure he may or may not admit to them—hell he may not remember—and by this point, who cares anyway; so, that statement out of the way, I am here to

Altered Statements #1

personally declare that MR. BILLY BLANK never came down hard on me and had always been a good friend to me. In fact he always treated me with respect and when the bigger picture called THE JOCKEY CLUB got rolling he was the one who grabbed me and said, "Here, Jerry, get your ass in the little club and interview these people." I interviewed a lot of people and for everyone I interviewed I met 10 more who were famous, infamous or wanted to be famous. My only regret now is no cameras and not many autographs—But IT HAPPENED. Dana and I found ourselves chugging beer with STIV BATORS telling us about his Manhattan experiences with MADONNA for quiet the while before he went on stage with THE LORDS OF THE NEW CHURCH. I had THE FALL—told me more or less, "Go get fucked before we beat the piss out of you." People like JOHNNY THUNDERS were actually more subdued. He chatted for a while but was more interested in chasing women and well I guess, the dragon, but he still came off really low key…so anyway, I interviewed many local and regional bands but some of the bigger people and bands were T.S.O.L., THE SUBHUMANS, KLAUS FLOURIDE, D.O.A., THE VIOLENT FEMMES, HÜSKER DÜ (that was the famous wrestling interview where BOB MOULD said he wanted to talk about wrestling and CLEM CARPENTER and I hit him with it and he was joking, he knew nothing of wrestling), SEVENTH DREAM DAY, RAGGED BAGS, and the list just goes on. Some of this even still exists on cassette and I plan to soon work with KENNY SIMS, JOCKEY CLUB archivist to get all of this shit together. Hell, there are some things missing from the A/S files…it was a long time ago and I am still friends with just about most people that were in the core crowd of the club. I even remained to become even better friends with JIMMY D!

AND…in the midst of all this unbelievable stuff there was Shorty and Tiny, the Mincey brothers. I had mainly talked with Tiny as he used to help run the door in the beginning and up until his untimely death, I really wanted Reagan out of office and Tiny had vowed not to shave his beard until Reagan was out, so we were always Reagan bashing and talking about the fucked up state of the government….

After that I had been travelling in the summers to France and to New Orleans to study French and finish my degree--what does a crazy hillbilly need with a degree in French anyway? I just kept taking the courses because yes, it was interesting but the possibilities for women and travel were actually great. I even went out partying with EUGENE CHADBOURNE in NEW ORLEANS Because I had met him at THE JOCKEY CLUB. So anyway, I'm spending one of my several summers in New Orleans and lo and behold, I'm deciding on whether or not to stay or move back to Cowtown--actually Pigtown--and I get a letter from STEVE BEDEL which says pack it up and get your ass back up here. Himself, MARK MILLER, myself and Dave DUNKUM were gonna start a band. Well, that's all I needed to hear so I put out an ad at NKU and came up with DALE KESTLER on drums and with the help of our consultant, SNARE STEVE ARNZEN, PEPPERMINT SUBWAY was born, and I'm talking about the original line up which lasted about 2 1/2 years. Then after the demise of the JOCKEY CLUB, Dale and I kept it going another two or three years with some other local musicians like MIKE SETA, DAVE RUDISHAUSER and KAPTAIN KARL BRINKER….so after the BIG FOUR RAILROAD BUILDING burned in 1984 and DUNK (who ran off and joined the carnival recently) and I found our photo on the front of THE CINCINNATI ENQUIRER in front of the smoldering building, we had no studio left and through the graciousness of SHORTY and BOB HALLIS/HALLIS SOUND, we had a new home and that's when it really began with SHORTY. By this time we were on a first name basis as I had moved back to NEWPORT, yet another four blocks away from The JC and just being more in the loop than I had been it became apparent that "SHORTY" HALLMAN MINCEY was a more complex person with even more human qualities than anyone ever expected. He was a good friend and had a big heart but if you thought for one minute you were getting a free beer, that wasn't going to happen--at least not too many times. It got to the point where besides JUGHEAD and JIMMY D doing their things there, that

BILLY had to go on a couple of hiatuses out of town, on tour or something, that DAVE HILTON, DAVE DUNKIN and myself helped out doing whatever was needed to keep the place above ground until it—which we hoped—could get back on its feet all the while SHORTY was getting too old to sink a bunch of money into a building which the city was dogging him on code violations like the leaky roof…so now between practicing there, playing there, drinking there, DUNK and I inherited the infamous a.m. clean-up. Which was a pretty good deal. I think Shorty gave us both 20 bucks each, A FREE OIL CAN OF FOSTER'S and would buy us lunch. So by this point we were stopping in on weeknights ribbing SHORTY that we just stopped in to take his pulse and see if was dead and if we were gonna get into the floor safe and you could realize his salty reply. So between BILL the cab driver and a couple of SHORTY'S old school friends and of course his new following, we started stopping in and going to pick up his dinner, just making sure he was eating and generally hanging out there watching his 13-inch black and white TV and drinking beer. At one point we were even meeting him and BILL the Cab driver up at PAYTON PLACE for a breakfast of biscuits and BULLDOG GRAVY.

No good thing lasts forever. BILLY BLANK was back and back at the main stern, giving it his best and I had fathered my firstborn, gotten an almost full-time job at the CINCINNATI ART MUSEUM and was going to finish my last work at the NKU graduate program, was still playing in PERRERMINT SUBWAY and on top of all that, married someone else from THE ART

Altered Statements #3

ACADEMY (now my first ex-wife…) and my time and responsibility became more and my time with SHORTY became less. I left NEWPORT and moved to CLIFTON and WALNUT HILLS and then it happened. The news broke. What else is there to say? HISTORY, right before our eyes, fucked. I only saw SHORTY two or three times after the club closed and I had no idea where his apartment was located. As you know, he had lived in the bar, i.e. the club itself, sleeping on two chairs. SHORTY DIDN'T GIVE A FUCK ABOUT A LOT OF THINGS BUT TREATED HIS FRIENDS WELL. So, unfortunately the last time I saw him was for a stint at PAYTON PLACE for some BULLDOG GRAVY. He was a little salty with me and I was honest and said, "Look, Shorty, I'm keepin' up as best I can." And this is something I have had to live with and will have to live with the rest of my life. I didn't even find out he had died until about a week after the funeral, so that wasn't good either. Everybody hates to lose a friend and SHORTY MINCEY went out of his way to befriend me and hey, I guess it's an Appalachian thing, but I've always had this attrition to hanging out in crusty bars with even crustier clientele. We were always quizzing SHORTY about which bands he liked and which ones he hated. Now I cannot tell you if his answers were totally financially driven but I think they weren't. He hated the MEAT PUPPETS. "Yeah, I know where they got their fuckin' name." After their gig, he told them to get out of the little dressing room, flashlight in hand. SHORTY'S favorite band was THE RAMONES and he was serious about that! My favorite memory of "SHORTY" HALLMAN MINCEY, besides his personality, wit and wonderful wardrobe from HOUSE OF NELSON is this: one morning after mopping up the club and hauling out the trash, DUNK and I were there drinking our beers, SHORTY had paid us and he said, "Jerry, I need five dollars of that money back." And I replied, "SHORTY, what do you need money for? You're the one who has all the money." And SHORTY says back, "Just give it to me!" So, I fork over the five and ask, "Now, what's that for?" SHORTY replies, "I'm saving you a seat in hell next to me because by the time you get there it'll be standing room only. Now you got a reservation next to me and a place to sit…" Well I am truly honored and I never got my five back either. See you there, Shorty, and keep it warm for me. Remember, IT'S A FREAKSOW OUT THERE, ACE!

It's a Freakshow Ace

Freakshow
It's a freakshow, it's a freakshow,
it's a freakshow every night
It's a freakshow, it's a freakshow,
ain't a helluva sight
See the winos, see the bums, see the
whores and see the scums
The freakshow goes on all the time,
it's all for free don't cost a dime.
See the hillbillies, see the hicks,
see the preppies showin' off to
their chicks
See the faggots, see the maggots
ain't it a helleva mix.
Guitar break—circus music bass brea
The freakshow will never end,
but sometimes I wish it would, but
it's always there
Doesn't cost anything and the circus
was never this good.
—Snare and the Idiots,
lyrics by Steve "Snare" Arnzen,
Dave Dunkum and Bill Leist

Mike Gregory (passed out) and Corbett Stepp (seated), Jockey Club foyer.
Oil on canvas, 1991 (Mike Gregory)

Joetta (Lickteig) Sez...

Once upon a time walkin from Covington to Newport weekly across that damn bridge we never knew which or what band we were about to see or what redneck would try to take our mohawks out. We never hardly had any money but we always made it in somehow. Gettin ice at the carry out...feigning off creeps...Shorty lettin us in and givin

At the JC bar
photo by Sarah Kuhl

us oil cans...plus it was always sweet when Bill Leist or one of his lackeys loved our nuts nuts nuts...Be honest with you I really can't recall when or if I ever paid...Lookin back on it I was just another punk who just happened to live next door.

Sittin on the carpet, hangin in the front if you couldn't get in they would still let you sit in the front if you couldn't pay...

The music and the shit I've witnessed I won't name bands or names but...

I'll tell one story only...One of my favorite Jockey Club memories is seeing Black Flack when Henry Rollins whipped out his penis and showed it to the crowd. He really took his pants off and wiggled his dick to the audience. I was up front with my mohawk and grabbed it. He got SOOOO PISSSSED!!!!! I told him he was a retard for whippin it out in my face...Arrogant prick.

Once upon a time there was the Jockey Club...then there was Bogarts... I became just another mohawk but the Jockey Club taught me to be tough and I will always love Shorty...Thanks for all the oil cans buddy!

PS to Bill Leist miss ya mean it

You want more? I got lots...

The first time I went to the Jockey Club
by Becky Baldock Powell

I remember that night.

Cathy (Walker-Lakes) and I had been told by some skinheads that Black Flag was going to play at the Jockey Club. We had heard of the place but had never been there before. Black Flag was playing and we were gonna be there. We jumped in the trusty little grey Datsun and were on our way over the river to Newport.

Fans outside the JC with "friends"
photo provided by Becky Baldock Powell

Cathy and I had been spending our time in Clifton and were getting to know people and feeling pretty confident, then we went to Newport. Things were different there. We walked up to the door and this little mean looking man, with a stub of a cigar hanging out of his mouth, was standing there looking at us. Small but intimidating. Music blasting, people yelling, glass breaking. Cathy and I looked at each other and decided we needed to go back to Clifton. We never did get to see Black Flag.

Well, next time we tried, we made it thru the door. Shorty wasn't really so scary as we had first thought. I remember getting in free sometimes. I remember sometimes we had to pay a dollar and say sausage. I still don't know what that was about. We kept on going back as much as we could. We saw a lot of good bands, we met a lot of really crazy people, and had a lot of great times.

I still have a piece of the wall from the last night we were there. Cathy has a toilet seat. We still talk about our times at the Club. Great memories.

Stacy Adkins

I've often said that punk rock saved my life. And I believe that to be true. If you were to look back at my situation in my young teen years—I probably would have gotten married at a young age, pushed out a bunch of babies, and ended up a divorcee with a dead end job—and in my opinion that is death! And on that note, The Jockey Club is probably what really kick started me on a new life. It's hard to look back and reminisce on any one event there. Maybe because I was drinking a LOT of Foster's oil cans, but mainly because so much shit was going on there in the mid-80s! My friends and I seemed to end up at The Jockey Club at least 2- 4 nights a week. We were, pretty much all of us, under-age. Everything was explosive and exciting! I can remember Clem hiding certain people under the stage when the cops came in looking for runaways. Or standing in line, passing back the same ID, from one person to the next, so they could go through the motions of carding us at the door. One time, a 15 year-old girl friend of ours brought in her brothers' ID. Bill Leist looked at the ID, then up at her without a word. She said, "I got a sex change". They just laughed and waved her in. I remember part of the ceiling falling, and later catching Lux Interior's gold lame` glove, during The Cramps. I remember meeting Cliff Burton from Metallica, with Steve Schmoll and Ric Hickey, and being crushed against the barricade during The Ramones until they pulled me out of the crowd to sit in front of the band and Marky Ramone shaking his head in disbelief. Afterward everyone waded through sweat and beer and who-knows-what, ankle deep on the floor. I remember going to White Zombie, on their "Soul Crusher" tour, with Bill Weber and he yelled, "More hair in the monitors!" during their soundcheck. I remember meeting The Damned at the Record Bar, in Tri-county Mall before the show, and later at the show getting a kiss on my soaking wet forehead as they left the stage. I remember drinking St. Pauli Girl's with Modern English and my friend Astrid Heller, on their bus, out back. I remember fighting with some guy that was taking apart Daniel Ashes' spotlight before Love and Rockets took the stage. I remember the first time I saw a brooding Henry Rollins sitting alone in the hall, before a Black Flag show. I remember sitting in the front bar/ green room with the famous glass coffin and G.B.H.. I remember Shorty dragging Aaron Graham out of the girl's bathroom by his hair. I don't remember seeing

Big Black there, but I somehow ended up with the board tape. And for some of the other shows I don't remember so well, I still have a few ticket stubs and my good friends, like Sarah Heidler and Kurt Froehlich, to talk about it. The Jockey Club was more than a music venue to us. It was a second home. A family. A sanctuary to some of us that had no home or family or anyone to understand us. There were fights and laughs had there. There were life-long friendships and memories made there. And, DAMMIT!, there were bad-ass punk shows there to boot! A lot of people have scattered, and some have moved away over the years, but no matter where I go I always tell people that I was very lucky to have had The Jockey Club when I was growing up!

Chuck Byrd

I'm thinking I was 16 years old when I first met Billy Blank at The Record Alley. It was this really cool music store in Northern Kentucky on Dixie Highway. Billy noticed I was fingering my way through the PUNK section unsure of what to buy. He came over and suggested I check out Sham 69's "Hersham Boys" LP. It was this really sweet gatefold album that included a free 12 inch single with "Borstal Breakout" on one side and "If the Kids Were United" on the other side. It was Brit Street Punk at its finest. I still have that slab of vinyl in my collection and it's still one of my all time favorite punk records. Bill also told me about this new punk venue called The Jockey Club down on York Street in Newport. That kind of scared me a little because in those days the Newport area was pretty seedy. I remember going to the Thrift Store on Monmouth Street with my dad and gawking at the strip clubs as we passed along the way. But this 16 year old who was struggling his way through Catholic high school was about to break out and the Jockey Club was the place where it was going to happen. I would eventually spend many drunken nights with Bill and friends talking about music and life on the edge. Some of those nights we would wind up at Sylvia's Mexican Restaurant trying our best to sober up enough to get back home and to bed. To this day I'm not sure if Billy is the one to be blessed or to be blamed. Our friendship has been renewed for this project and I hope it continues long into the future.

John Haynes, "Handsome" Clem Carpenter and Chuck Byrd in front of the JC
photo by Sarah Kuhl

It was also around this time that I discovered "Handsome" Clem Carpenter and his now infamous "Search and Destroy" radio show on 88.3 WAIF here in Cincinnati. In those days Clem's weekly program was the lifeline of the Cincinnati Punk Scene. He spun the records of all those bands we read about in Maximum

Rock and Roll and Flipside magazines. I was lucky enough to be on his show a few times. I would bring some of my vinyl to play and I would answer the phone for him. People would call in just to say hi to Clem and get updates on shows at the Jockey Club. It really made you feel like you were part of something new and different not to mention the music was full of angst just like we were. I didn't realize earlier on that Clem lived at the end of our street or the beginning depending on which way you drove through. One thing I did realize was that this dude had some kick ass vinyl in his basement and I was bound and determined to steal all of it. Clem and I would share a lifelong love for underground music, professional wrestling and roller derby. I have called my good friend the master cylinder of the Jockey Club stage. We all loved to see him up there introducing the bands he loved, and then he would come down and do some skanking with the gang. I miss him saying …."and on the horizon". He is and will always be and institution in this town.

Chuck Byrd stage diving

In those days there was no internet or email or Citybeat, only the radio, awesome flyers and word of mouth. If you hung out on Short Vine in Clifton you could hang out with other Jockey Clubbers and find out about upcoming shows and parties. Mole's Records was a great place for digging up hard to find used vinyl. Around the corner was Another Record Store. Nick Stavale and I used to go in there on the weekends and race each other to snatch up the latest releases. I remember us fighting over the JFA record when it came out. He beat me to it and I ended up getting the Canadian Subhumans "No Wishes No Prayers" record. I'll never forget that Misfits "Walk Among Us" poster hanging up on the counter. I would drool over that damn thing every time we went in there. It was a great place to meet people and find out about Jockey Club shows.

Everybody's Records in Pleasant Ridge was also a major pulse for the music arteries. Tim and Nolan Benz were the professional art geeks of the music world. I use that term with a tremendous amount of respect. They taught us about weird and quirky noise to make the ears bleed. Both of them were always open to help out and talk about something new and exciting on the underground horizon. The Cincinnati scene and The Jockey Club history would not be the same without the mighty BPA. In those days the punks hated them, nothing personal but to us it was just a racket. Boy, were we wrong! Now we worship them for their longevity and musical prowess. They were way ahead of their time and their LP on Hospital Records is still a classic.

Nick Stavale and I used to frequent Sight 'N' Sound Music at the corner of Queen City and Grand Avenues in Fairmount a lot in the old, old days. Hell, I think I was still in middle school and Nick was in high school when we first met a gentleman by the name of Jim Davidson. That was even before we would affectionately call him Jimmy D. I remember ordering the early Clash records from him. He turned us on to the SKA movement by ordering the Dance Craze soundtrack. It was our first introduction to The English Beat, The Specials and Madness. Jimmy was an encyclopedia of our kind of music. The Jockey Club past would not be the same without Mr. D. He was in The Rituals, The Reduced, The Highwaymen and later on The Libertines. He ran the sound board and was Shorty's right hand man at the infamous money and ID table. Let's be real here, we all have an "ID" story to tell. Jimmy has a million Shorty stories to share, he could have his own book to relate them all. This guy is good people.

When I first thought of writing this piece I wanted to talk about my first Jockey Club show. It was so long ago that I couldn't remember the date. That weekend I found myself at Jughead's annual cookout. I ask him if he could

John "99" Haynes, Nick Stavale, Dave Fry and "Johnnotto"
photo by Chuck Byrd

remember when The Zero Boys first played the JC. He shouted out October 1982. I almost shit myself! Holy Fuck, in the fall of 1982 I was still in my first year of having a drivers license. I can't even remember if I had sex for the first time or not at this point? There was no way of telling how much my life would change after this night. The simple fact that Nick and I were in Newport Kentucky and about to enter the soon to be infamous Jockey Club for the first time was scary as hell. It also had the same excitement as when you first rode The Beast rollercoaster at Kings Island. This was going to be a little bit different than seeing a band cover "Slow Ride" or "Free Bird" at a school dance. This was fuckin' Punk Rock and there was no turning back. I can still remember walking into that dark and damp hallway for the first time not knowing that I would become part of its treasured and checkered past. You bet your ass I was shaky scared and ready to run out the front door just like I did the first day of kindergarten when I was missing my mommy. But I didn't and I'm forever grateful. If I would have wussed out and gone back across the river I would not be part of this historic punk rock legacy. As far as the Zero Boys go all I can recall is they played all of their seminal punk anthems from the Vicious Circle LP. Songs like "Livin' in the 80's", "Vicious Circle", "Civilizations Dying" and "Dirty Alleys/Dirty Minds". They tore up that small stage and opened my young and impressionable eyes to new music and a new lifestyle that would stand true to this very day. I broke out the old turn table the other day and dropped the needle on that crusty, scratchy vinyl masterpiece of memories and almost started skanking around the kitchen. I didn't want to break anything so I grabbed a cold beer and started singing my ass off.

The Jockey Club would become my second home for the next five or six years. Those damn clove cigarettes would tickle my nose every time I would be at a show. That pungent sweet stench would become imbedded into the wood paneling. That cool ass checkered floor would become our skanking pit and we would sweat out all those beers we snuck in. Our usual m.o. would be to grab a six pack of Ballantine or Old German and suck it down in the parking lot. Sometimes sneak in the last one or two if the show was starting. You would have to guzzle them so you wouldn't get a Shorty flashlight upside the head. Then it was time to order up a Foster's Lager Oil Can and be set for the night. Those damn things would get warm quick so you would have to hammer them down. You would be off your ass the first half hour. The rest of the night was an oasis of great music and great friends. It wouldn't matter if you were seeing local favorites like SS-20, The Edge, Musical Suicide, BPA, Sluggo or Lexington's Active Ingredients or punk kings D.O.A., you knew the camaraderie of crazy haircuts, thrift store clothes, broken homes and lasting friendships were the order of the night. That place was a therapy session for poor kids and suburban kids alike. It didn't make any difference because we were all there for the same thing: the love of underground music. Everyone was accepted, it was the people that made the club what it was. Only at The Jockey Club could you see punks skanking to Dementia Precox or Junta. I remember local legends SS-20 when they opened up for Charlie Pickett and The Eggs. Who the hell was Charlie Pickett? It turns out he would become a Jockey Club favorite. I remember getting on stage with John Haynes and singing with Charlie on "Overtown" and "If This Is Love". The next show you went to see could be Toxic Reasons and you'd be singing and stage diving to "War Hero" That was the beauty of the place. One minute your yelling into Jughead's microphone "He's got a regular job"… and the next you could be singing the Leroi Brothers, "d.w.i., the national past time of the average guy".

Twenty years later I have come to realize how much of an affect the JC has had on my adult life. I still seek out new and unusual underground music. I still have most of the records on my shelf and break them out from time to time to relive all those special moments from the past. I have to mention that most of my political leanings stem from those great SS-20 songs. Now I enjoy e-mails discussing politics with my buddy Jughead. One day I would like to share a stage with him in the political arena. "Handsome" Clem still turns me on to interesting music and we still chat about wrestling and roller derby. I'm looking forward to hearing more tales from Jimmy D and get a kick out of hearing Billy's voice on my answering machine.

I saved my memory of our man Shorty for last. I can picture him taking bets in an old black and white mafia movie from the fifties. People say Iggy Pop was the first punk rocker, I say Fuck You! Shorty was and always will be the first punk rocker to me. My wife Betsy recently uncovered a song I wrote about Shorty when I was a young Jockey Clubber. Here it goes…

Stories for Shorty

SHORTY   Chuck
                Byrd

① Cigar smoke, King Edwards brand
Cigarollas, Blunts, Demi-tipped, any kind he can
Dirty ashes cover his clothes
He's the big little man everbody knows

"Give me your money", "Let's see I.D."
"I'm the man they call Shorty"

② The Flamingo is what it used to be
With Chuck Berry, old drunks and Jerry Lee
The lines on his face tell the story
Those were the days of Shorty's glory

"Give me your money", "Let's see some I.D."
"The man with the piece, I'm Shorty"

③ It's 3:0'clock time to close down
A grubby old face with a sinister frown
Sit and smoke, count the dough
Easy come easy go

"Give me your money"
"Give me your money"

Dee Snyder

It all started with "Handsome" Clem. I had just come out of a three-day coma from a failed suicide attempt when I was 17, and I discovered Clem's radio show on WAIF-FM. He played music I knew, and new, exciting music I didn't know. I listened to him regularly in my bedroom in the suburb of Forest Park. I taped his show on reel-to-reel tape! I called him up to request songs like "Rawhide" by Dead Kennedys. He played Flipper all the time. Flipper was funny. I got excited when Clem said over the air, "Dee called to request this." Then, when I was 18, I met Clem in person at Bogarts, when Bogarts was booking a ton of punk and new wave bands. I double pogoed with Clem and, there met other regulars on the scene.

Pabst light, JC
photo by Sarah Kuhl

And THEN, the Jockey Club opened, or should I say, the key players involved started booking punk bands at the Jockey Club.... and it was there that I really felt I found a home, and, hokey as it sounds, a family.

One thing I liked about the scene is a lot of people had their "punk" names. You never got to know their real names unless you got close to them, and sometimes, not even then.

When I eventually became a punk rock drummer and started my very own show on WAIF-FM, my stage name was Dee DeVoux, because I thought it sounded exotic...but, in retrospect, not a good punk name.

Another thing that struck me about the scene, and influenced me, is the sense of humor the local punk bands had (Snare and the Idiots - "Pimples") and also this political, twisted, dark humor of the bands (11,000 Switches- "Haitian Vacation", SS-20 - "Car Won't Start" etc.) I'm convinced that the whole Jockey Club phenomenon happened as a result/off-shoot of these many, talented local bands.

As a formerly shy, insecure person, hanging out at the JC with the guys, talking about music for hours and hours gave me courage, acceptance, and a TON of happiness. In a largely male scene, I was a female treated with respect and equality.

Here's a few of my JC stories:

Bill asked me to put up a speed metal band from Boston at my house. I thought they'd be there for one night, but they stayed for four days, drinking my beer, eating my food, and one of them fucking my girlfriend. I didn't really mind. Then they left, and the phone company called to say the band had made hundreds of dollars in illegal phone calls from my phone using a stolen credit card. The phone company was sympathetic. I wasn't charged.

I took a date who happened to be a psychologist to the Jockey Club one night to show him "my world". He only lasted about 20 minutes. He looked around and said, "All of these people need my professional help." He insisted that we leave. I didn't want to leave.

When the band I played drums in, Alien Pleasure, played the JC on 4/10/87, I wore my mini skirt with the zipper up one side. As I was playing drums, a guy stood by the side of the stage just watching me and my creeping mini skirt. I was scared to death the thing was going to fall off of me. My shining moment playing at the JC.... in front of about 20 people, I'll never forget it.

There are so many stories!

The JC, the regulars, the people who became my friends, and, especially, the people who made it all happen, will always live in my memory.

You CAN put your arms around a memory!

Brendan Halpin

In tenth grade, our school was rocked by two new arrivals: Karl and Andrew. At first they talked incessantly about something they made up called The Neue Program, which they claimed was some sort of scientific breakthrough about making giant chickens to cure world hunger. They had photocopied flyers they used to give us.

It was pretty clear that they weren't serious, but they always acted like they were. We really had no idea what to make of them.

They further confused us by being in punk rock bands. Karl played bass and Andrew played drums for a band called Sluggo.

Hardcore at the time was a very fringe genre of music that was not about the crunchy cords and low, Cookie-Monster-Style growling that goes by the name "hardcore" today, but, rather, was punk rock played really fast, with the singer essentially shouting amelodically in order to spit out words fast enough to keep up with the insistent beat.

Sluggo

Anyway, Karl and Andrew were in one of these bands. The rest of us were into bands like the Kinks and the Who that had basically stopped putting out decent music before we got to kindergarten, or even, God help us, bands like Genesis and Yes that had never put out any decent music. It is safe to say we had never seen anything like it.

Three times a week at our high school, we had all-school assemblies, and people could get up and make announcements. Karl used to announce Sluggo gigs, which were invariably at the Jockey Club in Newport Kentucky.

Kentucky is the place where Cincinnatians typically went to get their salacious entertainment. Cincinnati itself has all these anti-porn laws, but the city council could have their cake and eat it too by appearing to be righteous, yet knowing full well that anybody could just cross a bridge and get porn, strippers, or prostitutes. (Indeed, one Cincinnati city counselor was famously disgraced when a personal check of his was found in a Newport whorehouse. His name was Jerry Springer.) So, naturally, Cincinnatians had to go to Newport to get their punk rock, too.

I was sort of familiar with Newport—not because I went to its nasty strip clubs (at age 15, I just wished…), but because it had the only Mexican restaurant in the entire tri-state area that was operated by an actual Mexican, and a couple of blocks away was a place that would put a ball of soft-serve inside a sno-cone for you, which was a really great post-enchilada treat.

But I had never heard of the Jockey Club until Karl started making his announcements. One day he announced that Sluggo was opening for a band whose name he couldn't say. Naturally we all crowded around him after the assembly, where he revealed to us that Sluggo was opening for the Crucifucks.

All of this seemed kind of interesting and exotic (the only way to hear this music on the radio was on some community radio station that got in trouble for broadcasting a guide to good anal lubricants, and the punk rock show was hosted by two guys who called themselves "Handsome" Clem" and "The Hockeypunk") but, much like the Neue Program—some weird thing that Karl was into that would never really touch me.

And then I heard that the Ramones were coming to town, and that they were playing at the Jockey Club. Though every other punk band was completely unknown to me, I had been obsessed with the Ramones since the eighth grade. I went to Everybody's records, and they sold me a ticket without blinking, though you had to be 19 to get in to clubs in Kentucky at the time.

I asked Karl what to do about getting in, and he advised me to head over to this place called "Scarborough Photography" to get a fancy laminated card with my picture on it that claimed to be a "State Identification Card."

So a couple of friends and I headed over to this dimly-lit, grungy photography studio. The guy dutifully took down our information (we all used our real names and addresses. Morons), remarking when the third of us claimed to have been born in 1965, "hmmm…there's a lot of that going around."

Our transaction was interrupted like seven times while this guy got phone calls and yelled at people about how they needed to be in thus and such a place at thus and such a time, and get over there now, and we figured either this guy was booking a hell of a lot of wedding photographers on a Thursday afternoon or else he was into something slightly less legal than photography. We all walked out proudly with our "State Identification Cards. I carried mine proudly until I was really of age, and despite the fact that it didn't say which state, it worked a kind of surprising number of times.

The first of which was at the Jockey Club the night of the Ramones concert. My heart was pounding as I handed my ID to the scrawny, unkempt, barely-19 "bouncer." He stamped my hand, and as I went through the door, he said, "Just out of curiosity, what are you really—about 16?"

I pictured myself in the back of a Newport squad car (the Newport cops were such famous fascists that one of the local bands, the Edge, had a song called "Newport Gestapo"), being beaten senseless and jailed with a bunch of guilty-looking Cincinnati city councilors, one of whom would doubtless make me his bitch by the end of the night. Should I try to brazen it out? Well, shit, I was busted, and I was always a terrible liar. I didn't correct him and tell him I was actually only 15, but I did say, "Yeah," and almost held out my wrists for the cuffs.

"Enjoy the show!" he said to me.

And I did—sort of. It was a tremendous thrill to be in a real rock and roll club, even one as filthy and disgusting as this one. In the left hand corner was the bar, where five old men were sitting. They looked like unlikely Ramones fans. The folklore at the time was that some young con artist had talked the cantankerous old men who ran the place (they were known as Shorty and Tiny—Shorty was actually short, while Tiny was huge) into booking punk rock shows so as to keep the mortgage payments up, and I guess it worked, because this place looked like it should've been closed down at least a decade earlier.

I walked right up to the stage and waited for the Ramones to come on. Suicidal Tendencies opened, and they were ok—I liked the song "Mommy," but their snare drum broke before they could play their big hit, "Institutionalized".

Once the Ramones started, everybody started slamming (what's now known as moshing)—running around and throwing themselves into other people. I was constantly taking elbows and forearms in the back, and I was shoved so tight up against the stage that I had a caster from an amp giving me a kind of semi-Heimlich maneuver all night, but I was able to reach up and touch Dee Dee Ramone on his Chuck Taylors, which was about the biggest thrill of my life up to that point. (If that statement makes you question my success with the ladies up to that age, I must admit that you are correct.)

Though I ended the night bruised, temporarily deaf, and feeling like I had only just barely escaped serious injury, I was sold on the Jockey Club, and ended up going there many more times. I cannot understand for the life of my why my mother let me do this. I mean, I didn't even bother to lie—I showed her my fake ID and told her I was going to a club in Kentucky, and she told me to have fun. I should point out that I had to lie to go to high school parties. I guess she figured (correctly) that a trip to the Jockey Club was really all about the music for me, whereas a party in one of my classmates' giant, can-get-loaded-and-have-sex-even-if-mom's-home-because-she-never-leaves-the-east-wing houses would probably end up being about something else.

I became friends with Karl, and my friend Danny ended up being in a band, the aforementioned the Edge (group motto: "No, not the guy from U2") with him, and so I went numerous times and saw them play by themselves, or as part of a local triple-bill (my memory is that I once saw one of these local triple bills with the Edge, Human Zoo and SS-20, all of which featured Karl Meyer on bass). Only once did I have problems—a bunch of us got there early, and Tiny, who presumably knew that on any given night fully half of his clientele was underage, came over and shined a flashlight in our faces and busted our balls about being underage. We all produced our State Identification Card (known affectionately as "the Scarborough"), and Josh, who was 14, and I, who looked 14, got kicked out. We went over to White Castle to wait for everybody else, and ended up leaving, because the place was full of vaguely menacing drunks who were saying things like, "I want my coffee black—like a nigger!" and laughing hysterically.

I saw Squirrelbait (the show ended prematurely with a fight in the crowd and Squirrelbait's lead singer took his pants down in protest, or something, and just said, "fuckers!" over and over) and Hüsker Dü , and, senior year, the Ramones again. This time we brought along my "little brother" (this was more

of a hazing thing than the friendly mentoring it sounds like) Jonathan who...
well, Jon was 14 and looked about 10. Karl, who by this time was actually 19,
gave Jon one of his spare drivers' licenses, and though Jon was about five feet
tall with blond hair, and Karl was about 8 inches taller with brown hair, the
bouncer took the ID, stamped Jon's hand, and told him to enjoy the show. He
got a few puzzled looks from the other patrons, but most of them looked like
if they'd only known, they would have started coming here when they were
ten.

I went to the last show at the Jockey Club, which was torn down in order
to make more parking for the taxi company located next door. Basically
everybody who had ever been to a show there was there, but I left before the
night ended—I remember standing there with Karl and The Hockeypunk as
Doc and the Pods played and morons tore the paneling off the wall in big
sheets and threw it around and deciding that it was really time to go.

Ric Hickey

In 1984 when I was 17 years old, I started working at the Record Bar in Tri-County Mall. While I was working there I became close friends with a co-worker named Paul Horton. Paul was a few years older than me, took me under his wing and started calling me his "protégé". I always thought of him as Dylan's "Napoleon in rags" and a hilarious bastard who loved putting people in awkward situations. Paul was raised in East St. Louis in the early 70s, so he was not an angel or anybody's fool. He had great taste in music and took immense pleasure in steering me away from the cheesy Heavy Metal that I had been listening to up to that point. My taste in music, my sense of humor, and even my very personality all owe more to Paul Horton than anyone else I have ever known, with the possible exception of my father.

Paul was good friends with Bill Leist. I'd met Bill at the record store on several occasions and he and Paul painted a pretty vivid picture of what was happening at The Jockey Club. They told me that any show that I made a flyer for they would let me into for free. I studied art in high school and made flyers for my friends' bands all the time so I took Bill and Pauly up on their offer. I cranked out a flyer for the May 1st, 1985 Dead Kennedys show at the JC so I could finally go down there and see what all the buzz was about. This was about a month before I graduated from high school. I had been to Bogarts once or twice and a number of arena shows, but I had no idea what was in store for me at the JC.

On the night of the show, my dumb ass was down there at like 7:30 or some shit, thinking the music would start around 8pm. Needless to say, I waited around for a while before the first of 3 opening bands even did their soundcheck. Also on the bill that night was Sluggo, SS-20, and Musical Suicide, all great local Punk bands that I would eventually see dozens of times over the years at the JC and elsewhere around town. Sluggo's one-song soundcheck was curiously hypnotic. The singer stood totally still and kinda mumbled, hanging on the mic-stand like an old rag on a stick. They were loud and fast and reminded me of something Paul had told me, comparing The Stooges to all the crap Metal I had been listening to. "Rickie," he'd say, "There's a big difference between speed and intensity".

Two hours later Sluggo started their set proper and the same singer dude was wailing and leaping all over the stage, totally unlike his corpse-like demeanor during soundcheck. It kinda threw me at first and I wasn't sure I liked it. David Coverdale seemed like a million years ago all of a sudden, on a distant planet inhabited only by primitive mouth breathers. But I didn't have time to decide whether I liked Sluggo or not, as a giant mosh-pit appeared out of nowhere and snapped my twig-skinny frame up against the wall where my head was nearly impaled by a wall-mounted coat-hook. Sluggo's sense of humor ultimately trumped my corn fed inhibitions and I felt like I was finally in on some cosmic inside joke.

The crowd kept up slam dancing and stage diving and fueling the untethered energy coming from the stage for the rest of the night. Musical Suicide was funny too, and SS-20's brand of "Punk Rock" was illuminated by sublime pop hooks and a defiant stance not unlike Johnny Cash. When they went on, well after midnight, The DKs nearly ruptured my suburban brain with their black humor and sick chops that I did not expect. It made me immediately realize what bullshit it was to think that Heavy Metal musicians were virtuosos while all punks were just punks. Guitarist East Bay Ray, in particular, drove the final nail in that thought's coffin.

I started going to the Jockey Club on an almost-weekly basis, to see what was happening down there and to loiter just half a sniff away from that magic stench as often as possible. Between 1985 and 1988, I saw dozens of shows there. I'm sorry to say I missed the infamous pair of appearances by The Replacements ("first time sublime, second time shit shower" was the consensus). But I was fortunate enough to catch Black Flag, H.R. (from Bad Brains), an early gig by Love and Rockets, MDC, The Lazy Cowgirls, Tex and The Horseheads, The Mentors, Charlie Pickett, Jerry Dale McFadden, and others too numerous to recall.

Charlie Pickett
photo by Chuck Byrd

Two of the best shows I ever saw at the Jockey Club were The Ramones and The Cramps, both of which were within a 2-week period in the summer of 1986.

Cramps flyer

The Ramones show in July was way oversold and the club was blazing hot. Two guys from Metallica were drinking at the bar, having just come to the show after opening for Ozzy at Riverbend that night. The Cramps show that took place at the JC in the first week of August still ranks as one of the best shows I have ever seen in my life. It was so hot in the club, I went out to my car and stripped down to shorts and gym shoes. Onstage, Lux Interior started out in a gold lame' suit (including elbow-length gloves) and gradually removed it all except for gold skivvies and pumps. Poison Ivy looked, as always, like an Egyptian goddess that night. Lux destroyed a mic-stand with his head (you had to be there) and dangerously climbed up on the Jockey Club's teetering speaker columns. Lux writhed on top of the speakers with the microphone shoved in his mouth and poured red wine all over himself. Back at center stage with broken mic stand in hand, Lux started poking and prodding loose the ceiling panels just above his head. He tore up a huge portion of the ceiling and flung the pieces of broken ceiling panels like Frisbees out over the swarming sea of raised hands. Lux flung his wine bottle up into the ceiling and when it didn't come down the crowd roared with depraved approval. (Days later I thought of dragging a ladder out in the middle of the dance floor and trying to retrieve the bottle but I heard somebody say that Bill Leist had already done so himself.)

Earlier that same year I had the good fortune of seeing Johnny Thunders twice in the same weekend at the Jockey Club. On the last day of February 1986 Johnny finally appeared at the JC after several cancellations and bogus bookings. I was sitting on the floor in the lobby when Johnny made his entrance, loudly bossing around some hapless roadie in his unmistakable New York accent. The show that night was a glorious mess and I took a bunch of pictures. Two days later a round of phone calls spread the news around town that Johnny was passing through Newport and would play another show

Poison Ivy at the JC

that night, Sunday March 2. Still working at Record Bar then, I went across the mall on my lunch break and had a couple 8"x10"s made from the Thunders' show of 2 nights previous. Down at the club real early that night, I nervously lingered in the lobby, hoping I could get Johnny to autograph them for me.

Just off to the side of the main lobby inside the front door there was a dusty old barroom that occasionally served as a makeshift dressing room. I paced around the lobby trying to get up the nerve to just push the curtain aside and go in to say 'hi' to Thunders. It was, as I recall, Paul Horton, appropriately enough, who physically shoved me in to the room. Suddenly I was in a dimly-lit side parlor, the back of Johnny Thunders' head seated in a chair right in front of me. I sputtered, "Hey Johnny, do you think I could get an autograph?" As he slowly spun around in his chair I saw a large tray in his lap that displayed an array of pills and powders. The man was clearly doing some shopping. Having just witnessed his Italian temper in the lobby only minutes earlier, I braced myself for a razor sharp tongue-lashing. To my great surprise and even greater relief, Johnny simply said, "Yeah kid, sure. After we get this together here I'll sign whatever ya got." He was really kind and patient with me, a dumb ass kid from Ohio that interrupted his drug deal. In retrospect I always found it cute and curious that Johnny was keen to display his entrance by making a scene when he arrived, but in truth he was a sweet and soft-spoken guy. It also probably made him look really cool in front of a drug dealer and other druggies that the man couldn't even get through a quick purchase without somebody asking him for his autograph.

I ducked out of the dressing room and approached Johnny onstage about 30 minutes later during a lull in the evening's soundcheck. He was kneeling at the edge of the stage and graciously talked to me for about 10 or 15 minutes, signing one of my pictures and begging me for the other picture so he could send it to his girlfriend in Sweden. Who could resist that? Johnny Thunders wanted one of my photos! For me, Johnny signed a picture I'd taken during Friday's acoustic set and I gave him the shot of him playing his Les Paul Jr. with a fat joint hanging out of his mouth. Fair trade. Johnny remains one of my all-time favorites and I will never forget that.

(I have a soundboard tape of both Thunders' shows from that weekend, if anybody wants a copy.)

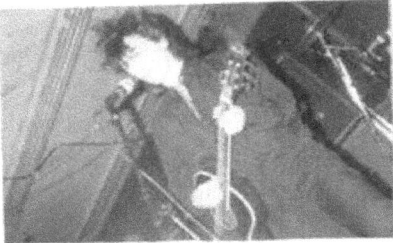

Johnny Thunders
photos by Ric Hickey

Angie Rawers

"What's the Jockey Club?"

How did I first hear about the Jockey Club? I moved to Cincinnati from Dayton in 1983, a few months prior to starting my freshman year in high school, to live with my father. A few months later, I began dating what seemed to be a typical rich suburban boy, but who later turned out to have a very impressive Punk and New Wave record collection. It was Lords of the New Church, the Sex Pistols and X for me.

I was at the kitchen table one Sunday in early '84, reading that day's Cincinnati Enquirer and the Jockey Club article in The Enquirer Magazine, when my father said to me, "Don't get any ideas!" and promptly threw it away. I knew then that the JC was the place for me, even though it would take me almost two years later and a move-in with my mother (who had then moved to Cincinnati) to get there.

A Girl's First Time

Moving in with Mom proved to be beneficial to my Jockey Club aspirations, as she was one of those I-want-to-be-your-friend-more-than-your-Mom types. A few months later, in November of 1985, I met Kevin (now Churchill) Brauninger and we began dating. Our first "official" date was the Love and Rockets show in December of '85. Kevin, my best friend Michelle "Machete" Thompson, and I crammed into his VW Bug and headed to Newport. It was my and Michelle's first time

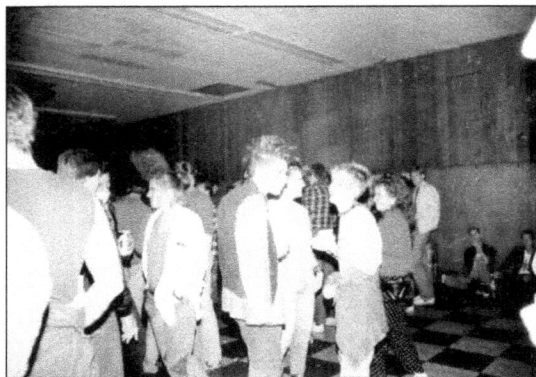
Angie at the JC

there…I don't remember if it was Kevin's. It was going to be a packed show, so there was a ton of people outside. Michelle and I were so excited we could hardly contain ourselves.

142

We had heard a million different stories about how to get in if you were underage, which was part of the charm of the JC. Ways to try: "note from Mom" saying you're 18, someone else's ID (even of a different gender or race!), etc. We decided to go with the tried-but-true method of Kevin showing his valid legal-adult driver's license and then passing it to me and then me passing it to Michelle. Voila! "Just run out the back door if the cops come!"

Although it wasn't a punk show, we were all instantly addicted to the place.

Girls On Stage

Like several other girls at that time, I'm sure, I also went through the obligatory female JC rite of passage…boys pushing an unaware chick up on the stage and when she'd try to scooch off, pushing her back on the stage until she had no choice but to dive headfirst into their more-than-willing-to-"catch"-her hands. Fortunately for me, at least it was two of my male friends with whom I was in attendance who grabbed my thighs and threw me up there that first time at the Gang Green/Squirrel Bait show. Stage-diving fever…I had caught it. I don't remember a ton of girls doing it, but I do remember that teeny-tiny Bentley, who was a good friend, was absolutely voracious at it.

Ring It In

The best memory I have of the Jockey Club is a somewhat romantic one (yep, romance DID happen at the JC). On December 31, 1985, Kevin and I had been hanging out downtown earlier in the evening with Brian Falls, et al, at the Milner Hotel, before heading over to bring in the New Year at the JC. We apparently lost track of time because it was around 11:50 when we headed over there. Kevin and I parked the car and booked it into the lobby, where we were frantically trying to pay and get stamped as we heard the crowd start the countdown…10-9-8-….holy shit….we weren't going to make it in time! With one last burst of energy Kevin and I sprinted into the main room and entered just as the clock struck midnight. What better way to bring in 1986 than smoochin' on your man at the Jockey Club? Love, Jockey-Club style.

Here and Now

Unfortunately, my initial time at the JC lasted only three or four months. After I had broken up with Kevin and started dating Jerry Wells, my mother wasn't feeling it (since Jerry was 25 and I was 16). In April of '86 she threw me in the cultish hellhole called Straight (even though I didn't do drugs) for a year. After I got out of her grip in early 1988, I began going to the JC again, but it wasn't the same experience for me because of having been out of circulation for a year.

I had so much fun in those initial months that thoughts of what I missed during that one year dogged me for years. Some kids went through their "punk phase" as just that: a phase. For others, like me, it was an early acknowledgment of the person each of us really was and is, which is why the Jockey Club meant so much to me.

A few years ago, I had the good fortune of snagging a full Jockey Club "dinette" set from Pat Patton; the great red-topped tables with the heavy circular base and the heavy wood chairs with red vinyl seats and slatted magazine racks on the bottom. It sits proudly in my living room, where my 16-year-old son Zeque sometimes does his homework. I have three tables in my living room, all of which are in fairly close proximity to each other. Hence, the Jockey Club table is referred to as just that to distinguish it from all the others. "I think I left it on the Jockey Club table." "We need to replace the bulb in the lamp on the Jockey Club table." The tabletop is peeling back a little and most of the legs of the chairs are worn to almost a pencil-point, but to mend what seems like imperfections to others would be anathema to what the Jockey Club represented and to the memories of those who loved it: imperfect people coming together for a perfect musical cause.

Thank you, Shorty.

Allen Lee Scott II

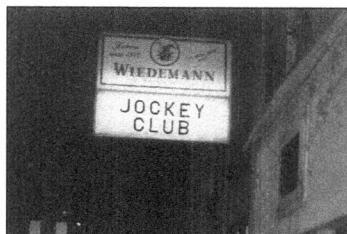

Jockey Club sign
photo courtesy of James Bramlage

There was a stern warning—

With every trip down York street,

To the dangers of a rundown bar

Given the name of the Jockey Club

On the avenues of a more wild city,

That brought angst and rebellion

To the fears of single mothers lives

I heard my own Mother's words to—

"Avoid that place of freaks and punks"

From hair stained red and safety pins

Foster's, Dock Martens, Liberty spikes

'An the violence of an age that was raw

145

With the promise of change forthcoming

The music spilled forth into the gutters—

I close my eyes and see the punkers dive

Into the Wiedemann dumpsters for beer

Lager, piss, and blood mixed into swarms

Of the disenfranchised breaking the mold

Over cracked skulls and fractured nights

Amid the riot of spirit and corrupt police

I learned music from the alleyway graffiti

That brought me bands like the Exploited

Soundcheck, Dead Kennedys, the Subhumans

Gifts like acid that burned into my dreams

'An led me further away from my youth"

Newport or Bust: Roads Scholars All the Way from Athens

by Spike Vrusho

The road itself, somewhat like our destination in Newport, carried a certain level of intimidation. Traveling the Gov. James A. Rhodes Memorial Appalachian Highway from Athens, Ohio to the Jockey Club in Newport, Kentucky was not for the mild-hearted.

Not that the road was paved with the bodies of slain Kent State students, it was more like the pork-barrel type-A personality sweat of Rhodes and his cronies rolling up sleeves and building a transportation network that would supposedly save the hayseeds who dared live south of the boring capital "city" of Columbus. Ironton, Belpre, Franklin Furnace—these were just a handful of the scary towns situated not far from this lonely road. It sucked, yes, having to drive on it, but god bless Jim Rhodes for allowing us college students to go see some kick ass bands during the mid-1980s at the one and only Jockey Club, which, apparently, Neil Young does not remember.

There were potholes aplenty, faded stripes, poor signage and a sense that you were being watched by Bosch figures on the horizon—spear-toting skeletons aboard horses.

If it was "all about the journey" then the journey was geared around a case of Goebels in the back seat of a rusty Subaru DL sedan with a dodgy clutch and a Black Flag bumper sticker. Progress was not to be measured until we could smell the paper mill stench of Chillicothe to the north. Through the windows there was the inky blackness and menacing strip-mine scenery of a towns like the funny ha-ha of Beaver, the gun-toters of Winchester and the Biblical overtones of Mt. Orab, which meant we were getting closer and closer to Newport. It was a tough 150 miles for the driver, and for inspiration we would tape the flyer for the show we were to attend onto the cracked dash. The fog of time and the haze of memory seem only to be pierced by the U.K. Subs, a venerable act from across the pond that seemed to adopt the JC as its American roost. No arguments from us Ohio University undergrads, we didn't mind. Our goal was to get through the forgotten southern shelf of the Buckeye State to stride triumphantly (but without swagger) beneath the eyeball white glow and red vein script of the famous Wiedemann's sign above the club. It was Valhalla for kids who wanted to see live punk rock in a seedy setting. You watched your ass in Newport, and those of us who piled creakily out of cars after a two-hour drive could recognize fellow refugees from Columbus, Indianapolis, Lexington, Granville and sometimes Cleveland.

We played the role of outsiders. We recognized the locals who were lucky to have the privilege of attending every JC show by simply riding a bus or driving a Ford Pinto a few blocks.

There always seemed to be taxis near the front, and there was the time the local cops were busting people out front for "vagrancy." That is, if you were loitering on York St. and didn't have more than a dollar in your pocket, off you went in the cop car.

So we dutifully paid the guy with the cigar, got our Foster's and then marched to the hexagonal jut of the stage to marvel at the girth of "Handsome" Clem, the amiable MC for most of the shows we caught inside that perfect rectangle of warped paneling and groaning linoleum. We gathered flyers for future shows, stickers and 7-inch vinyl from opening acts like Active Ingredients or Sluggo and argued over who would take the wheel and cart us across the state to see Discharge or T.S.O.L. There were sometimes fanzines to distribute filled with Reagan imagery.

A guaranteed sight, and one that warmed my heart and still does to this day: a lonely goth girl would ALWAYS be slumped in the corner (like a tired black swan) smoking a clove cigarette. It was not a Jockey Club show without the smell of her cloves, and even now some 20 years later, when I smell a clove cigarette I think it is time to get another Foster's Lager and maybe some earplugs before G.B.H. takes the stage. Wherever she is, I thank her, and yes, I wanted to marry her but she could never hear my muttered proposal over the amp-blast of SS-20. Her name might or might not have been Oktobriana and she might or might not have been going out with one of the Dementia Precox fellows.

Oddly enough, some of us even had girlfriends who hailed from tony Cincinnati suburbs like Wyoming, where basement crashing space awaited after the show. But usually we were so filthy in so many ways after a Jockey Club show that we wouldn't dare show our bruised faces for any respite in the 'burbs. No amount of Glade air freshener could right our wrongs, so we would aim the Subaru east, maybe even with a bootleg cassette tape of the evening's musical program for the heavily-stickered boom box. Prayers were said to avoid wrong turns or sleepy wheel syndrome outside Waverly.

We had to survive the return trip to Athens, lick our wounds and prepare to make the trip again, maybe arrive earlier next time and check out the graffiti on the back loading dock area of the club, or pause in front of the Brass Rail or get some of that infamous chili.

D.O.A.
photo by Witt

One return trip after a blockbuster D.O.A. gig featured a flat tire and a creepy encounter with a Jehovah's Witness who came to our aid. He invited us into his house and then hit us with the literature and the spiel. It was 2 a.m. Jonestown was fresh in our memories, so we hightailed it out of there and waited for the tow truck in the rain along the Rhodes highway. The trigger-happy Governor would have packed a spare tire. We did not.

Of course we would occasionally stray into the "civilization" of Clifton for shows at Bogarts, but there were always parking tickets and other annoyances. It was the kind of place where you would bring your girlfriend along. It just wasn't the same as the Kentucky experience of 633 York St.

A few years later, having left Athens and Ohio for parts Northeast, I chuckled during the Robert Mapplethorpe shut-down hype in Cincy. What, the Jockey Club wasn't available for his show? As Clem might have put it: "Get that bullwhip out of your ass and use your noggin' next time, son."

Margie L. Garrett

The trip to Cincinnati was always a raucous rendezvous. The Lexington crowd would talk about it at parties or at the small bars and pizza places that we were able to go see local bands and the occasional out of town band. The Lexington crowd is a pretty close group. We didn't listen to cover bands at the big disco places and we didn't attend the Cheers bar on the corner for polite conversation! We had a great time dancing and slamming and being pretty RUDE in Lexington! Now, Bogarts wasn't really too bad, but it was definitely subdued. Pretty drinks at pretty tables, but thank goodness it was there! Then a new club started showcasing the music!

The trip to Covington opened up a whole new possibility for us to enjoy the music and yet still not worry so much about the upholstery! We'd get into town early and maybe grab some food then meander over to The Jockey Club.

We don't talk much about Covington history in Lexington, but when we visited town, there was a lot of questions about the intrigue of the old city. Talking of stories of gangsters and high-rollers that we would share over dinner.

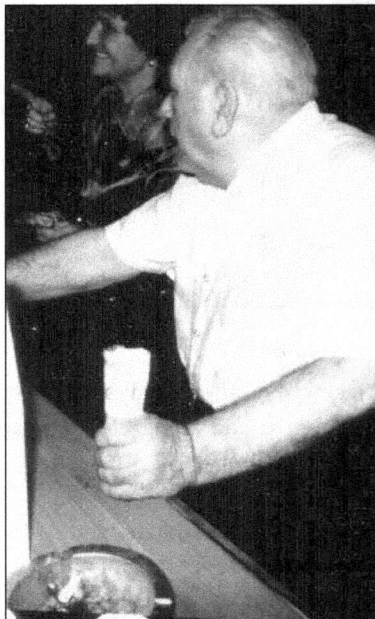

Shorty
photo byWitt

Then we'd often get to the club early because we didn't have anywhere to go and the traffic was better than we thought. The best part was getting to chew fat with Shorty. We knew that he didn't know us, but he was willing to tell us about the place if he had time. I only say we because I went up there with different people most of the time, but a certain band member from Lexington a lot of the time. I had a great, good time and appreciate having a venue for all the hundreds of bands that I saw at the Jockey

Club! I have a whole bunch of pictures from that time, but as it was before the era of digital anything, no way to show them! Appreciate the memories. Those memories are forever. Good thing there are some on YouTube! That Suicidal Tendencies show, I remember. DKs, GBH, Violent Femmes, the Cramps... well, I am sure somebody wrote them all down. Enjoyed the local shows, too! Seems like yesterday, yet a whole different life away.

Amy Miller

Amy and Shorty

I was 15 when I first walked in the door. I had a bad fake ID, but my money was good…though I got in on borrowed food stamps once. There were bands I had to see. Even if I had to walk across the bridge and panhandle, I was going to get in to see the band. In later years, I would walk in to cries of "Talking dirty about Amy" or be tackled like a football player by Chuck Byrd. There were so many great bands that played. Local bands were just as exciting as bands from other places. My friends and I use to scream along with all the bands. The people made the Jockey Club. Half the fun was the people who went there. The Jockey Club was full of characters. People once met you could never forget. Though some have since passed, they are never forgotten. They are still alive in the memories of those who will always remember those crazy JC nights. Sometimes it was almost empty and at other times it was over flowing. There were bands with amazing props and bands that paraded to the stage. There were bands that threw things at the crowd and bands that gave us things. There were bands that came to the parties we had after the show and bands that had parties in hotel rooms. There were bands that came to see bands at the JC after they played somewhere else. The Jockey Club was more than a club; it was home to punk rock in the area.

The first time I went to the JC, the stage had a sort of catwalk runway thing. It was rather awkward. Things improved greatly when they redesigned the stage. The dance floor really opened up. It was easier to stand against the stage and get giant bruises on your hips watching the band. (Or in the case of Black Flag, a face full of Henry sweat. ACK!) The place always smelled like stale cigarettes and beer. In a big crowd, it was rank with sweat too. Once some idiot let off some firework that filled the place with red smoke. I didn't actually care what the place smelled like. I was there to damage my ears with really loud music. I am still amazed that I didn't have any lasting hearing damage. These days I wear ear plugs when I see really loud bands. In the 80's, I would not only not wear earplugs, but I would stand right next to the really big speakers, where

Billy Brady was usually curled up inside. Hardcore punk is always at its best with the volume cranked up.

There were so many excellent shows as well as memorable shows. When Minor Threat played, I convinced my mother the flyer that said everyone welcome meant all ages. They let me go. It was on a week night and none of my friends could go. I had to take a bus and walk across the bridge. The stupid part was I had to take the last bus home. The band had barely started when I had to leave, so I didn't get to see the whole show. I was there early sitting by the bar when all the lights were on and I had to leave before they were more than a few minutes into their set. It was cold outside; it couldn't have sucked worse for me. Tracy Hooks and I got on stage uninvited and helped Dementia Precox play. Some girls from out of town hated our audience participation and wanted to fight. When Myra stepped in, the girls decided it was best avoid a confrontation. I miss Myra. When Agent Orange played, Tracy Hooks and I were smoking in the boy's room. The girl's room was too crowded and no one ever went in the men's bog unless they had to, so we were smoking in a stall and laughing. There was a knock on the stall door and it was some unknown guy asking for a toke or two. He said he would do stupid human tricks for us, so we let him in. Just as we finished smoking, there was a call from the stage, the band was missing a member. It turned out we had held up Agent Orange by way laying one of their members. When the Dead Kennedys played I was pregnant and they let me sit on stage against the speakers. It was the best seat in the house and a great show. When Hüsker Dü played, my youngest sister was there. She was only 14. I was dancing and stage diving, but at one point I realized she was sick. Too much alcohol can do that, I tried to move her to somewhere comfortable, but I kept finding her hugging a toilet in the girl's room. I think she had fun, despite the being sick portion of the evening. I personally loved when D.O.A. or Toxic Reasons played, both bands were always amazing live. Some bands got worse each time they played, Black Flag for one got worse each time I saw them. I think that may be, because I am not a fan of their later albums. I was a huge fan of STD, out of Knoxville, TN. I went to all

Amy and friends at the JC
photo by Sarah Kuhl

their shows. They always put on a fantastic show. Plus they were nice guys. I was also a big fan of SS-20, a local band; they totally rocked out every show. Everyone would sing along with SS-20. It was always a lot of fun.

Some nights the lobby was like a casualty ward, so many injured laid out. Lost teeth and broken limbs, I was lucky and never got hurt badly, a few bruises at most. I never hit the floor when I stage dived, I did get a beer bath once though.

The first after parties I ever went to were at Terry and Amy's on Walnut street. They were all so great that I found I loved the idea of the after party. I loved the idea of people getting to know the band. I learned a lot about the scenes in other cities. I met Legal Weapon before they played, I was sitting on the sidewalk drunk outside Terry and Amy's place and they walked up looking for the apartment. I am sure it was a wonderful first impression. I finally got an apartment in 1984 and I had a few after parties. The only reason they are remembered at all is weird things happened at some of my parties. Plus I only had a studio apartment so half of every party was outside the actual apartment. I was so excited about seeing the Exploited I wrote stuff in glow in the dark nail polish on my shoes, clothes and arms, I had a big party after the show. It was summer and the band was sweaty so I took them out to the pool. They jumped in and the pool turned purple. It was like 2 am so half an hour later the apartment manager ran us out of the pool. Someone stole my cat named Mouse at that party. I was pissed. There was also an argument between some Kentucky guy and Wattie when Wattie wouldn't pass him a joint.

All in all, it was an eventful night. The JFA show was so fun, I didn't want the night to end so, I had a party. The band skated down Riddle Road before coming to the party, but the Sun City Girls kept us entertained. I liked the JFA show so much I saw them again in Knoxville a few weeks later. Nothing odd happened at the party after the Necros, but it was so crowded that I had to sit on a table and

Tammy puts makeup on Dave Fry
photo by Jakki Repellent

there were people sitting under the table. It was fun! The party after Black Flag was the biggest. The funny thing is, it was not Black Flag that initially caused me to have the party, it was my sister Robin's birthday week. It was a party for Robin and I accidentally made it too big. I had friends in from out of town and invited too many people. Robin was supposed to meet my Mom on the street after I took her to the show and she was at the party a bit. She was supposed to be picked up on the street by my parents. Mom drove past her. The parking lot was full of partying kids and my Mom figured out what I was up to. She came in… and Black Flag had been wondering in the building removing the covers on the lights in the hallways while looking for the party… and Henry walked into my apartment right behind my mother. She was going off about my sister who was not in the apartment and pushed Henry and everyone behind him out of the apartment. She shut down the party. I was only 17 and the apartment was only good when she had no idea what I was up to. It was her answer to me running away. It all ended that night. I got evicted and lost everything. I went to Knoxville. I loved the scene there. I use to run away to Knoxville often when I was younger. I had many friends in STD. I still miss Camp. He used to bring me Pop Tarts. When I got back to Cincinnati, I eventually ended up staying with Jolene, the armed prostitute, she was not a punk. She was nice enough to let me stay at her house. She worked at truck stops and was gone for days at a time and I had parties at her house when she was gone. At her apartment, I had parties for Fang and 45 Grave. Fang remembered some of us from the first time they were here. Hard to forget being stuck in Cincinnati for a week when you are supposed to be on tour. Everyone in the scene had time to hang with Fang when they got stuck here in 1983. They stayed in Terry and Amy's attic. They got invited all over. Everyone got a chance to play quarters or

Agnostic Front
photo by George DuChaine

hang out. It was automatic that I would have a party for Fang at an apartment that wasn't mine; they had made so many friends from the first time they were here. They tossed bottles from the roof that night. Hell, it was just at Acropolis, they didn't even hit it. It was fun to hang with them again. I loved the 45 Grave show the next week even more. I was happy to have them come to Jolene's house. Toxic Bob remembers who set who on fire, but I all remember was there was a debate about whether hair mousse is flammable. Luckily, the mousse was piled on to a skinhead before it was set on fire. It was put out fast and I was standing there freaked. I was in charge of the apartment, not mine. Funny thing is I left with 45 Grave, fuck the apartment. I took them to Tammy's the next day. She was ill and missed the show. She also had vodka and drugs. She was injured. I brought her the band she did not get to see. They gave us a record and toys. I put up Tammy's Mohawk and we hobbled around Clifton. It was the best day. In 1985, I let Agnostic Front stay at my house on Stratford. It was a small after party, but I let the band write on the walls, so it is forever remembered in pictures. It was just after my 18th birthday party. They were very nice guys. They didn't even make a big mess which was a rarity when it came to bands. Tammy and Bob stayed over that night and I got a lot of bad pictures in the morning. No one looks good in the morning. On Stratford, I didn't have parties as much as let bands crash or bathe. I had roomies on Stratford so I had smaller gatherings in my attic instead of all out parties. Though someone showed up uninvited with a band needing a bath once and I did let them bathe. I did not encourage people to show up uninvited. I had roomies. It turned out that my sister staying at my house when I was in DC got me kicked out. I was a horrible roommate; I deserve to get kicked out. I did a lot of dumb ass things when I was young; luckily none of them killed me. I know there is more I should have written, but this is all for now.

Tammy Zienau

Tammy and cat
photo by Jakki Repellent

I was fifteen years old in 1983 when I first stepped foot into the Jockey Club. I wish I could say I remember who was playing that night. What I do remember is seeing a Mohawk for my first time and being so completely blown away by the strangeness of it all. Strange, but wonderful. I had found my kind. I thank Jeff Stewart and Helen Greenburg for that. They were the instigators that showed up at my house one day and decided it was time to turn my metal listening ears onto some harder and faster music. It worked, and I was hooked.

One year later, I was sporting my own Mohawk and throwing back Foster's. Of course it didn't take me a year to go back, I was there every weekend. I still don't know to this day how my friends and I managed to get away with being underage and in a bar. What I do know is the few times the cops decided to raid the place, Bill Leist would shuttle us out the back door until the coast was clear. That didn't happen often; the local fuzz stayed away most of the time. They didn't know what to think of us.

All I could think of was how I was going to get money to see a show. Hell, I have no idea how I got into most of the shows; I don't think I had a job then. Once again, Bill was there to take care of that too. The times that I didn't have money were the times my partner in crime, Amy Miller, and I would sit on the stump, begging for change, until we either had enough, or Bill felt sorry for us and let us in.

The Jockey Club soon became my second home. I couldn't wait for the weekends to come so I could arrive early and bullshit with my friends, drink some Foster's, smoke some ganja, and eagerly wait for the band to take the stage. The group of people that I hung with in that time frame were the most wonderful, quirky, and unique people. I'm so proud and honored to have been a part of that group. Some have since passed away but they will never be forgotten. They will always live on in our hearts. Having the technology of the internet, notably MySpace, makes it easier to remember…even for those of us who have a few brains cells missing.

It's hard to pinpoint my favorite show. It's amazing how many bands I saw in the two years that I hung out there. The band that turned me around and caught my ear is D.O.A. "Fuck You" was my theme song. Seeing Joey Shithead was definitely a highlight in my life. The Dead Kennedys and the Ramones were probably the biggest acts that played. If I remember correctly, I think the

Tammy with JC friends Greg Cull, Dave Fry and John "99" Haynes
photo by Amy Miller

DKs played two nights in a row? Or was it the Ramones? The most memorable bands were Charlie Pickett and The Eggs, Tex and the Horseheads, and Tupelo Chain Sex. They were out of the norm, a bit off the beaten punk track. Who didn't play at the Jockey? Seems like I saw the best of the best: UK Subs, T.S.O.L, D.R.I., Suicidal Tendencies, Violent Femmes, Hüsker Dü, the Dickies, and Black Flag. One of my favorite bands I saw there happened to be playing the same night I went to Riverbend to see Ratt. After the Ratt show I went to the club and caught a band from Chicago called Discharge. I remember meeting the lead singer and wearing his leather jacket and how impressed he was that I had just seen Ratt. I was the impressed one…they shredded!

Not only did I see some great bands in my youth, but I also went to some great parties, mostly hosted by my friend Amy. It was a treat to hang out and party with the band. In my experience with Metal bands, they were so cocky they didn't want to give you the time of day. That was another thing that I loved so much about the punk bands; they were so personal. They never put on airs; they were just real people. Hell, a lot of times we would sit on the stage and listen to them play.

Let's not forget stage diving. Stage diving and moshing eventually all bled through to the metal world and punk and metal fused together through thrash. I still remember my metal friends giving me a hard time for listening to punk, although my punk friends didn't care. The one band that bridged the gap between punk and metal is Motörhead. The only time I ever saw my punk friends come to the metal bars was for them and nothing pleased me more. Long live Lemmy!

When I moved away in '85 I had no idea that when I returned, the Jockey Club would be no more. My only regret is not being there for the final night; it still saddens me to this day. If I had known I would never set foot in the Jockey Club again maybe I would've moshed a little harder, drank some more Foster's, and hugged Shorty? Shorty was the owner of the JC. He probably had some ties to the Mafia...who knows? I do know he liked the ladies! I remember his damn flashlight he used to carry. I'm sure he probably knocked a few of us on the head with it too…what a character! I didn't really get to know the other owner, Tiny, too well. He died not to long after I started going there. I'm grateful to Shorty and Tiny for putting up with us misfits, who knows what went through his mind. Maybe he was a closet punk? Something to ponder. There will never be another Jockey Club. I can proudly say that I was part of its history.

Long live Hardcore!

"Toxic" Bob Butler

If I gotta fix this fucker, tell me 'ow to fix this fucker...the DEADLINE! the DEADLINE! OH SHIT!

Damnit, I need a Beer. How else am I to knock loose a few brain cells to humorously produce an anecdote or dozens and smash it all back in order just to contribute slightly to these Jockey Club Memoirs. But now, I don't drink, so all I have is the Haloperidol I just took so let's see where this thing goes.

"Toxic" Bob photo by George DuChaine

The memory of what preceded a particular night is all in a fog. Perhaps I was rolling out of band practice, intent on going to the JC. The JC regulars I knew around UC didn't mention any show for that night. A flyer I'd seen in the lobby beforehand had subliminally stuck in my head there was indeed a show. I was bored so FUCK IT I went. Billy Blank, I think, was working the door so I asked what kind of bands, what kind of music. "Psychedelic" was the descriptive I recall, and I thought "Oh great, hippie shit."

This was the same night "Figures on a Beach" was playing at The Metro and some people sitting at the JC bar were complaining that The Metro got all the Jockey Club's clientele that night. I didn't know who the fuck "Figures on a Beach" were nor did I care, never heard of them. Neither did I before hear of the bands playing at the JC that night, one local band's debut and an out-of-town band nobody around here has heard of. I was thinking it was going to be another one of those boring nights, where I end up walking all the way across the central bridge to Cincinnati to catch a late bus, or at least getting a cheaper cab fare than going to the Cab Station next door to the JC. I was wrong.

There were 30 or 40 people at the club, when I arrived, enthusiastically awaiting the debut of the warm-up band EL KABONG! Stunning, Loud Garage Rock. Like a crunchy sonic sandwich made from the 13th Floor Elevators and The Ramones. My boredom was gone. I was at that elevated state where you just wanna yell "Bring it ON!!"...slam my fists on the table, make the cans and ashtrays rattle. My head was roaring even after the last few chords of the last song. Then that was over. I wanted more.

So now there's that period of time between bands. The bands packing up equipment, some people shuffling around, looking for their friends. Now you can hear the old-timers arguing and chuckling at the bar. Sitting in the darkened Ballroom area, it seems the two shades of brown on the checkerboard tile floor just radiate translucently upward, filling in the void of space with this..... returning boredom. It grew, and manifested a life of its own, and I started to wonder if I should just go. I wasn't the only one feeling that way as people were leaving. The next band was setting up, so there had to be MORE...was there even a board-tape to play through the PA? The darkness was closing in... And just when I thought I couldn't take another minute of it, the headlining band took the stage. The guitar player was a stringy-haired 'record store' type. The drummer was the jock-type. The bass player had that UK MetalPunk hair and wore a clown's outfit. The lead singer was a spellcasting beat-poet, who looked like Adam Ant's skinny gothic evil twin brother, complete with the sideburns.

"Yeah, we're from Phoenix, OUR NEIGHBORS SUCK, and here's a song about doing too many hits of acid..." and I was hurled into this quirky rollercoaster of sound, jumping back and forth from fast Hardcore into these inventive grooves with weird time signatures. Watching and listening was like flipping music video channels. Just the schizoid type of thing I've been looking for. I was blown away. The guitarist stooping over and kicking this mountain of effect pedals, making every sound possible...while the lead singer changes stances from break-dance mockery to a sorcerer. I was so spellbound that I didn't notice that they had shortened their set, probably less than 20 minutes, because, apparently everyone had left before they started. I was the only one in the audience. I looked around and there were just a couple of old-timers at the bar, along with a couple of New Wave debutantes who were drunkenly conversing about cosmetics or whatever New Wave debutantes converse about. Metro rejects perhaps.

Well as it goes, the band was on the road, had no money for motels. I let them crash at my cramped apartment on Short Vine. I made up several skillets full of French Fries, cause that was all I had to offer for food, maybe a few multivitamins, as they were flipping through my Record collection. They got into a hilariously typical argument about what to play. The guitarist wanted to hear Hüsker Dü's "Flip Your Wig", the drummer wanted to listen to Yes' "Close to the Edge", and the singer seemed strangely pissed that I didn't have any Bachman-Turner Overdrive records, so he went out to my fire escape to do bong-hits, in full view of the 2700 block of Vine. You call that a fire escape? I'd have to jump 15 feet to SuperX's roof.

Well, after trying to figure out who sleeps where and who's on the floor, still couldn't get to the john without tripping over somebody and I was keeping them awake by trying to study in my kitchen area. There was a bit of going back and forth from their van to my apartment, so I don't think anybody got any sleep. The drummer wanted to know where's a good place to get breakfast, but the singer insisted they couldn't afford to go out and went to the grocery store. This is when I discovered the 'punk rock diet.' He came back with a bag of apples and a dozen packages of Ramen noodles. I'd never heard of Ramen noodles 'til then. Well I was a bit impatiently overly-patient by this time as I had already missed two classes, but for whatever reason didn't give a shit.

There is no climactic denouement to this story, but my rant to the JC regulars... WHERE THE FUCK WERE YOU?! You missed a PHENOMENAL show. I wish they'd put out more records.

...and now three dizzy spells later...that's all done. And to all, a good night.

Jon Dameron

I had started hanging out with Bill Leist, Dave Hilton, and Pauli, and the rest of the Newport boys in 1980. When Bill started booking the bands at the Jockey Club, we used to drink beer in the parking lot because it was cheaper than buying the beer from Shorty. One night I was in the Club and I yelled to Bill that I was going to run up the street to the liquor store and get some beer. Well Shorty bitched at Bill, and then Bill bitched at me for saying that in front of Shorty.

One of the most hilarious times was when the Violent Femmes played at the Club. Gordon Gano, the Femmes singer came in the front door and Jim Davidson was working the door. Gano said he was in the band, but Jim did not believe him. Gano said something like, what do you want me to do sing a song. Jim said yes, and Gano started. I think it was, "When I'm a walking I strut my stuff and I'm so strung out ..." Then Jim let him in.

I remember when the Fucking Cunts played the Club, and bill talked them into letting me sing the Heartbreakers song, Let Go. In true Thundersesque form, I forgot the words part way through and just winged it.

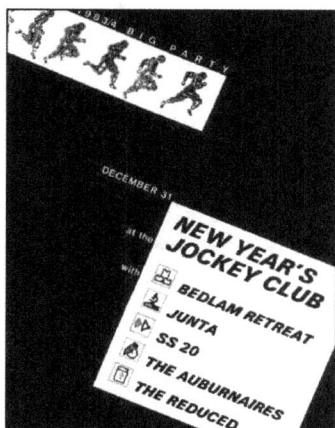

JC flyer, New Year's Eve with Bedlam Retreat, Junta, SS-20, the Auburnaires and the Reduced

Speaking of the King of Rock n Roll, the highlight of the Club was seeing Mr. Johnny Thunders and hearing the opening chords to Personality Crisis, and then seeing him for free on Sunday night. I remember being in the wet room with JT, his band and other JC'ers, while Johnny was rolling a big spliff, when Bill came in with dad and kinda startled Johnny.

Fav local bands: The Reduced, The Thangs, The Auburnaires, Snare and the Idiots, SS-20, Doc and the Pods, El Kabong. I am sure I am missing some people.

Fav touring bands: The Ramones—the place being packed and me telling my friends we need to get back inside before the fire department comes and does not let anyone else in, The Damned, The Lords of the New Church—seeing Stiv Bators walk in right in front of me, Tex and the Horseheads—she was good, and sexy and funny.

But mostly, I just remember how cool it was to have our own club. It was great to see so many great bands, local, national and even bands from the U.K. But it was also so cool to know that you could go down to the Club, knowing that no matter what band was playing, you would see a bunch of people that you knew, and that you would have a good time. I remember playing pinball with Pauli, hanging out in the corner where you could do whatever you wanted. I remember slam dancing and pogoing, and the freak show as Snare would say.

I remember The Reduced and Snare and the Idiots letting me sing a song every now and then.

I remember going to the bingo at the Club with my mom in 1969 or 1970.

I remember Bill introducing me to Sherry Johnson on April 5, 1985, and us getting married six years later. People, especially the women, are always impressed that I remember the date that I met my wife. But I can date it easily, because it was the weekend after we came back from New York City after seeing Johnny Thunders play three nights in a row at Irving Plaza, and pretty much seeing the New York Dolls, with Thunders, David Johansen, Syl Sylvain and I think Killer Kane playing.

I remember the cops coming in and checking IDs, and going to eat at Sylvia's or the Pepper Pod very late at night.

I just remember it being a great fun time in my life. Like the Boys said, in "Brickfield Nights", "On summer nights, like a sauna, we always met by the corner lights, Brickfield Nights (Jockey Club Nights). And it seems so long, those days are gone, dark nights down Brickfield (Jockey Club)."

Jake Ashcraft

Dazzling lights! The glitter of an awesome marquee! Elegant dance floor!

Okay, so that is pure bullshit and not at all what our favorite memories of the Jockey Club are all about. Thank god!

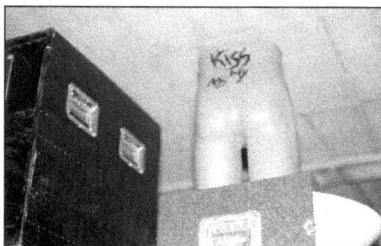

Kiss my ass

The Jockey Club had bad lighting, smelled like years of beer, piss and sweat, and the floor was usually filled with garbage and filth. But for all of those seeming "drawbacks" it was the best place the Cincinnati music scene has ever had.

From my first show at the JC (Gang Green...1980...something...memory fried from...well let's just leave it at that!) to the final night when everyone literally tore the walls out prompting Shorty to come after us with a ball bat, this club has represented not just great music, but the bonds of lasting friendships born of a unique subcultural phenomena that I am privileged to have been a part of. It was at this club that I did most of my growing up. I had my first serious relationship with a girl I met at the J.C. I had my first heartbreak from a girl I met at the J.C. And I had my first serious hangover from the beer at the Jockey Club. I met a girl at the J.C. who became much more than a simple friend, but a confidant, mentor and teacher. (Thanks Bryna!) And I saw my best friend who I met at the Jockey Club buried.

Last night
photo by Dee Snyder

The Jockey Club represents more than just a place I hung out. For me it is akin to the hippy Summer of Love; it wasn't merely a club- it was a happening. When you said "The Jockey Club" it was an action word. Looking back on it I can understand why some of us began

165

tearing pieces off the building on the final night it was open. In a sense those pieces represented parts of our lives-memories and emotions invested in the very foundations of the place. How could we just say goodbye? How could we just let it go?

We had to keep to whatever we could of the life we all gave the Jockey Club. In doing so we also celebrate the life that the Jockey Club gave us.

Betsy Young

Like a million other kids shadowboxing their way out of adolescent purgatory, I emerged on the other side scathed but still searching. I'll admit I did troll around in souped up cars for a time—bored as hell—with pot smoking, 40-ounce drinking, Lynyrd Skynyrd listening kids who were also trying to escape their pain in the only way they knew how. Looking back on it, the only thing we had in common was the pain. We basically loitered and I tried hard to identify with their brand of angst but their preferences in playing it safe and staying within carefully guarded boundaries made palatable with Pink Floyd records, bottles of Mountain Dew in 16-ounce green glass and meticulously packed down and counted Marlboro cigarettes felt pointless and tiring, even for a 14-year-old. While they stuck to their uniforms of bell bottoms and concert tour shirts, living out the rest of their lives in suburban Dayton, Ohio, I left for greener pastures.

The night I finally turned my back on that world for good was right after friends stood me up on my 14th birthday. I remember the humiliation was almost more than I could bear. Instead of staying home alone feeling like a fool, I went to see the movie "Times Square" with my mom because she felt sorry for me. What I didn't expect that night was that the movie's mood and look with "The Sleez Sisters" Nicky Marotta and Pammy Pearl would have such a profound impact on me. It instantly inspired me to quietly go it alone. Plus the soundtrack from that movie, which I bought the very next day, gave me the ammunition I needed to do it. Exit classic rock, enter the Ramones' "I Wanna Be Sedated", XTC's "Take This Town", Patti Smith's "Pissing in the River" and the best part—there was more! It seemed like overnight the music I was listening to before became non-relevant.

Once my eyes were finally wide open, it didn't take long for me to start cutting my teeth on great Dayton bands like the Toxic Reasons, Dementia Precox and the Delinquents. And with the help of my partner in crime, Amy Kreitzer, who I began just casually talking to in homeroom one morning, I discovered thrift store fashions, how to fuck with people's social expectations and best of all, her uncle's record collection! We spent hours plucking records from his stacks just to hear what they sounded like, everything from the Dead Kennedys to Lydia Lunch to Fingerprintz.

One night, for $3, we went to see the Toxic Reasons and The Delinquents open up for D.O.A. at Brookwood Hall in Dayton and for the first time I saw leather-jacketed punk boys slam dancing. For some reason, this thrilled me so thoroughly I laughed the entire time I watched. The Toxics, then fronted by Big Ed Pittman, showed me that rock could be pure, it could tell the truth and it didn't have to exploit. Without being too haughty or intellectual, that music was actually saying something to me, something that I was dying to hear. While Ed angrily raged at the boys who threw beer bottles at the Toxics' P.A., just the human act of Ed getting pissed off and walking off the stage felt like I was a part of a drama that was unfolding, not just an observer. What I saw that night was not like anything I had seen up until then. The rage and aggression I observed fed my rage and aggression but only to help me manage it better. I stopped turning it inward, for example. Because of that, the Toxics will always be my favorite band from that era.

At that point I was hooked as my taste seemed to evolve daily. For example, one major revelation happened when I was introduced to the vast and far-reaching power of punk from Maximum Rocknroll. Up until then, I didn't understand how un-alone I was. There really were others out there! I fully understood the power of D.I.Y. after I scurried home with MRRs in hand and devoured them all cover to cover. I even read the letters! But one issue in particular caught my attention. It had a scene report from Ohio in it (July 1984). This issue happened to feature an article about what was going on in and around Cincinnati but more specifically, Newport, Kentucky just across river. The first line read, "Cincy's "freak show" is better than TV nowadays." The report was written by some guy named Bill Igerent. Anyway, "Bill" described a city that sounded to me like an oasis if you yearned for something other than what was being spun on the radio or offered up at the local arena. Record stores with indie records galore, do it yourself 'zines xeroxed by hand, "Search and Destroy" on WAIF hosted by "Handsome" Clem Carpenter and The Jockey Club. Oh, the Jockey Club! He talked about the local bands that played there: "Cincinnati's most hated band" The Edge, the "highly charged and politically influenced" SS-20 and his own Musical Suicide with the "infamous Jakki Repellent on bass" among others and he made all of them sound like superstars. I knew instantly I had to go there!

Wiedemann Fine Beer

Circumstances brought me to Cincinnati in the late summer of 1984. I had a whirlwind of an end to high school and I left Dayton feeling like I crashed and burned out of there. I skipped graduation, I broke up with my boyfriend but the worst happened. My grandma died. I was 17. Wiping the slate clean in a bittersweet way was somewhat cathartic but I was never so glad to see Amy when she visited me in Cincinnati. One night during the visit, we decided on a whim to drive around Newport, Kentucky until we found the Jockey Club. I didn't know where it was and up until then, I had never set foot in Newport, Kentucky. It took driving around in circles in Covington and Newport without a map before we spotted the fairly innocuous "Wiedemann Fine Beer" sign with "Jockey Club" below it. There weren't any bands playing that night but that wasn't the point—we made it! I'll never forget my first look at the lobby hallway that recalled the glamour days of the Flamingo Club long past with its faded topography I've forgotten (palm trees maybe?) but now saturated with layers of black grime, spilled drinks and crushed cigarettes. The whole vestibule smelled like mildew and smoke. What I liked about it was it lacked any pretense of glamour at all but somehow I knew it was just a dirty pearl.

Once through the door though, the Club itself opened up to reveal a beautiful wooden bar as I recall, but no matter how hard I strain, it doesn't quite come back to me as it should. Oftentimes I noticed the Newport townies sitting and drinking there, oblivious to the freak show around them. I remember

JC, a view of the stage
photo by Jerry Adams

being surprised at the size of the Jockey Club, with its wood paneled walls, drop ceiling and linoleum covered floors. It looked like it had been refurbished at one time to look "modern" but it really looked like a honky tonk with its jukebox, decrepit pinball machines and "bar" tables and vinyl covered chairs.

I went to the JC alone many times in my mom's little blue Honda. I just couldn't stay away. I was equally excited and intimidated every time but I continued coming even if it meant standing in the shadows chain smoking and speaking to no one all night long. But what was different than the few shows I saw anywhere else was a willingness to accept anyone into the fold. "Regulars" at the JC embraced me over time because they just kept seeing me there. I remember being in awe of Jakki Repellent—I've always LOVED girls who rock--as she took command of the stage behind that seemingly huge bass despite her petite stature. One evening after once again arriving too early for a show with too few people there, I was trying to "hide" my alone-ness by sitting at a table by myself and chain smoking. In the corner of my eye, I saw Jakki head in my direction with a cigarette and a glass in hand. I remember thinking, nah, she really isn't coming over here! No…no…no…, hi! Jakki graciously introduced herself to me and her boyfriend Billy Brady (who I'm also still friends with today) and said, "you remind me of me" or something to that effect and I proceeded to nervously hang out with her the rest of the night. I roll my eyes at my nervousness now because she ended up being a close friend, one of the few I could ever trust with my full self. But coming to the JC alone in those early days I realized there just wasn't any posing and thankfully, I wasn't alone for very long thanks to people like the guy I eventually married, Chuck Byrd. That was something that I had never experienced before. Not because of how I dressed or what I did or who I knew (hell, I didn't know anybody!). At the time I felt lucky and relieved. I never felt fear there.

Just like the stories we all heard when it was the Flamingo Club about the Mob hanging out there when the heat was on, the JC with its urban decadence and crumbling beauty was the perfect place for punk. Not just for its size and Shorty's shrugging acceptance of the whole craziness but that punk was really well suited for a place with the Jockey Club's history and current state of decay. Even though for punk the decay was part of the expected landscape, it was sort of beauty reclaimed and redefined to me. We were all messing up the pretty picture but not because we wanted to fuck it up exactly. It was ours, a room of one's own so to speak. The dirt and the graffiti on the JC was the thing that made it a beauty. The camaraderie was the thing that made it special. Sure, the Jockey Club could be dark. There were "dark" nights where the neighborhood had a living, breathing vibe (or was that just me?!), like someone was trampling on my grave. The Club itself sometimes felt like it would get in a bad mood. Those big cans of Foster's Lagers that we shared on hot nights before they got too piss warm, just couldn't always bring the fun or chase away the shadows. And sometimes as much as I loved it there, I just had to get the hell out.

This would not be complete if I didn't talk about Shorty. I never knew him in the way that many did but I recall seeing Shorty and his brother, Tiny, mulling around the crowd from time to time and feeling unsurprised by their presence. It was like, oh, yeah, the old guys! Shorty and Tiny were just part of the woodwork for me. Still, I've always been a pro at dealing with curmudgeons coming from a long tradition of grumpy drunks on my dad's side and ethnic grouches from my mother's. Shorty's presence with his sturdy black slacks and starched white short sleeved button down shirts with the front pockets came from the old school style of dressing purposefully and not "throwing something on" like we all do now. With Shorty everything is tucked and belted and tied. Meanwhile, Tiny with his enormous beard, would shuffle past.

Shorty was this grunting grump who would occasionally grab my hand when I wasn't paying attention and shine his flashlight on my beer to see what brand I was drinking (well, he did this to everybody!). Luckily, I was always drinking something from the bar. I never did find out what he did if it wasn't from the bar. I remember the first time he did this, I actually felt honored instead of offended—albeit a bit startled at first—it was like getting Shorty's attention was a weird privilege since he always seemed so unaffected. And it was funny how I was never concerned if he "approved" or not. I guess to me he was no different than my grandfather gnashing his teeth and swiping his cane at us as kids, barely missing our butts. I never took offense to that either.

I always heard Shorty was packing. I never saw Shorty's pistol but I somehow learned early on that he carried a gun. The mere idea that he could have a dangerous side just lended itself to the mystery and infamy I created in my mind. Even though I tended to romanticize the thought, it turned out to be true. In fact, he had a summer gun and a winter gun, I now know. But the thing I think about when I remember Shorty was he was ours. That dangerous, snarling, old man that I knew was an intrinsic part of JC Land and we were lucky to have him but we didn't know it at the time. It wouldn't have been the Jockey Club without Shorty.

I always had the Jockey Club to go to and I will always have it in me. If your life passes before your eyes when you die, I think like an old film noir movie, images from the Jockey Club will come back to me in black and white movie stills. My old life for what it was worth was wiped clean in favor of something that defined me better then just as the Jockey Club years have been wiped away for something else now. It embraced me as much as I embraced it. And what was different is it didn't belong to any one person. It still doesn't. The JC was mine and it was ours. There were nights when people traveled from out of town to see bands or "outsiders" visited the JC to bust heads or whatever and it felt like your home was being invaded but it also contributed to the whole thing imploding which it had to do. Big shows got out of hand some nights with the toilets flooded, bloodied boys dragged out of the pit by friends, when the place didn't even resemble the Jockey Club that I knew just as I heard it did on the last night. Thankfully I missed its destruction. But what makes us lucky is having that place exist at all, to feel like we belonged somewhere. This was the place where punks didn't beat up hippies. Where skinheads didn't beat up punks. Where it was OK to like metal, for instance. "Normal" looking people mingled with the extreme but it really didn't matter. As corny as it sounds, it was the music that brought us all to that place at that time. After years of being a freak, the freak was finally home! Plus I could do it in the same room as Musical Suicide, Hüsker Dü, Toxic Reasons, Ramones, Active Ingredients, Damned, SS-20, Dead Kennedys, Dickies, Minutemen, Black Flag, the Edge, Samhain, BPA, D.O.A., Circle Jerks, Subhumans, Legal Weapon, Scream, Dickies, the Reduced, Descendents, Johnny Thunders…!

Amy Kreitzer

1984. That was when I went to the Jockey Club for my first, and, unfortunately, only time. My submission probably does not belong in this book, but I went to JC with Betsy Young, the editor of this text, and it was definitely not her last time.

Two girls, freshly escaped from Centerville. That town was perhaps the most conformist, soul-sucking environment in SW, Ohio. I had joined the Marine Corps a few months before in order to leave Centerville (Dayton was my hometown, where I was born), not realizing that the military was perhaps the worst option I could have chosen. I was back in Ohio on leave; Betsy moved to Cincinnati with her family several months before, and was attending U.C. We met at Centerville High School a couple of years before, and our shared love of music helped forge a strong friendship. We were both smart, funny, cute and outcasts in the land of those whom hate all things different and good. Without Betsy, I know I would have run away (again). Together, we found humor in our shared predicament of living in oppressive Centerville. Together, we also both loved the punk rock music that told us: 1). Yes, this world is messed up; 2). It's OK to not be like "them".

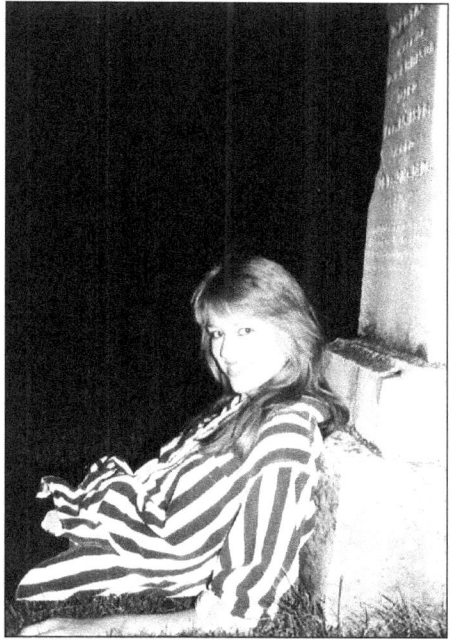

Amy
photo by Betsy Young

Night on the town. I visited Betsy in Cincinnati and was so excited because, though Dayton had a really great (though small) alternative music scene, it always seemed like the Cincinnati area got more bands, and I was eager to see what that was all about. That night sort of reminds me of my several trips to Seattle in the past, always anticipating an exciting night of amazing music, only to discover: you have to plan ahead. There were no good bands that night in Cincinnati. So, we decided to check out the Jockey Club in Newport, KY, a hop-skip-and-a-jump away.

`Jockey Club memories.` I have a foggy recollection of the JC. I can't even recall Shorty, and this is a tribute to Shorty. I do know we were not carded when we entered and ordered drinks. We did look a little older than our ages. Make-up can do that (and that effect is why now, at 42, rarely wear any at all). I can't remember what clothing we wore. I probably had on the "Toxic Reasons" (great Dayton punk legends) sweatshirt an aunt made, but luckily left at my house when she went into the Navy a couple of years before then. Maybe I had on my "Last Cigarette" jeans, two different pairs of jeans, sewn together, the tops from one (sans bell bottoms), and legs from another (pencil thin), replete with punk patches and a zillion holes. Most likely Betsy had on some cool, spiked, punk bracelets, and black Levi's topped by leather motorcycle jacket. Oh, and both of us would have worn our treasured "buttons". I know Betsy had long hair then, though in the years before she normally wore short, punk styles, and I recall I was in awe of her gorgeous, thick, dark hair which framed her cute, face with that Snow White skin. I'm sure I had one of my vintage lunch boxes or doll cases with me for use as a purse, and I recall at that time I had recently discovered cat collars made for excellent bracelets on my (then) rail thin arms, my favorite one a black velvet band with several, pearly white beads sewn across the front in a row, and a wee tiny brass buckle. Most likely we both had on "found" items, converted to jewelry, just weird stuff, like chains "borrowed" from various fixtures in old buildings. This attire sounds sort of ho-hum these days, but back then, we had just endured years in Centerville, being horribly ostracized for being so daring as to dress (and listen to music) far different from the norm.

`No band.` Just my luck, no good, live music anywhere for our night on the town(s). It wouldn't have mattered what band would have been playing at the JC- we were absolutely dying to hear some live music and, of course, dance wildly, until we simply collapsed. Instead, we sat at a table in a bar with perhaps less than 10 other patrons and we drank. I can't remember how much. We were tipsy, I know that much. What I do recall is at some point, so very disappointed that our reunion from several months of not hanging out would not include music, that we would be the music! We went outside to Betsy's car to retrieve the Fisher Price xylophone. We were going to take turns: one of us would play, while the other made up a song and sang. We were ready to go back in and climb onstage, but it dawned on me, or maybe her, that we were quite trashed. What if—worst case scenario,—we were told to get off the stage? Would they then find out we were under-age and had been served alcohol? That ended that. Now, I regret it, as I think they would have enjoyed our little show, and most likely nobody would have asked for IDs. Later in life, I always felt that Betsy and I should have had a band, a great creative outlet during our perceived oppression. That could have been our first gig, unpaid (and uninvited).

No going back. That night was the last time I would see Betsy for a couple of decades. I "found" her online a couple of years ago. It's so sad we missed all those years, because our friendship is as strong as ever. I've tried to live my (adult) existence (anyway) with no regrets, yet I yearn for the years without Betsy in my life, and feel a horribly wrong turn was made somewhere along the line. Those years can't be retrieved, but I sense Betsy and I will always have a connection and will never again lose contact. Right now, I'm pining for that xylophone, 'cause I sure feel a song coming on…

Heather Prescott

You know, the 80s pretty much sucked for everyone else but us. Talk about make your own fun. Cincinnati had the perfect mix of personalities back then to create and give birth to a scene that at the time, while we all enjoyed the shit out of it, we didn't know how lucky we were. Such freedom within the scene. One could drink or not drink, smoke or not, take drugs or not, dress however you like. Everyone was accepted for who they were, and enjoyed the shows and scene side by side. With such a volatile mix of music, personality, drugs, alcohol, etc., it could have been a lot messier than it was. I only remember trouble from busloads of Indy folk, and the Newport Police, but I'm sure plenty got past my radar. I did have to miss the Circle Jerks "Golden Shower of Hits" tour because it was a school night. Serious bummer.

Now on to the man himself! What a guy. Good thing he warmed to us. I think he actually preferred us to the locals. A cigar in one side of his mouth and a fistful of dollars. He measured everyone up as they went past. And he had his own personal guest list. Johnny Ruzsa and I, as well as many others, got the short sharp wave to go through on plenty occasions. Always made you feel like it was your lucky day.

With a night out at the Jockey Club, whether the slew of opening bands were terrible or brilliant, it didn't matter. Plenty of Foster's Lager, Jim Beam, and socializing more than made up for it. Fun Fun Fun Fun Fun. The surrealism of the men's (I use that moniker loosely) bathroom. Tiny and his cattle prod (I've seen him use it, especially on the last night). Amazing acts coming in and looking around with shit eating grins on their faces like they just died and went to heaven. Well, I think Brixy thought it was a nightmare, but so what. Absolute magic. A privilege. The healthiest, most well rounded springboard into young adulthood I could imagine. Lifelong friendships (fiendships) forged. I show the Ho-Ho Records site to backpackers who come through the farm to stay and work. They are amazed and sooooo jealous. Seriously, even by today's generation it is considered to be the crème de la crème of punk clubs ever. A fantasy that actually existed. And we all got to enjoy it to the last drop. Sssssssay sssssssausage!

Greg Borman

It was the early 1980s, and Reagan was in office. I was a teenager living in a relatively affluent Cincinnati suburb. My parents had PhDs in Psychology and Sociology. Politically speaking, they veered solidly to the left. Around this time, I began sensing that something was changing in America. It seemed like pushy, Type A personalities were taking center stage, while those who valued intellect and reason were being swept off to the side. Sometimes I voiced these perceptions to my family, but sitting around and agreeing with parents didn't seem like solid teenage footing. Meanwhile, my friends and I were buying and borrowing records by the Pistols, the Clash, and other likeminded bands. Plenty of these friends were content to stick with stuff like Talking Heads, XTC, and Elvis Costello. In retrospect, those weren't bad musical choices at all. At the time, though, I wanted to dig deeper.

Further musical research came in the form of afternoons and evenings spent with my headphones on, listening to WAIF FM, 88.3 ("stepchild radio", the station's DJs called it). At first I gravitated towards programming like "Another Music from a Different Kitchen", appreciating its focus on post-punk bands like Public Image Ltd., New Order, and Killing Joke. Another program (its name escapes me) played '77 punk bands. These were groups that either originated during, or close to, that pivotal year. There were other WAIF shows, too – the station was a solid source of musical education. But more than just building on my audio knowledge, I felt a pull to participate in a music-based culture. It was when the WAIF DJs played the occasional track by a local punk or new wave group that I felt something akin to a "call to action". It was time for me to do more than just passively take in the music.

I'd been playing guitar for a while and had vague notions about forming a band, even though I wasn't the most likely candidate for such an endeavor. I was shy and not particularly interested in showing off in front of crowds. However, I met a new kid at my high school—he owned a bass guitar and amp. He also knew someone at a different school who played drums. The three of us started practicing in my basement. I began favoring WAIF's "Search and Destroy" show. The DJs, "Handsome" Clem Carpenter and Hockeypunk, focused on louder, faster punk and American hardcore. This stuff wasn't about musical mastery. It was more like, write some lyrics, use the same guitar chord, and hit some different notes with it. Of all the WAIF programs, "Search and Destroy" name-dropped the Jockey Club the most.

I started getting over to the Jockey Club pretty often in 1984. Leaving a D.R.I. show that summer, I remember noticing their singer hanging around near the exit. His hair was a pretty major statement—patches randomly chopped, revealing a good amount of scalp. I thought: What could I possibly talk with this guy about? I imagined that he lived a life completely foreign to me. Maybe he was a squatter back in San Francisco, where the band was from. Maybe he hadn't talked to his parents in years. The Midwest must have looked like a joke to him.

Meanwhile, the group I'd formed hadn't played outside of the basement. I eventually heard about another local band from "Search and Destroy" and other sources. A friend took me to the house where they practiced, and I was invited to join as a second guitarist. I was signing up with an already established entity, which made things easier. We played the Jockey Club once, in the summer of '84. Scream, a Washington, D.C.-based band on Dischord records, was supposed to headline. They didn't show. Still, we had managed to get up on the stage of those hallowed halls. About a year later, I was in another band that played the JC exactly once.

In the fall of '84, I went to the Jockey Club with a specific purpose – to interview Henry Rollins and take photos of Black Flag for my friend's 'zine. Having to ask Henry for an intervie—it didn't sound like the easiest thing to pull off. But it all worked out. I got some good photos, and Henry did the interview after the show. I had encountered a nationally known punk band and lived to tell the tale.

Then there was a Flipper show a little later that year. I'd heard their song "Brainwash" on "Search and Destroy" countless times. They weren't really the kind of band that inspired fandom, but for me, it was hard to not be intrigued by the song's mind-numbing repetition and mumbled lyrics. The night I saw them, Flipper managed to be deadpan, ironic, and menacing all at the same time. They didn't go through the usual punk/hardcore motions at all. It was strangely exhilarating, although I didn't go out and buy any of their records afterwards.

I suppose I qualified as a Jockey Club regular throughout most of 1985. I remember the front hallway where the guy who checked IDs, collected money, and stamped hands sat at an invariably wobbly table. This hallway was usually occupied by lots of show-goers stationed on the hallway's floor, backs propped against the walls on both sides. There was a hall in my high school where kids did the same thing. But the Jockey hallway was filled with people who were interacting outside of officially sanctioned spaces like schools. Going to the JC was something like an extracurricular activity for me. Instead of joining the debate team, I was gaining exposure to a subculture that seemed to gain strength from having nothing to do with respectable organizations and institutions.

While I could isolate and discuss those nights when I saw now-legendary acts like the Minutemen, Hüsker Dü, the Damned, and the Fall, right now

I'm mostly remembering the Jockey Club as a place where I learned to appreciate and interact with people who were open-minded, restless, and participating in something. It was definitely better than staying at home with the headphones on.

Hüsker Dü

Jimmy D

I like to drink cold beer in big cans. When people see me with my hand wrapped around a big blue Foster's Lager, I sometimes get a smile, a knowing nod or my favorite reaction, the gentle chuckle with a head shake that turns into a wistful sigh, then the words, "The Jockey Club". Next thing you know some stranger is telling me about their first time at the Jockey Club and the first time they ever saw a can of Foster's or "The Oil Can" as they're known by some. We then share our stories of speed drinking beer to keep it from getting warm and what band was the first show they witnessed/participated in. Or which show changed their life or rocked their world. The people they saw, the friends they made. The stage diver they caught (or side stepped). The "so, this is a mosh pit; I thought it would be deeper" kind of stories.

Then there are the tales of "I met my boy/girl friend that I married 10 years later". How I played my first gig ever on that stage. I had first my first orgasm in the parking lot. The I got/gave my first blow job in the bathroom with someone pounding on the door. People share tales of drunken debauchery with details of the distance they puked or the size of the puddle of piss they woke in. I get to hear some of the craziest shit from people when they split open their heads and let the memories flow like beer spewing out of a Foster's can dropped on that hard imported terrazzo floor. The Foster's Lager can. Especially the old style steel, made down under with a welded seam on the side and a lip top and bottom seems to be an icon, a touchstone of the good old days for some of us that can remember when Shorty and Tiny welcomed us in. Ok, welcome may not be the right word but they didn't kick us and our silly haircuts and thrift store finery out in the street. Bless them and their cooler full of beer with names we had never seen before.

The band of brothers, the bond you instantly have with others that know! A kinship, the sense of survival, the acceptance in the pack, blood brothers! You see it in veterans of war, ship wreck survivors, bikers. We may now be writers, bankers, cooks, bartenders, politicians, shopkeepers, factory workers, drunks in the street. But at one time, for just a moment, we were together. We gathered at 633 York Street to sing, to dance, to look cool, to drink, to try to get laid, to see the show. I may have taken your money, "checked" your ID, or mixed your band. I may know your name, maybe your face, or just shared a memory from the best rock and roll show you saw. Or maybe we passed out like drunks in a crowd unaware of each other's presence. We did our time at The Jockey Club (damn it!) all under the watchful eye of Shorty and his flashlight. If you were ever there you know you are my friend and I am yours. So buy me a can of Foster's and tell me your side of the story.

William Gilmore Weber

The origins of "Hoo-Weeee!" Yes, folks, 'twas I. At the time I was a big Benny Hill fan (shit...still am!). I remember one episode he was doing some kinda cowboy song. For one of the lines he looked directly at the camera and said, "Hoo-Weeee!" I thought that was one of the funniest things ever (well, at that time). So, anytime there was a lull between songs, or something stupid was going on, I would let out a loud "Hoo-Weeee!"

Bill Weber

Everyone back then threw at least one Foster's can at a band. If someone tells you they never did, call bullshit on them. No one was innocent. But THE best was when the Meatmen were onstage doing their worst metal shit...thinkin' they were "funny". I was at the sound board standing next to Tim Schwallie....and we both finished our Foster's at the same time. I threw mine first...probably missing the stage altogether. Schwallie does a wind-up, pitches it... and threw the most incredible shot. It went straight for Tesco Vee's viking-helmuted head... nailing him good. But it didn't stop there...it proceeded onward to strike the drummer square in the face. I felt like I was standing next to Lee Harvey Oswald...the "Magic Foster" theory. Back, and to the left, back and to the left. Schwallie jumped about three feet in the air in pride. I let out a "Hoo-Weeee!"

—William Gilmore Weber

Teresa Bowling

It was late in '83 or possibly early '84 (where is that damned diary when you need it?) when I heard that the Ramones were playing a gig at the Jockey Club. My high school friends, D. and M. (names have been omitted to protect the guilty) and I had been regular "fixtures" down at the club on Friday nights when it first opened in '82, but we'd become so tangled up in "college life" at three different schools that we'd drifted apart. In an effort to get us together again and to "scratch" another band off of our Punk-and-New-Wave-Bands-That-Must-Be-Seen-Before-We-Die! list from high school, I called them up and offered to pay for all of us! We'd already seen The Damned, The Germs, The Clash, Blondie and Generation X (but we weren't allowed to see The Sex Pistols!), so this show would be our "triumphal return" to the Jockey Club as well as to "the music scene". We just had to "make an entrance," so I designed "special" skirts for us to wear. Inspired by Debbie Harry, I made three skirts out of green garbage bags, snaps, studs, zippers, Ramones stickers and old razor blades in the hems (to weigh them down)! It took us a very long time to sew ourselves into our skirts and by the time we drove to the Jockey Club and found a legitimate parking space (tow me once, never again!), the opening band was wrapping up its set! The outside crowd was "on fire" with excitement (spontaneous "slam dancing" kept breaking out among small groups) and the slow-moving line snaked around the building. As we rolled forward, D., M. and I found ourselves next to a dim alleyway. D. was the first one to notice the burning tips

WEDNESDAY, JULY 23rd, 1986   9 P.M

JOCKEY CLUB

— Proudly Presents —

The Ramones

Admission $10.00   633 York St
                                    Newport, Ky

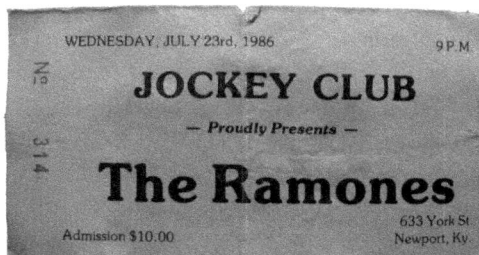

Ramones ticket, 1986
stub courtesy of James Bramlage

of cigarettes in the shadows. As M. guarded our place in line, D. and I went to investigate (safety in numbers!). We heard a disembodied voice greeting us, "Fuckin' cool skirts, girls! Where'd ya get them?" I answered clearly and directly, "I designed them based on something that I saw Debbie Harry wear at a concert and the three of us put them together to wear just for this show."

Then D. twirled around in her best impersonation of a Playboy Bunny strutting down the catwalk (D. was a natural platinum blonde with big boobs!). Almost at the same time, D. and I realized that "the voice" belonged to Joey Ramone himself and that the whole band was outside having a few beers and "smokes" before going on stage! D. and I desperately searched the pockets of our leather jackets for SOMETHING for them to use to autograph our skirts! I found a pen in my inner pocket and we had The Ramones sign our stickers (on our butts!). I flew out of the alleyway to get M. and took her place in line without explaining (couldn't alert the mob!). The line started moving forward, so I shouted for D. and M. They came "slinking" out of the alleyway, pointing at the stickers on their butts with "innocent looks" on their faces! We finally made it into the club and received compliments on our skirts (from guys and girls!) as we squeezed our way closer to the stage. The show was FANTASTIC! We were convinced that The Ramones "signaled" to us as they performed several songs: "Sheena Is A Punk Rocker," "The KKK Took My Baby Away" and "I Wanna Be Your Boyfriend" (my, M.'s and D.'s favorites!). We jumped up and down to the music throughout the show (there was no room to really dance!), but we didn't realize how HOT plastic garbage bags could be! By the end of the encore, we had rivers of sweat dripping down our torn fishnets into our ankle boots! We were so saturated that we made squishing sounds all the way back to my car! But that night at the Jockey Club wasn't the last time that we saw The Ramones. In April 1991, D. and I (M. had moved away, married and was never seen again!) went to Bogarts to see our favorite punk band. We were crammed up against the stage (another EXCELLENT show!) and we had to

Ramones autographs courtesy of Lindsay Belisle

hang around to wait for the crowd to thin out. We had "snuck" a Ramones poster in with us (it "fell off of a wall" at another show and I "saved" it!), so D. shouted up to a crewmember (while giving her best centerfold pose): "Can The Ramones sign this poster for a couple of garbage bag-wearing, Jockey Club fangirls?" Another crew member (a young kid) replied, "Youse girls don't sound like youwa from New York!" I asserted, "We're not, we met them at the Jockey Club, DOWN BY THE OHIO RIVER!" A look of recognition passed over the first guy's face and he took my poster backstage with him. After a tense 15 minutes (Bogarts "goons" tried to "hustle" us out, but the Ramones' manager's girlfriend told them that we were with her! Praise to the music gods!), the crew member returned with our poster signed in silver by the whole band! Although I haven't seen D. or M. in years, (and my skirt "disappeared" during one of my many travels), I still have my autographed Ramones poster and it's an irreplaceable part of my collection of concert souvenirs!

Thank you one million times, Jockey Club!

Peter Aaron
aka Pete Wegele

The Jockey Club had a reputation as being a violent place, but really it was the neighborhood that was rough. Most of the time you were okay going two blocks down on York Street to White Castle or next door to Sylvia's Mexican restaurant to eat, but early on the safest place was always inside the club. Inside it was pretty much the Wild West, you could do whatever the hell you wanted (use your imagination) as long as you didn't hurt anyone. But outside, because of the club's location, run-ins with the locals were always a problem. On one occasion my high school buddy Tom Turck—who I had introduced to punk rock, much to the chagrin of his parents—and I were jumped by a van full of rednecks that had followed us up from White Castle. Wuss that I am, I was all about running away, but ninja master Tom decided to take on all six or eight of them. I got out of it with a few punches to the gut—Tom, though, wasn't so lucky. We ended up driving to the emergency room, where it was determined that his jaw had been broken; he had to have it wired shut for two weeks. Boy, his folks were really happy with me after that. I still remember one of the pale-mustachioed, center-parted rednecks hopping back in their beat-up van and yelling at us: "Y'all go back across the river now—we're rock 'n' roll in Newport!" The shithead had no clue that the real rock 'n' roll was happening just up the street at the Jockey Club. But, then again, that gentleman is most certainly languishing in prison right now, giving himself more bad tattoos and surviving by being the girlfriend of someone bigger than him. Which brings a smile to my (and, I'd guess, Tom's) face. There was also the infamous standoff between punks and rednecks outside the club the first time the Circle Jerks played, which brought the cops in to shut things down, if I recall correctly.

I'm sure many other contributors to this book have rightfully gushed on about the number of amazing performances they witnessed at the Jockey Club. No doubt that Cramps show, in 1986 during the tour for A Date With Elvis, stands out. During the set, a bikini-briefed Lux Interior knocked a hole in the ceiling with the micstand and tossed the wine bottle he had just emptied on himself up into it—where it remained lodged until Snare retrieved it the next day. I've heard many people who were there say it was the best show they ever saw, which is hard to dispute. When I was the bassist in Sluggo, I got to open for some great bands like Negative Approach and JFA. But perhaps my favorite gig, which happened before that period, was Hüsker Dü's first time through, in 1983 on the tour for "Everything Falls Apart". The Hüskers absolutely blazed through a non-stop 45-minute set (no breaks between songs!) and then, as the band was walking off stage, (singer-guitarist) Bob Mould turned to the 10 or 12 of us still-reeling kids in attendance and said, "Okay, now it's your turn." He and (bassist) Greg Norton, handed their instruments to me and the other dumbstruck kids standing in front of the stage, one of us got behind Grant Hart's drums, and they actually let us jam for a few songs using their gear. It was incredible. I recall struggling to reach the neck on Mould's impossibly low-slung flying V as we did the Circle Jerks' "Century City" and then singing "Louie, Louie" while somebody else took a turn on guitar. Then they came back on played a few more songs—Donovan's "Sunshine Superman," (Minneapolis punk pioneers) the Suicide Commandos' "Mosquito Crucifixion," and some other spontaneous covers. Shows like that just don't happen anymore.

Neil Aquino
aka "The Hockeypunk"

Twenty years after the Jockey Club closed its doors, I still feel a mix of relief and gratitude that it existed at all.

Relief I was able to find a place I could fit in. And, gratitude for the many relationships I formed at the Jockey Club and still have today.

I don't know that I have one moment that stands above the others from my Jockey Club years. It was always fun.

Though I suppose a few do stand out:

*The afternoon I spent watching the People's Court and going to White Castle with Fang the day of their Jockey Club show. That was an education for a 17-year old.

*The time I was walking down York Street wearing a Vancouver Canucks hockey jersey and D.O.A. stopped their van to talk to me.

"Hot Tip" pinball

*Anytime I played, the Hot Tip pinball machine would rank as a good time as well. I recall the drawing on the machine of the jockeys fighting each other as they rode their horses down the race course. I loved that machine.

And I loved my time at the Jockey Club. Not just in a nostalgic way as life moves on, but with an ongoing appreciation of the chance to be myself for the first time in some ways.

It was great to be with people who shared some of the same frustrations I did with the larger world in the Age of Reagan. It clued me into the fact that if you look around, you'll find people to enjoy your life with.

Many of you, no doubt, know "Handsome" Clem Carpenter, who gave me the chance to be the Hockeypunk. I've never properly thanked him for letting me co-host Search and Destroy on WAIF for three years.

Thanks Clem!

Growing Up Jockey

by Matt Becher

I grew up at the Jockey Club, just another misfit that somehow ended up at that smoky, piss soaked, "nightclub" in Newport. I counted it up once and figured I went there about 100 times between 1984 and the end. The first show I saw was D.R.I. with Personality Crisis and The Edge in June of 1984—one month shy of my 16th Birthday. Some friends and I had gotten these comical fake IDs by mail order, but Bud or whoever worked the door could care less as long as you had the cash cover. I distinctly remember that Personality Crisis was great—good enough that I bought their LP "Twilight's Last Gleaming," with matching poster insert. D.R.I., by comparison, was terrible. My memory is fuzzy at best, but Big Black was one of the best shows I saw down there. It was a weekday with maybe 20 people in the place but the sound was solid that night. Albini's screams on "Jordan, Minnesota" stuck with me for days after that show. Other great shows that stick out in my mind: the Damned, Minutemen, Charlie Pickett and the Eggs, Agent Orange, Raunch Hands, Didgits, Toxic Reasons, and of course H-Bomb Ferguson with Big Ed Thompson and the All Stars.

The Boondocks: Bob Butler, Nick Stavale, Greg Cull and Matt Becher
photo by George DuChaine

Everyone who went to the Jockey Club has at least one goofy story. Mine was never making it to see Johnny Thunders. The night we had tickets for it was going to be packed and by the time we got down to Newport, there was nowhere to park for several blocks. Greg Cull was driving me and "Hüsker" (aka "Acid") Bob in his disintegrating VW bug. We parked somewhere up past 9th Street and started walking down the alley behind the club. About a block from the JC, these two late '70s land yachts came screaming up toward us from different directions, squealing their tires. Plain clothes cops jump out with guns drawn yelling "Freeze! Newport Vice!" One of us was drinking a Bud, which gave them a reason for the bust, I guess. They searched us, found the expected contraband and were going to take us in until I told them I was only 17. I could hear the gears in Serpico's head slowly turn, saying "too…much…paperwork." They took our stash and told us to "get out of Newport in 10 minutes and never come back." That kept us away until the next show—The Damned—2 weeks later.

Jacob Heintz

"Handsome" Clem and friends

I got my first taste of the early '80s punk underground scene in a downtown Cincinnati basement art show. A local band, The Edge, was running through a raw set of loud punk-tinged rock. After an hour of bashing it out in a small little pit, I was hooked. Around the same time, I discovered "Handsome" Clem Carpenter's great "Search and Destroy" radio show on WAIF. You would be amazed at the aluminum foil antennas that we had to create just to get some reception, but when the Dictators and Mexican Pig Torture came blasting through the little radio, it was worth it.

From there, I quickly started digging into Wizard and Mole's records, where John James and Darren (now owner of Shake it Records) would point me in the right direction. "In God We Trust, Inc." by the Dead Kennedys was quickly snatched up, and just as quickly thrown in the trash at home. Mom was furious, yelling at me that my generation just didn't appreciate who and what the Kennedys stood for. Not to be deterred, I grabbed the tape out of the trash while she wasn't looking, rolled it back up, and still have it to this day.

One day, I saw a flyer for the Dead Kennedys playing at the Jockey Club, and I just had to stick it to mom and catch them live. I walked my pitiful ass over in hopes of getting a dose of righteous rage, and then walked right back—no ID, no go. A few months earlier, I had caught Toxic Reasons (hint: "Killed by Remote Control", a lost classic

Toxic Reasons: Tufty and Bruce Stuckey

album) at an all ages show and when I heard they were playing at the Jockey Club, I decided it was worth another shot. I befriended a fella out in front of the Club who was grabbing a smoke and told him I was trying to sneak in, but had no ID. He handed me his passport, and with him walking in right in front of me, I gave it to the door man, who accepted it without question. It turned out the fella was Fefo Forconi, a short-time member of Toxic Reasons, and thanks to him, I finally made it in.

The décor was American minimalist, a few coolers of beer, a stage, P.A., a couple of beat up chairs, and Shorty. Just what you needed, little else. I flat out had a great time, and with posters for Active Ingredients, SS-20, Rhythm Pigs, Sluggo, Black Flag, Exploited, and D.O.A. floating around, I knew I had

to get back in. The next week, I heard tale of a place to get fake IDs. My long term partner in crime, Dylan, and I immediately went on a hunt for them. When we found them, they turned out to be typed up, kind of official-looking cards from a Church Supply store. Today, it would be laughed at, but in the '80s, it worked. Suddenly, I went from being 14 to 21 and found myself sneaking into the Jockey Club on a regular basis.

Die Kreuzen with SS-20 flyer

Some of the gigs were just incredible, like seeing Die Kreuzen and White Zombie with just a handful of other people, and sneaking in the back door to a sold out Ramones show. And some sucked, like when we waited hours to see HR on tour, finally giving up, only to find out the next morning that he showed up a few hours later and rocked the house.

The last night the Jockey Club was open before the cab company took over, I was there and still remember people ripping holes in the wall. I should have grabbed a piece; I bet you I could get a pretty penny for it on e-Bay.

How the Jockey Club Saved My Psyche
by Laura Harrell

JC at night
photo by Becky Baldock Powell

Being a little fat girl that wore the same sweatshirt day after day was not the way to gain friends or popularity at Walnut Hills High School.

I found the Jockey Club, or it found me, at exactly the right time. I was sad and depressed and then punk rock gave me life with enthusiasm.

Here was a whole culture of people that were real. I could be me, which was angry, without direction with nothing to focus all that pent up aggression on. It took a year or so of much skanking and drinking to realize that my problems were miniscule compared to the world's. I learned about the genocide happening in Central America from M.D.C. I learned about Big Mountain and the corporations dumping toxic waste on Native American land—what land was left after our government allotted them the worst.

Adolescents with M.D.C. plus SS-20 flyer

I grew so much between 1984 and 1989. I'm still growing. Still fighting. Still loving. The world hasn't gotten much better but never mind, I want to be an optimist. My memories of the Jockey Club are of friendships, a lot have lasted to this day. I woke up to the world, I love punk rock! It saved my Soul.

The Dead Kennedys at the JC
by Mike Stocks

In 1985 I was pulling my hair out trying to figure out how in the hell I would ever be able to go see the Dead Kennedys at the Jockey Club. I was 15 and had absolutely no money, no car, nothing. Three days before the shows (they played two nights) 97X was giving tickets to caller #9. I scrambled and won! I was stoked! I called my friend Kyle who had turned me on to punk and told him he was going and it was fuckin' on!

We got to the club and were supposed to get our tickets at the door. I tell 'em that I won tickets and this old dude (Shorty) asks us for our IDs. I tell him that I left it in my other pants, after rummaging my pockets, and he says "No ID, no entry". FUCK THAT! We stewed around in the hall for a few and I decided to try again. I went back and asked again and after the second no I started arguing. This wasn't working but it was something! It

Shorty

didn't look good until this other guy who probably sang for a band (still does) who was in with the old dude got into what was going on. He asked the old guy to let me in and it was no again. That seemed like the final word, but I persisted with the young dude and he asked again and it was no again. Then he says "You gotta let him in, HE WON TICKETS, IT'S THE MAGIC!" I saw the old guy's brain click and he said o.k. after a moment and then said "But no drinking." And it was fuckin' on!

The first band started playing and the singer/guitar player had a guitar with a round table leg split in half for a neck, tuned open and singing "When I look into your eyes, you look like John F. Kennedy!" in a kind of Crucifucks/Flipper kind of voice. I wondered if that was written for this show or if they had it for

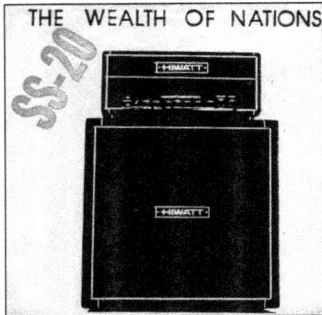

THE WEALTH OF NATIONS
SS-20

SS-20 "Wealth of Nations"

a while. Either way it was intense and heavy and fuckin' psycho, but right. I loved it! The band was 11,000 Switches and I didn't even know they were playing the show. Bonus!

The second band was Active Ingredients, whose 7" record "Bringing Down the Big Boys", had been in my collection for a while already along with SS-20's "Wealth of Nations" which came out at the same time. I love Hardcore and started slammin', PUNK FUCKIN' ROCK! They really got the crowd moving.

Kyle and I "got" some beers, Foster's of course, and soon the Dead Kennedys came on. The whole club exploded instantly! The pit went from the stage to the bathrooms and there wasn't much space left except the old timers at the bar and people squeezing between them to get drinks! What's that 15 square feet? Of the whole place!

In between songs later some guy was fucking with East Bay Ray about his Heavy Metal distortion pedal. Punks didn't do metal! Well, maybe Accept's "Fast as a Shark"! Everybody around him told him to shut the fuck up and that was that. Ray didn't have much to say, he was busy and launched another 150 stage dives! Then and there I knew that that was what I wanted to do. The magic was there, you could really feel the energy. That was my first show. My ears rang for three days after that and a boot busted a blood vessel in my leg where a little of the bruise remains to this day! There are some pictures from that show. I really like the one of Little Rich W. with the M.D.C shirt and liberty spikes all over. I spotted myself in a couple with an army green t-shirt and some goofy red high tops. It was fuckin' on!

p.s.-16 years later my band Rip, Rock "N" Raunch played a gig with the DKs and The River City Ramblers at Top Cat's in Cincinnati. Brandon Cruz from Dr. Know was singing for them and they were KILLER! That may very well be a full circle for me.

We Pilgrims Piggybacked the River, Instinct Puffy in Our Eyes

by William D. Waltz

JC parking lot
photo by Sarah Kuhl

The Queen City may have shimmered

mildly on the far shore,

but Newport is for foraging

and thus attractive in deformity.

A black eye's black sty

served alternative tentacles,

which we devoured, slowly

disassembling the unhistory

we'd memorized so dutifully.

Then the sound of fresh fruit

bursting over the throng

of rotting vegetables moved us,

damp and undulating, and one

by one by none we jackknifed

upstage. Entangled

in a snare of cords and cables,

Jello gently unnetted me.

Floating there

before the crescendo

I wanted to be

more than anything.

Then the surge and swell

passed me back,

a beatific insect

atop a mass of army ants.

Glasses lost amid the jubilee

until the last chord reverberated

in the four chambers of our hearts,

It's a Freakshow, Ace

and although my astigmatism is

much worse now,

my vision is not.

Permanently Altered

by David "Dook" Russell

July 22, 1985 – a day that would rank alongside weddings, births, deaths, and graduations. I'd been gobbling up all things punk for only a short time, and one night at the Jockey Club would prove one of the most pivotal of my life. Becoming a man would have to wait another year or so, though I don't really remember the date, or the year. The events I recount here would establish a life-long trend of favoring music over all things, even sex —tell me you can relate. Upon hearing my first punk rock song—Hüsker Dü's "Eight Miles High" —I shuddered and wept. My first lay registered but a brief, goofy grin.

I first heard punk rock in the summer of 1984, listening to the Adolescents, Descendants, Angry Samoans, etc. through the static on WAIF, listening at night under the covers, much in the way many kids listened to baseball games. Actually, I was 16 in 1984 and a little old to be hiding under the covers, but my parents were bible thumpers from way back (stopped just shy of taking up serpents), so I had to hide the music, especially this music. I had no musical influence growing up other than the disco my sister would force on me and my parents' two 8-tracks (Eagles and Doobie Brothers greatest hits)—no doubt gifts from a cool uncle trying to clue my parents on lightening the hell up. If only mom and dad knew what a doobie was. They thought smoking pot resulted in permanent and rudely unannounced flashbacks. Me, I'm still waiting. I still remember the day my dad bust into the living room ranting "Can your pussy do the dog? What kinda filth are you listening to son?!" After my brain processed the sound of my dad's mouth spewing "pussy" in a way that fell my adolescent wood for a week, I realized he'd found my Cramps cassette.

Anyway, I digress, and apologize in advance for further digressions, but much of my Jockey Club story is the path I took to get there. Immediately upon hearing and feeling real music, real emotion, real energy, real rock for the first time I closed the lid on the case that held my once-dear ACDC, Iron Maiden, and Judas Priest cassettes and gave it to a friend. I realized my mistake years later (hey, Bon Scott, Paul Di'onno, and Rob Halford are bad ass!), but I was young and in love. Next, I drove to the best record store I knew at that time –

Record Bar in Tri-County Mall—punk rock hub of the Midwest. Yeah, laugh it up, but I was living in Fairfield at the time (my parents moved us from St. Bernard in 1977 because it was becoming too "urban" and they wanted to raise the family with country values) and I only knew one other kid who'd ever even heard of punk rock (thus, I'm assuming this was before the famous Quincy and CHiPs episodes that introduced middle America to the evils of punk). In 1984, Rich Rooney was the only kid in Fairfield who owned a skateboard. He loved JFA and was so cool I dated his sister for a year just to hang with him… she was really cute too. Rooney was the only kid I knew who knew what punk rock was, so he and WAIF were all I had to go on. Armed with an iron will and paper sack comprehension, my trip to the mall would somehow result in a chance meeting that set the course for who I am today—one of only a handful of defining moments allotted in life.

Stepping up to the record store counter, I asked "Do you have any punk rock?" The guy behind the counter—tall, thin, early twenties, brown curly hair— looked down at me, smiled, and said "Man, are you lucky I'm working today." His name was Paul and he led me to the Ramones It's Alive, Black Flag Damaged, and Hüsker Dü Zen Arcade. Yeah. Hello, I've never tasted food, can you recommend anything? Sushi, mashed potatoes, and chocolate? Sure, why not? I could've stopped right there and had a pretty complete picture of what it was all about, but of course this only made me hungrier.

For several months, I visited the store regularly, buying Paul's picks and learning his work schedule so as not to waste a trip. One day we stumbled upon the greatest find ever to be unearthed in any mall anywhere. Paul didn't even know what it was at the time—an original copy of Agnostic Front's Victim in Pain (on Rat Cage Records) wrapped in what appeared to be a used sandwich bag. How it came to find me was either divine intervention or support for Paul's sainthood. While others had come before, to me, Agnostic Front represents the birth of the NY hardcore scene and the real transition of CBGBs from the art crowd to the uglies.

And so I came down from the mountain holding the tablets, ready to spread the word of sonic salvation, the alpha and omega from which all future relevant music would spawn. Unfortunately, I converted few and managed to draw the attention of those who remained violently zealous in their defense of AC/DC, Iron Maiden, and Judas Priest as the true word. Luckily, I was big, mean, and in love—a combination with which few would fuck. Mostly, people would listen and say "The music is OK, but I can't understand what they're saying." Fools! They're singing about fighting and fucking, details don't matter. I'd try to explain, but you know how that goes. If you don't get it three notes in, you're not going to get it. Discussion is either unnecessary or completely futile.

These were the early days of punk—no message necessary or even welcomed. Anything positive was preachy. The Minutemen and a few others got a pass, but these were the days when MRR judged a band on their music rather than their message. We're not changing the world here people! Screw the world! Cram your message and play or we're coming up there! On another note, there were no crews—nobody needed a crew because the whole fucking scene was a crew. Those in need of a crew played a sport or joined 4H and generally stayed the hell away from us.

So, a few weeks or months after meeting Paul, I spotted something new on his counter—a flyer for a place called the Jockey Club in Newport, KY. It listed bands—punk rock bands—and gig dates for summer and fall of 1985! I was floored by the thought that the bands I'd been listening to knew where Cincinnati was, could rent a van, and would actually come here. At the same time, I was distraught with the realization that I was only 17. It was then I heard Paul utter the magic words—"I work the door." However, having never been to a bar or club or anything requiring a human to control entry (save Kings Island or the movies), I wasn't sure what that meant, so I asked how it worked, the legalities of a 17-year old entering a drinking establishment where music with curse words would play, no doubt at insane volume. "I work the door, kid. I decide who gets in. You come to the door, I see you, I recognize you as Dave, you show me your ID, I ignore it, I let you in." Saint Peter himself had not only showed me the way, but he was going to let me pass through the studded gates. I couldn't believe my luck. I still can't.

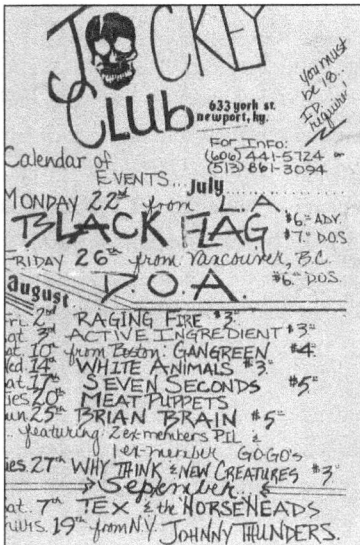

JC flyer courtesy of David "Dook" Russell

To recap, I was living in the then countryside of Fairfield, OH in 1984, somehow discovered punk rock through the static, went all in, found the only guy within miles (except Rooney) who knew what the hell I was ranting about, and he turns out to be the door man at the Jockey Club. I don't play the lottery today because I hear the odds of winning twice are fairly ridiculous.

July 22, 1985—first time at the Jockey Club—BLACK FLAG, from Los Angeles, California. I borrowed my parents' car and headed toward Mecca, toward Newport, KY. The drive was a daze. My first memory is that of walking down the sidewalk about half a block from the club. Something sounding like a giant chain saw brushed me as it sped past on the sidewalk, jarring me from my daze. It was a huge dirt bike ridden by a guy with a huge ax head and a black leather jacket that read "NO FUTURE" on the back. Mr. Future almost snuffed me 40 yards from the club door. Man would I have haunted the hell outa someone had I gotten that close and bit it.

Walking up to the front of the club, I thought to myself, "This is it?" Such a small, unassuming little place, with a small, unassuming little sign—I envisioned horse jockeys lounging around inside. Of course they would be wearing their race uniforms. I waited in line, fully expecting to get up there, get rejected, and likely ridiculed by whoever was no doubt filling in for the sick, dead, fired, or pissing Paul. I was betting on pissing—I'd be denied due to bodily function. I'd have to turn around, go home, and face whatever vanilla future lay ahead. But, when I got to the door, ID in hand, an arm reached out and pulled me in followed by a familiar voice that said simply, "Enjoy."

I looked down the long, narrow entrance way, littered with people sleeping, making out, puking—one long dog pile with little visible floor. Though I walked through nervously, trying not to step on anything important, I already knew I belonged. I belonged because I was there for the only thing that mattered – the music. However, I did realize, with equal parts pride and amusement, that I'd completely overlooked the fashion element of the eighties punk scene. I was wearing what I wore every day—jeans and a white undershirt. At that time, the only visual I had on the scene was from the few cassettes and MRRs I owned. I'm not sure I knew punk had a look, let alone what it was. I mean, for me, it was all music. Hell, I listened to the Bad Brains for two years before I realized they were African American. I made a copy of their Roir cassette from a friend, so I didn't have the band's picture. Anyway, I wasn't there to make a fashion statement. I would've gone in a grass skirt. I didn't care what I wore and neither did anyone else. This was my place.

Passing through the entrance way, I entered a larger, darker room that opened up into what looked like a post-apocalyptic cavern holding a couple hundred crazed survivors from our civilization. I stood, slack-jawed, absorbing the scene as it unfolded—the place was a human stew, stock of beer, sweat, spit, piss, blood, and other random bodily fluids. I was wading in a pool of piss, water, and random 'solids' that spew from a pitch black room to the right—the bathroom. Luckily, I was in the shallow end. The place looked like a prison riot, with a stool-mounted elderly gentleman fueling the inmates with Foster's oil cans from behind a bar to the left. The show hadn't started, but the crowd was warming up, getting ready. The gentleman behind the bar, Shorty, sat expressionless on his stool as he continued to supply fuel and shrapnel to what was about to detonate.

Shorty's oil cans were the original all-steel cans. Not the limp, hippie Canadian oil cans they sell these days. The Jockey Club may have sold other beer, but I never saw it—would've been like taking nail clippers to a knife fight. No —the Foster's oil can was the perfect instrument of war or peace. You could offer it to the parched throat of a friend of five seconds or to the tender skull of an asshole. Mostly, you just got loaded and chucked them at whoever was playing. A really bad night (or a really good night) would see a shower of the communicative cans, many full, resulting in momentary clarity between act and audience…but I'm jumping ahead.

I went to the bar to arm myself, found a wall, backed into it, and waited. Suddenly, I saw the band enter from the right rear of the stage: Gregg Ginn, Henry Rollins, Bill Stevenson, and Kira. I was in shock. This was Black Flag! This was the Gregg Ginn who wrote Nervous Breakdown, Jealous Again, Thirsty and Miserable, and invented a punk rock sound. Based on the ensuing shower of cans, spit, and vulgarities, the crowd was less impressed, or very impressed, I wasn't sure. The music started with a singular crushing impact, igniting the place—that's when the riot really started. Every limb in the place shot out in search of a target. I rushed the stage to join in. As the stew boiled, I became covered in sweat, beer, and spit. I lost count of how many times I hit the floor, got kicked in the head, or was otherwise battered in a way that would've had me on my back had I not been in adrenaline drive. The sensual assault was unlike anything I'd ever experienced.

The show was a blur of sheer brutal ecstasy. At one point, Ginn turned the neck of his guitar on some asshole who'd spit on him one too many times—

planting the butt of the neck in the guy's forehead, sending him to the ground. He put his boot into the tonsils of another for the same offense. Some poor bastard got up to stage dive, appearing as though he'd just wandered in off the street on a three-day drunk. He leaped out in total horizontal commitment… the crowd parted in cartoonish unison. Even over the din of the riot and its soundtrack, I heard the guy hit the floor. A couple of people were nice enough to drag his limp body off the floor before he got trampled. A chubby skin in a Fear t-shirt asked if I'd boost him on stage so he could kick Rollins' ass. For a second, I considered it, hoping Rollins would beat him shitless. He finally drew Rollins to the side of the stage where they were pulled apart before anyone got hurt. Through it all, Kira hammered away on a bass that appeared twice her size. (More than thirteen years later, I would name my oldest daughter Kira in tribute.) And the music—it was everywhere—it was overwhelming—like I was hearing it for the first time. Words can't describe that show and what it meant to me. The music, the club, the atmosphere—it changed my life. Radio no longer existed. Life became a constant search for undiscovered sound and experience.

What I remember most about the Jockey Club is that as soon as my ass hit the ground, there was a hand pulling me back up. A mutual love and respect existed between everyone in the place that stemmed from the fact that you had the passion to come out and guts to enter in. You didn't end up at the Jockey Club by mistake. You didn't pop in for a latte. You didn't drop by after work for a Michelob and potato skins. You didn't go there to be seen or to stir drama. You walked in and you held on. You didn't control shit. A trip to the Jockey Club was the purposeful pursuit of, and guaranteed return on, a life-changing experience. You were signing up to be permanently altered.

Thus are the recollections of someone who went to numerous Jockey Club shows, but could never be considered a regular. I was a pretty drab article, coming and going in my jeans and undershirt without being noticed. I made no friends or enemies, had no impact on the place or its events. No one would remember me. And yet, 23 years later, the place remains a critical part of my DNA. I saw the Cramps, D.O.A., Suicidal Tendencies, and a few others before heading to school in Athens, OH to be part of another amazing scene. The Cramps show remains the best I've ever seen in my life—played as if they knew they were dying that night. I can still see Lux swaying back and forth on top of a stack of amps, lying on his back in a leopard print G-string, smashing a hole in the ceiling only inches above his face with his now-empty wine bottle, all while crooning like a ghoul with the mic halfway down his throat. It was rock, it was art, it was blues, it was glam, it was go-go, it was gospel, it was porn, it was horror…it remains the benchmark.

I could go on, but I've gone too long. I've found that the few things about which I'm passionate enough to write—my wife, my kids, and my music—are those with which few can relate. You can relate.

Thanks to Paul.

Lux Interior and Nick Knox/ The Cramps
photo by George DuChane

Judi Rothenberg

One of the only times I was at the JC: It was 1987-88 and I was a senior in high school. I went with Aaron and we saw White Zombie. I was able to get into the club somehow and the show was awesome. I didn't get all fucked up that night; I was too in awe of the whole scene. I was 17 years old. I remember Aaron hitting on the girl in the band, Rob Zombie's girlfriend at the time.

My Favorite Concert Tee
by Lisa Nichols

I recently wrote about the first concert I ever attended and a comment I received got me thinking about a related artifact, rarely seen outside of my home, but greatly revered and worn regularly: my favorite concert tee.

My favorite concert t-shirt has some holes in it now, and has grown soft from many trips through the laundry, but the band's name still burns as brightly as my memory of that night. It still fits me perfectly, and it still makes me smile every time I come across it in the wardrobe.

Circle Jerks flyer with Hillbilly Trash flyer courtesy of Art D

At the beginning of my sophomore year of high school, I had just moved to the Midwest from the West Coast and found myself floundering, that first year, feeling out of my element and looking to make new friends with common interests. It happened, quite by accident, when a beautiful senior girl (with an even more beautiful faux-hawk) turned around one day in class and caught my amateurish notebook sketch. "You like Suicidal Tendencies?" she asked, and right then, I knew we'd be friends.

We quickly dispensed with the formalities (getting me an ID, introducing me to the other club kids in town) and headed off to the now-defunct, but still infamous, Jockey Club in Newport.

The band playing that night was intense. Too shy to jump into the mosh pit, I volunteered to help collect pull tabs from beer cans to benefit dialysis patients (the sponsoring group in turn recycled them for cash and donated the money to the cause). I worked at a booth in the back of the club, sipping Foster's and actively soliciting tabs from passers-by.

By the end of the night, I'd managed to talk almost everyone in the bar to donate all of their tabs, and had amassed a bagful. Then I heard: "Thank you so much for all of your hard work. What's your name?"

I turned to find Keith Morris, the lead singer of my-then favorite hardcore punk band, the Circle Jerks. I introduced myself and he insisted on giving me an over sized Circle Jerks sticker, autographing it personally, again thanking me for my help.

And then he reached behind the booth. And handed me my favorite t-shirt.

Cathy Lakes

We used to go to the Jockey as much as possible. My photo has been on the jockey website for quite a while. The only remaining flyer I have is HR, but is in bad shape and I have a White Zombie and C.O.C. ticket stub. Most of the time they just had raffle tickets, or nothing at all. I used to go with my best friends Jesse Zimmerman (RIP), Becky, Sheri S., and Paul Smith (Grace). We used to have a blast. Turns out that Snare (Snare and the Idiots) and Sheri knew each other from school. Any time SS-20 played we were there. I have been on stage and sung with them several times, but so did a lot of people. It was cool as the stage was low and you could just sit on the edge and listen and sing along. The bands just walked around and you could talk to anyone—D.O.A. was always very chatty, fun guys. We also saw The Reduced, Haunting Souls from Dayton,

Cathy (far left) on stage with The Auburnaires

C.O.C. and many, many more that I can't think of or remember, including the Mentors. When HR played it was a nightmare as they showed up so very late, but they were awesome when they got going. It was just a great place to hang out, have fun. We even got a couple of hookers to come inside one night and hang out with us. The photographer dude that used to walk around has those photos. That was a fun night. Our friends included Amy (big hair), Sherri L., Danny, Gumby, two Michelles, Brendan, Joetta, Mike Stocks, Roy and a ton of others. We were never unable to find a friend there. And the music was great. We would then go crash at Sherri's house in Bellevue. If anyone remembers Jesse Zimmerman (Danny, Gumby and the countless people that I never remembered their names) I wish I could find someone to tell me exactly how he passed. Jesse used to have a sweet black trench coat with a Misfits album cover painted on it. He was a great artist, and eventually opened his own tattoo shop many years after the Jockey closed. We were all there on the last night. I got a toilet seat and a chair. Who knows why? Becky got some of the wall. Some of my best times were spent there. I do know how the sink in the bathroom got broken, but am not at liberty to share that. When there were no bands playing, we would sometimes just hang out there. A buck for a can of Foster's was a great deal, I think it was a buck, maybe two, memories are a little fuzzy. It was a place to be free, to be accepted. I don't' remember any fights; I know there were a few little ones, but nothing major. On the last night, watching people destroy the place was hard. We were sad at losing a sacred place that can never be replaced, but at the same time I wonder what was Shorty thinking watching that. I did not tear anything apart, but did abscond with some stuff.

Paul Smith

Cincinnati almost killed me....but before this Midwestern river town turned to shit for this former country bumpkin, it was the center of my musical universe for a nanosecond.

Black Flag
photo by Sarah Kuhl

I spent the first 10 years of my life on a farm, and suddenly after a divorce, found myself in the heart of the city. Luckily for me we settled in Pleasant Ridge...home of Everybody's Records. Call it marketing skills, call it bad influence, call it whatever you like, but when I was 12 years old fishing around in the record bins looking for the latest Rush or Devo record, some long haired guy that had a twin brother working there as well, said, "You like that?". "Yes, I said...it's kinda cool and I really like their hats." He put his mitts in the bin and pulled out a record with a fist and some broken glass on it. BLACK FLAG. DAMAGED. "Try this," he says..."I think you'll like it". "What is that?" I asked. "Punk rock from L.A... not like that wimpy stuff that you usually buy," says the walking mountain range.

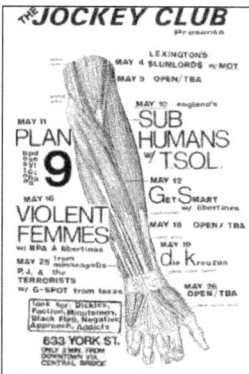

The Jockey Club presents
flyer courtesy of Mike Stocks

I pay my hard earned lawn mowing money on the record and go home.

I contemplate what I know as punk rock on my way home. I felt like I have a piece of pornography in my hands. I remember hearing about Punk rockers like SID VICIOUS one Christmas years before, about murder and death and drugs...bad people these punks.

When I laid it on the record player and the drum intro started and then this buzz saw guitar and then this gruff snarling voice...RISE ABOVE! I was scared, really. More scared than when I heard helter skelter the first time... more scared than I was of the boogie man Himself Charles Manson. These guys sounded violent and angry. I LOVED IT.

Fast Forward to 1984 (maybe...my memory is hazy). I had been sneaking into this dive called the Jockey Club, and for all my knowledge that I had acquired up until this point, this was the coolest place on the planet. I tried to get in and this small, stocky, shriveled up Cigar with a face won't let me in. I go to the back door with a bunch of other frustrated pubes, and the old dude lets us in with the warning," if the police come you go out the same way you came in, and if I catcha with booze, you're outta here". I'm stoked, because the band that started it all for me is playing tonight. BLACK FLAG.

Jules at the bar as usual
photo by Mark Kerley

Being the naughty kid that I was, I ignored Shorty's booze warning and promptly found somebody to buy me a beer. FOSTER'S LAGER....the can was bigger than my head. "What's that?" I asked. "Try it...it's not like the wimpy beer that you are used to" the bearded dude says. It was hot as fuck in the packed club, and I can still remember how delicious that beer tasted as I type these passages. I get another monster beer from my new pal, and move my way to the front to feast my eyes on the band that legends are made of. This must have been one of the first times I was drunk...I had butterflies in my stomach waiting for the show. As Greg Ginn started the first riff, I felt like someone slugged me in the stomach with a fist made of granite. I was focused on him for the first few minutes and was perplexed by the gyrating and grimacing. It seemed that he was suffering at the hands of his Plexiglas guitar that looked as if it was shoddily held together by a few strips of duct tape. "I gotta learn how to do that" I say to some numb nut standing next to me. His amp had the logo SOUND CITY, and all I could think of is it should be called sound planet. I was expecting the singer to be some cue ball head having goof, but when the animal hit the stage, all I saw was a mane of hair, tattoos, and a pair of black swimming trunks...and LOTS of sweat. More sweat than I had ever seen in my life. I was being slammed against the stage from behind from some unknown force, but couldn't be bothered to turn around and see what was causing all the pain and bruises. I was hypnotized by the sheer brutal power of what lay before me. I was smiling a toothy slack jawed mouth breathing grin, and about three gallons of sweat from Henry flowed into my drooling gob. It was disgusting, but I couldn't stop gaping.

Somewhere in the middle of the set something beautiful and moving occurred that sticks out in my mind to this day. It sort of sums up the interesting mix of people that would frequent this club.

In the midst of all the leather and spikes and flannel, a woman who looked sort of like a local redneck jumped on the stage and started trying to grind on Henry's leg. He graciously accepted her mating dance for a few seconds, almost embraced her then put his palm gently on her face and pushed her away, it all seemed to happen in slow motion and didn't look brutal, painful or malicious, and she disappeared back into the fracas.

When it was all over I was exhausted and in pain. The single most impressive live show I have seen in my entire life. I went against the wishes of my father and stopped playing clarinet in the school marching band, and got myself an electric guitar. I never had the chance to play in the Jockey Club, but the sights sounds and smells of the joint will never leave my mind, and every time I play in a smoke filled dive, the memories of those first experiences with true rock and roll fill me to the brim with joy and ecstasy.

The G.B.H / Cro-Mags Show
by Mike Stocks

I ran away from home to see two of my favorite bands. I went downtown to a friend's house on Court Street and we had a six hour pre-show warm up.

This was the era of the "birth certificate ID". Type your name and birthday on a sheet of paper, cut it out and glue it over the original, xerox it and you're on your way!

When we got in the club, some members of the bands were hanging out in the private bar off of the hallway. People were getting shirts from G.B.H. and Harley from The Cro-Mags kept complaining about his toothache. After a while they took off and we stayed there. I had been feeling queasy on the way to the club and the heat inside really did it. I puked over

Cro-Mags at the JC

the bar into an empty ice chest while a few people threw beer cans and it was good fun in a punk rock kind of way. As bad as it seemed for me, it didn't seem that bad to anyone else. I felt better and went and sat at a table and waited for the Cro-Mags. Ten minutes later, Colin from G.B.H. comes over and gives me a Sprite and tells me it will settle my stomach. Cool! Thanx! He sat down and we watched most of the Cro-Mags set together! He got up and told me that he had to get ready to play and said see you in a minute! The Cro-Mags smoked heavy duty and the Sprite really did the trick!

When G.B.H. came on you could tell that something was wrong, they weren't happy anymore. They announced that their drummer (Wilf) was on his way to the hospital and anybody that knew any of their songs could get up and play with them. After a minute someone got up there and did a couple numbers, then somebody else, then the bass player went for a drink and somebody

Charged G.B.H. and the Cro-Mgs flyer

else played bass, then someone else, then he came back and the guitar player left for four or five songs, then the singer left for two songs and the fans kept it going for 45 minutes! Then they were all together again with their favorite drummer that night and played great even though you could tell that they were upset and would rather be somewhere else.

They pulled off a bad night in pure punk rock fashion and totally made it work. There were probably 20 people the next day telling their friends that they played for G.B.H last night and they probably still do. That was the Midnight Madness and Beyond tour and Kai their roadie mate took over the drums after that night. Wilf is doing well.

Stage Diving

by Bentley Davis

Nick Stavale
photo by Chuck Byrd

Friends lift you up

heave you above themselves

onto the stage.

Quickly gather your Raggedy Ann self

boots beneath

head above.

Skip little girl way up high on the stage

but kick your feet out a little more.

It's a Freakshow, Ace

Don't hog the time –

two or three bars suffice.

Stretch out arms

parallel to floor

and fall forward with an outward push.

Hands reach up to catch you.

Though two or three pair would do

to break the fall,

several are there

holding arms legs torso

above heads of crowds.

They pass you back

to where the throng thins

slowly lowering you to your feet.

Ready to begin again?

It's an exercise in trust, you know

like the actors' game

of falling backwards

Stories for Shorty

to classmates' waiting arms.

But unlike the actors

you were

on stage.

"Stage diving" was previously published in the e-zine, Zygote in My Coffee, issue 14, July 2004. © Copyright Bentley Davis

Jenny Bennett Leist

If you lived in Cincinnati in the 80s and liked almost any kind of music that wasn't mainstream, chances are the Jockey Club was your mecca. The east coast had CBGB's but we had the JC, and that meant some of the best punk bands in the states and England were coming through our back yard. I discovered it thanks to Billy Blank's radio show "Out to Lunch" on WAIF. I lived for those couple hours a week. I'd call Bill all the time (nursing a raging crush on both him and the music). I loved how he'd juxtapose Black Flag and Buddy Holly, Sid Vicious and Syd Barrett. I'll never forget lying in my bed in suburbia and hearing Johnny Thunders ordering his audience to 'kick over the fucking tables'. I thought, hell yeah! I wanted more of that real, raw, dirty, dangerous thing that punk rock had. It made me feel glad to be alive, and in the midst of my awkward, angst-filled adolescence, I needed it.

I didn't set foot in the club for a long time because it was in Newport which my overprotective parents deemed officially off limits. I eventually learned to drive and learned to lie about where I was taking their car though. I'd tell the folks I had a night shift at Steak n Shake and drive to Newport, changing out of my waitress uniform on the way. My friends were too timid to join me and thought I was nuts to go alone, but I didn't care. I was a little nervous the first time I walked in by myself but I knew Bill would be there and thankfully he took my naive self around that night, introducing me to Guinness and pot and some of the JC regulars. H-Bomb Ferguson was playing. I had never seen

Jen and friends at the JC
photo courtesy of Jenny Bennett Leist

or heard or smelled anything like the Jockey Club in my sheltered life so far and I thought it was perfect in all its filthy decaying glory. I remember thinking the graffiti in the bathrooms looked just like the photos I'd seen of CBGB's which I thought was very cool. The stories I heard about its past as a casino frequented by gangsters and movie stars just added to its allure.

So I was hooked after that first visit and basically lived for the time I could spend there, even though it meant leading a kind of double life, letting my parents think one thing and doing another. When I found out Johnny Thunders was coming to the JC at the end of February, I was beside myself with anticipation. I had been listening to the NY Dolls, the Heartbreakers and all of Johnny's solo stuff over and over since I heard him on the radio. I figured I'd be able to swing it as I had been managing to get away with sneaking to the JC and back without getting caught a couple times, sometimes bumming rides from Bill's friends. Getting into cars with strange older men didn't faze me when the destination was the JC.

The Friday night Johnny played with his band was one of the best nights of my life. I was right up front leaning on the stage and in heaven. Johnny was so great, everything I'd imagined and then some. I remember standing next to this guy who kept screaming out 'I'm a Boy, I'm a Girl'. We were so stoked to be there, we were just grinning at each other all night. The next time I saw that guy he was singing for 9 lb. Hammer, one of my favorite local bands.

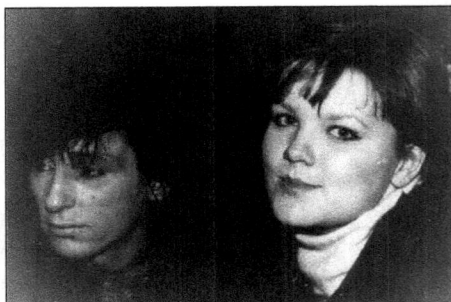

Jen with JT

When Bill told me he had finagled an acoustic show that Sunday from Johnny there was no way I was going to miss it even though I didn't have my handy night shift excuse to fall back on. I hadn't come up with any other viable alibi, so I just left, quietly walking out the front door while the parents were in the other room watching TV and taking the car to Newport. The show was just as incredible, more intimate since it was just Johnny plus the crowd was smaller. To top it all off, I got to meet Johnny before the show and have my picture taken with him. To this day that photo is one of my most treasured possessions. Johnny couldn't be bothered to look at the camera but I didn't care. I was standing next to Johnny fucking Thunders!

Coming home to a police cruiser in the driveway afterward wasn't enough to mar that night for me. You see, my parents had reported their car stolen even though they knew I was the one that took it. My punishment was removal of every item of mine that represented punk rock to them. My boots, my black clothes, my concert shirts, my records, posters, British punk zines, everything including my stereo went into the trunk of their car and I never got them back. I guess this was supposed to cure me of my punk rock addiction but their plan backfired. All that just made me more determined than ever to hang on to the music. I felt I could count on it not to let me down like I felt they had by not trying to understand my love for it

.

So the JC would become like a second home to me. I could be myself there (or be someone else) and no one would try to stop me or tell me that was unacceptable. Maybe that could be a bad thing, but regardless, I was going to do things my way (usually the hard way) and somehow this unlikely spot was a safe haven. It kind of felt like a family there, however dysfunctional. Bill (Leist) and Rick (Simms) were a little like indulgent big brothers to me and Shorty was like the disapproving dad, running me out of the men's room with his flashlight waving when I was trying to avoid the line in the women's and get back to the band faster.

Lux Interior
photo by George DuChane

The attachment I had to the club was so strong that I would go so far as to leave home for good when my ability to go there was threatened. I was supposed to live in my parents' house while I went to UC in the fall, but I had broken curfew the night that MDC played the club and I knew they'd put me under house arrest. (I had no choice really, I mean would you pass up a chance to go to a party with MDC?) I also knew that the Ramones and the Cramps were coming to the club in the next couple weeks and there was no way I was going to risk missing them. So without a thought about blowing off college or what I'd do without a car or my parent's money or blessings, I left. I managed to convince the girl having the party to let me move in even though I just met her that night. She got evicted soon after which led me to a fleabag hotel downtown where I had to share the bathroom with old winos. Of course this was a small price to pay to have the freedom to go see the Ramones and the Cramps!

It's hard to put into words why I felt and still feel the Jockey Club was such a great place. I guess telling the lengths I went to for it is the only way I know how to express how special it was. I lost a lot of brain cells there, my virginity too, as well as the higher frequencies of my hearing, but the memories and friends I took with me are irreplaceable. Twenty years later, no place can compare. To cop a phrase, it must not be forgot that once there was a punk rock Camelot!

Suicidal Nite

by Joetta Lickteig

The cage, JC's rear door
photo by Sarah Kuhl

All I wanted was a Pepsi, just one Pepsi…

Yeah, it's a damn shame

When some stupid band comes to town

Already famous with a MTV countdown

Has to get a chick drugged just to get laid

Yeah, I thought so too

But that's what happened to me

Stories for Shorty

And it was a Suicidal Nite

ONE TWO THREE FOUR

I let my guard down

When they asked me backstage

Too many Jockey Club Foster's

Got me in a rage

Onto the bus, Heineken and weed,

No Pepsi for me please,

What was in that fuckin drink?

Why do I feel wheezy?

Why is that the engine running?

Why are we getting on the freeway?

Where's my purse hat and shoes?

Why are you doin me this way?

Don't push me out the window

30 miles away

Shorty warned me about your kind

It's a Freakshow, Ace

Date rape drugs are not OK

This song is dedicated to Louiche and Mike

See ya'll on youtube

The Last Night

by Mike Stocks

The Jockey Club is the place where I saw my first five shows and ten all together. It was a place that would leave an indelible influence on me and others forever. You could be the first person there, sit down at a table, roll a joint (if you were known) and nobody would say anything! A friend of mine stage dived at C.O.C. landing on the floor suicide style so many times that I made him sit down and he got up and did it another six times! Dave the singer from M.D.C jumped off the stage to break up a fight. The Adolescents played the soundtrack

"Handsome" Clem Carpenter
photo by George DuChaine

for the "Kids of the Black Hole". Flipper cancelled because their singer Bruce Loose died. White Zombie's first tour sounded more like Misfits-y slop metal than a rap group with guitars. Modern Vending tried to talk people into going to Las Vegas with them, drumming up a road trip while on a mini-tour! Skinhead security, Newport Gestapo and "Handsome" Clem and sometimes Gorgeous George too! The best of times indeed, but the last night that the club was open was the definition of end all, be all.

The last night's bill was all the local bands I think. Even though they weren't the hardcore shit I liked, they were definitely entertaining. I brought a guitar bud who had never been there. We dug on BPA, rocked and surfed with Doc and the Pods (great version of Spider Man!), Victor Garcia from The Edge doing acoustic Edge songs. That was anti-climatic and got people rumbling. My friend and I were sitting at a table in the middle when beer bottles start whizzing around and breaking. That's when I told my friend that this was the last night that the club was gonna be open. He said "That's too bad. I was really

Spray paint on the walls, last night
photo by James Bramlage

starting to like this place!" Then people started throwing chairs at the wall on the right side of the place and some girl got up on the mic and plead with the rowdies something like " This is our place that we love, let's leave it with love and dignity and not tear it up...that went on with quite a bit of resistance for probably a full 20 minutes before totally going over like the Hindenburg. I think the Auburnaires were right after all that, they definitely closed the night out and that was pinnacle Rock "N" Roll shit. I've seen tons of crazy shit and as far as shows go; nothing has topped this yet. The Auburnaires are playing and bottles are thick in the air, mostly directed at that wall on the right. Chairs and tables, in the air, against the wall. Bathrooms, what was left anyways already, gone. The wall that was the target of a lot of the destruction was paneled with plywood to the ceiling. 25 of the 30 feet of the height of that wall was stripped bare of the paneling and then of the framing right down to the cinder blocks! And nobody got on anybody's shoulders or anything! Then the last chairs and tables were smashed against the wall and I don't know if anyone got a picture of this, but the damnedest thing was when someone winged a chair and stuck it by one leg into that last 5 feet of paneling that was left near the ceiling. Shorty was running around with his sawed off aluminum baseball bat but he couldn't be everywhere at once and probably said the hell with it after a while because the building was going to be leveled anyways. The Auburnaires played through it all even though I think they quit two songs early because it was so hairy and not in the get a haircut kind of way either! When they stopped it was pretty much all over anyways. Some headed for the door because it seemed like there was no way that the cops weren't coming and they didn't want to get nabbed for the destruction. Some stuck around collecting pieces for souvenirs and telling stories. No one wanted the club to go but it did and the world will probably never see anything that could hold a candle to it anywhere, ever.

The Last Show

by Max Cole

BPA
photo by George DuChaine

Todd Witt came on stage to play the last song from the BPA set. We had just played four new songs and for the last night it was not only appropriate but necessary for Todd to play drums on the last song. I helped him switch the drums covered in Weekly World News headlines from a right handed to a left handed kit... something we have done most every week to date since then in the BPA / Wolverton Brothers / Gordy Horn (just to name a few) practice space. He said to me "You got your feet wet, now jump on in"... something I later told him as he began his lead singer, guitar playing career with Go To Hell...but I digress for good reason. It's quite amazing how many bands the Jockey Club has spawned during and since its closure.

When the set was done I loaded the drums and headed home to my seven and two year old children. I didn't witness the interior implosion that night, nor the complete demolition later. In my mind it is still a cavernous, smoky, mildewy, pleasure dome of music, attitude, friends, and culture. Just like visiting a childhood home, I'm sure today it would seem much smaller, more narrow, shorter and the Foster's oil cans not so gargantuan. The graffiti was not the art form it has become today, but its statements made clear that this was not a place for the weak or weary. There was a purpose to all that occurred there. A vastness that swallowed you up and spit you out at closing time.

My only conversations with Shorty were ordering beers. If I could go back in time I would thank him for his seemingly effortless contribution to the Cincinnati music scene. It didn't matter that the Freon in the coolers merely helped keep the drinks slightly above room temperature, or that the pisser's smell made even the most ardent of punkers' gag. The place had no limitations and we were all dangerously safe there.

This is not a missive of sentimental memories... it is a testament to a man who enabled a culture which had no home to flourish, and helped me to become who I am as well as countless others.

Thank you Shorty... for everything.

Peter Aaron

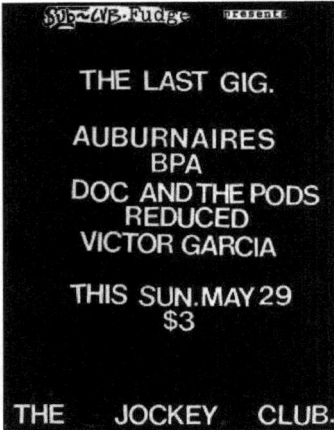

SUB-POP-PUDGE present

THE LAST GIG.

AUBURNAIRES
BPA
DOC AND THE PODS
REDUCED
VICTOR GARCIA

THIS SUN. MAY 29
$3

THE   JOCKEY   CLUB.

flyer by Pete Wegele

The last show at the Jockey Club was, ask anyone, totally insane. Toward the end of the club's existence, I had gotten involved in doing its booking with Bill Leist, a partnership that continued when we booked shows at the Top Hat in Covington, and Murphy's Pub and Shorty's Underground (named for the great man himself) in the Clifton area of Cincinnati. Working with Leist, I helped to bring Big Black, the Lazy Cowgirls, Green River, and other cool late '80s bands to the JC. Anyway, we found out from Shorty at the last minute that he had sold the club, so we had to throw together a closing-night bill really fast. I think we had maybe a week to promote it, but word spread like wildfire and the place was beyond packed the night of the show, mostly with people who had obviously never been there before but wanted to say they had. The bill, was, naturally comprised of regular JC acts: the Auburnaires, the Reduced, Doc and the Pods, Victor Garcia-Rivera from the Edge, and I can't remember who else (I'm sure someone does, though, or maybe they have a copy of the rather grim all-black flier I made). At the end of the night the crowd went crazy, tearing up the club for souvenirs

Bathroom, last night
photo by James Bramlage

with Shorty chasing them around and hitting them on the heads with his flashlight as he tried to save what was left for the cab company that bought the place. Of course, I didn't partake in the destruction, but I did manage to grab one of the chairs from the club, which I still have. After the dust settled at the end of the show, William Weber (with whom I would later start the Chrome Cranks and who is still my best friend today) and I did the only sensible thing to do in honor of the venue's last night: We went to Perkins in Clifton and stayed up 'til the sun came up drinking coffee, bullshitting, and reliving the innumerable and absolutely amazing rock 'n' roll shows we saw at the Jockey Club. Long may those wild memories live.

The Night My Job Ended, Part 29, or How I Attempted to Work Sound That Last Night at the Jockey Club

by Uncle Dave Lewis

(NOTE: This piece was written for the short-lived publication InkWire, with whom I published some other writing. They asked me to write about the last night of the Jockey Club. The typescript I found of this long lost text isn't dated, and I can't recall if it was right after the Jockey closed or maybe a year after, but it was not later than a year after. They wanted a nostalgic puff piece about the Jockey, but instead I gave them what really happened that night, and appended a note saying basically "I don't think you'll want this." And, not surprisingly, they didn't. I have edited it very slightly; otherwise this is the same text that would have run in InkWire if they had decided to go ahead with anyway. —Uncle Dave Lewis)

Diary Entry Sunday, May 29, 1988

"Woke up three-ish. Last night a tough one, went way too long and too late. Rumor has it SS-20 plans to play (again?) at the start of tonight's ordeal at the Jockey. If so, I will extend to them no more of a soundcheck than any other band tonight. Just set 'em up and let 'em fly. I've had enough of rock band egos this week to last me the rest of my life…"

I scribbled on. It was about 4:30pm and I was in a blue funk over my coffee. Over the previous three nights I'd mixed something like 13 acts including my own—thank goodness Pete (Aaron) was there to watch the levels! All in addition to acting as middleman in several squabbles between warring personalities and struggling to make peace with the Jockey Club sound system. It had been sputtering to a halt for some time and now was finally breathing its last. Good thing we close tonight, I thought. I was dead exhausted.

My mind travelled back to an embarrassing, accursed memory that dated from the Friday before. A good band was up there, I don't recall which one, crankin' away. The system liked them and the sound was virtually running itself. My boss, Bob Hallas, walked up and was very complimentary.

"Sounds really good, Dave." He then paused, and said "You know Dave, one of these days I've gotta get a real board in here."

I thought he was joking. I answered in my usual, dry manner, "Well, if you're planning to do that you'd better do it soon since we close on Sunday."

Bob's expression was one of shock. No one had told him. Soon I was bombarded with questions. Are you sure? Did Shorty say so? Bob was stunned. As it turned out, clubs were dismantling his systems left and right and he hardly had a gig left in town. Then, I was speechless.

I was staring into the bottom of the coffee cup, watching the grounds drift about. The throbbing The Didjits left in my skull the night before refused to go away, I continued to make chicken scratch in my diary though I was playing little attention to what I was writing.

"Tonight shouldn't be too bad. After all, The Auburnaires will be playing and Shaun Norton will have them set up on a system completely independent of mine. I talked to Victor last night and all he's going to do is sing and play acoustic guitar; that should be a breeze. Doc and the Pods I've mixed several times and I don't remember how many times I've mixed BPA. Hallas will probably do The Reduced himself. So after The Pods are done I can probably relax and enjoy the remainder of the show, break down, collect my pay and bid the Jockey Club a fond adieu."

I laid down my pen and hustled out the door.

I arrived at the Jockey at about 8 pm, about a half an hour past my usual time. As I came in I was informed that SS-20 wasn't going to play, so I breathed a sigh of relief. My dance card was already full. Even at this early hour there was a bustle of activity going on. I went straight over to Bill Leist and laid down my conditions for the evening, all of which he accepted. As I had figured, Shaun Norton was already there, set up and ready to go. He quickly explained the manner in which he has set up his snake and I saw nothing unusual about it. We both agreed that, at least sound-wise, things should run as smooth as silk.

Although Victor Garcia-Rivera was scheduled to play first, I went ahead and set up BPA's mikes first in order to establish a standard arrangement on the board for the instruments. By 10:30pm the crowd was already sufficiently plentiful to start the show. Victor went up and did several of The Edge's songs on acoustic guitar. The audience received the act with polite applause. Things were going smoothly.

Perhaps a little TOO smoothly. I was being approached by various curious crowds-people and being graced with near celebrity status by some. All of them asked the same question, "Did you really play the first punk shows at the Jockey?"

"The first three as a matter of fact." I was temporarily basking in the spotlight. "BPA and 11,000 Switches played here to nobody on April 3-4, 1982, which was a few months before Bill Leist came down to start booking this place. Then in September, when Bill started booking here, he was having trouble finding bands that'd come down to Newport to play, with its reputation and all. So we came down and played to no one again. But eventually things picked up."

BPA soon took the stage. To say that the BPA mix went off without a hitch would be dishonest. I had some problems. But overall I had no complaints. This was the first appearance by BPA since their disastrous show at the Southgate House an August ago. Since then they'd lost a drummer, gained a new one and worked up a whole new batch of songs. The crowd received them warmly. It was like an old friend had come home. It sure was good to see those guys onstage again.

To this point, Bob Hallas had been in and out, shuttling back and forth between the Jockey and the "Taste of Cincinnati" ceremonies. He looked tired and pale. I felt sorry for him, momentarily forgetting how tired and numb I'd been feeling the last couple of days.

The Jockey Club snake—the patch bay that takes inputs from the stage and feeds them back to the mixing board—had a couple of dead channels. Channel 5 didn't work, so we substituted 15 for it. There was no "9" on the snake at all, so you had to count 10-12 as 9-11 and then it was okay up through 16, except for 15, which was 5. Somehow, when I made my set change from BPA to Doc and the Pods my lines got crossed. My assigns back to the board didn't match what I had thought I'd put together up on the stage. Attempting to rectify the situation during the performance is damn near impossible. Bob took control of the board while I attempted to untangle whatever it was that I had tangled. Working under such stress I never do well, and managed to further complicate matters, though eventually, they got straightened out. About this time I heard the first in a series of increasingly louder crashes.

I looked around. A couple of the people in the crowd were tossing chairs against the right wall of the Jockey. I'd heard rumors that something was going to happen at the Jockey this final night. I'd heard that it could be anything from a small scale riot to the burning of the club right down to the ground. In any case, there it was, manifesting itself right before my eyes.

Torn paneling
photo by James Bramlage

It all started with just a few guys tossing chairs against the wall. Then more joined in. Before long it was a full scale melee, and the right wall began to splinter away under the force of the attack.

The paneling started to come down, revealing the studs and cement wall beneath. More were attracted into the destruction, and soon tables, chairs, wooden boards, paneling, records from the Jockey jukebox, bottles and beer cans became airborne en masse. There was so much crashing, bashing and shattering going on than the good-timey garage psychedelia of Doc and the Pods could barely be heard.

I went to Bob for instructions. All he said was, "Stand by the speaker stacks and make sure nothing happens to them."

It's a gig, I thought. Either I get brained by falling masonry or a stud with a nail in it goes through my neck. If the speaker stacks do tip over I'm supposed to break the fall with my body. Either way I'm a dead duck. Nevertheless, I go and stand stage left and watch the line of splintering wood and flying chairs creep gradually towards me.

If a speaker cabinet did happen to fall on top of a 15-year-old girl who'd used a fake ID to get into this place I'd feel pretty bad about it, and the random mass of dust and flying splinters and nails was getting pretty close to me. So I began to wave my arms back and forth like a racetrack ref in hopes that the destruction wouldn't get past a certain point. Suddenly, I felt a sharp and intense pressure against my left ankle, followed by a spray of little bits of glass embedding into my leg. Someone had nailed me with a bottle, but good, and my ankle was moist, warm and sticky.

The waving must have done some good though, because the destruction almost magically ceased. Doc and the Pods were no longer playing at this point. Several of the Jockey Club regulars were at the mike, haranguing the crowd for their bad behavior. Impassioned speeches were made. It was over, though. Along the right wall of the Jockey was a pile of rubble waist high and about 20 feet long. Broken boards studded with nails. Twisted remains of chairs; shattered and shorn fragments of wood paneling. The interior of the club was smoldering in a cloud of plaster dust; broken bits of records carpeted the floor. For the remainder of the night, none of the frightened crowd went anywhere near the right side of the club, preferring to huddle to the left, and left middle.

The rest of the show is rather a blur to me. I remember joining in on the mike and making some idiotic comment about Altamont. I guess the Reduced played; I remember trying to help Shaun Norton do his gig in any way that he needed me, but my heart wasn't really into the night anymore. I broke down the mikes and cables and collected my pay. Most of the Jockey Club staffers were standing around numb and perplexed and when I offered my goodbyes, hardly anyone noticed. Shorty, however, didn't charge me for my drinks, and left me a tip besides—gee, thanks!

The next day I skipped making a diary entry—I went to Columbus, and Greg Fernandez—who'd also played the Jockey long ago—and I made tapes and barbequed all day and I had a chance to stretch out.

Back in Cincinnati a few days later, I was getting in a heated disagreement with a friend over the phone.

"Why are you so upset about those guys tearing up the Jockey?" she asked. "They were just having a bit of fun; besides, they weren't doing anything the cab company isn't going to do to the Club eventually."

"Perhaps not" I answered, but added, "A couple of people walked out of there with head injuries and other complaints that was the direct result of that madness. They didn't go there and pay their money to get hurt. They went to see the bands, their friends and maybe to have a good time. Also, some of them may have felt the same way I do about the Jockey."

"I've worn a number of hats at the Jockey over the years, first as musician, occasionally as a booking agent, and mostly running sound," I continued. When it looked, at various times before, like the Jockey was going to close I was out there lobbying for it. I've played down there at times when there were five people there besides Shorty and me. At other times, there were 500 people there, and I was lucky enough to be on the bill that night."

"The bathrooms were awful. The cops would harass you when you tried to buy a drink, yet when you were getting your ass kicked in the parking lot by a bunch of rednecks they were nowhere to be found. But if you just wanted to play a gig—ANY GIG—the Jockey was always there. You might not get a great gig, but if it wasn't, then you merely played for yourself. Either way, I did a lot of growing at the Jockey Club, and nobody ever harassed me there for playing the kind of music that I play, nor being the kind of person that I am."

"I've had both good times and bad times there, but I've never felt compelled to trash the place. That last night I just wanted to say 'goodbye and thank you' to the Jockey just by doing my own damn job the best way I know how. And as I extract these little bits of glass from my leg I know who to thank for them —thanks for making my last night at the Jockey a living hell."

There was a silence on the other end of the line—then a sigh—and then she said, "Well, they didn't trash your memories, did they?"

A little later, I got out some tapes from the Jockey; some of my own shows, some by other bands. As I listened, it slowly began to come back—the musty smell, the crumbling walls, the discolored ceiling drooping towards the floor, the squeaky chairs. The essence of the Jockey Club; it all began to come back to me.

I award the argument to my friend on the other end of the line; No—no one can trash my memories.

John Rapach

JC at dusk
photo by Bob Butler

i was never a punk
i was a suburban kid
whose friend's big brother and
his older cousins from norwood were.
i remember watching them.
that crazy arms pumpin', legs stompin'
march thru the crowd
gathered all around the stage
at the jockey club.
But like many suburban kids
i was and still am
a punk in spirit
that whole sense
of the decline of western civilization,
of the darkness to come,
of the darkness that was left
in the wake of the rise and fall
of the civil/social/human rights
movements of the 60s and 70s.
and here can ronald ray gun
and the rise of the christian right
and the politics of fear and division

still alive and well
(and ignorant as ever)
today.
and there was the jockey club
and me and my suburban friends,
there to bear witness
and participate
in the protest of disgust
at what had become
of the idealism
of those 60s times.

so many of us as we got older
so easily make peace with,
and participate heartily in,
all the societal garbage
we were being fed (and still are).
This politics of fear,
all this us and them thinking,
all this politically correct bullshit.
shiny, happy people
going to hell as it were.
well i for one
approaching my 45th year here
am still here to say
fuck wall street
fuck the "establishment".
shit still ain't right
and. the decline of our western civilization
continues unabated.

I remember stage diving at the ramones
at the jockey club. multiple times
and never once losing my glasses.
i remember going outside
between sets
and wringing the sweat
out of my JOB rolling papers shirt
in the dead of winter

It's a Freakshow, Ace

steam rising from my body in the cold.
i remember drinking foster's oil cans
and making pyramids on the table
and the music
all that righteous anger
where has it gone?
i have a friend who lives in manhattan
and he and i went to check out CBGBs
last time i was there
and it was closed/boarded up.
gone just like the jockey club
gone just like the righteous anger
they'll probably put up a christian mega-church there
complete with starbuck's a kohl's
and the national jimmy swaggart museum
just to highlight the absurdity
of how far our larger society
has gone down the path of greed
and lies and unchecked power of the few.

MLK jr. used to say
that now is the time.
now is the time
to make justice
and freedom
a reality for all of god's children.
and i say that just like back in the early 80s
when this social trend
of greed and ignorance
(blissful though it may be)
and fear and distrust
began to flourish, that
now is the time for the jockey club.
now. in 2008. right now.
where are the bands
like all those great punk bands?
where are the people craving it,
and willing to support a club,
and attitude, a way of looking

at the good old u s of a
that includes a hearty f-you
to all the garbage we are handed daily
by the larger society?
MLK jr. also once said
that he was not satisfied
and that he would not be satisfied
until justice rolled down like water
and righteousness like a mighty stream.

now that's the kind of
punk ass attitude
that's so sorely missing today.
i've never been a punk
still don't have any tattoos
or piercings
hair is still the same color its always been.
but don't think it was all about
"punk fashion".
i think it was more.
i think that punk attitude
has sadly, largely gone away
just like the jockey club.
but my non-punk ass
still hasn't lost the faith.
and i look forward to one day
going to that glorious, dingy
jockey club in the sky
to stage dive
and drink foster's
and wring that heavenly sweat
from my JOB rolling paper t-shirt
once again.
to be a part of a collective, massive
middle finger thrust up
right there in the middle of heaven.
and to know that the lord
that god of all that is right and true

will be right there with us,
adding the considerable weight
of his (or her) omnipotent, omnipresent
middle finger to ours.

freakin' out all those goody two-shoes angels
havin' lunch at the heavenly panera bread
in their heavenly stylishly fashionable heaven wear,
or havin' triple caffeine lattes at the heavenly starbuck's
with their heavenly laptops to keep them company,
or havin' nice get togethers
in their heavenly, immaculately manicured
heavenly estates. gated. sterile.
and fully alarmed for their heavenly protection.
for god surely loves all of his (or her) children.
but i have to believe
that there is a special place
in the heart of truth and justice
or the punks. For places like the jockey club.
for without the righteous anger,
how can we experience the blissful joy
and without the darkness
how can we truly experience
the awesome radiance of the light.

In
Memoriam

Ben Shipman

To Those I Love and Those who Love me

by Myra McKee

When I am gone, release me and let me go, I have so many things to see and do. You mustn't tie yourself to me with tears, be thankful for our many beautiful years. I gave to you my love; you can only guess how much you gave to me in happiness. I thank you for the love you gave me but now it's time I travel on alone. So grieve awhile for me, if grieve you must, then let you grief be comforted by "god". It's only for a time

Myra
photo by Sarah Kuhl

that we must part, so bless the memories within your hearts. I won't be far away, for life goes on, so if you need me, call and I will come. Though you can't see or touch me I'll be near and if you listen with your heart you will hear all my love around you soft and clear and then, when you must come this way alone, I'll greet you with a smile and say, "Welcome home."

Steve Hull

Steve Hull was my best friend. We went to school together, rode bikes together and, most of all, we went to the Jockey Club together. I can't remember the number of bands we saw but it was in the hundreds. Most nights we scammed rides from anyone we could or took the METRO and walked across the river.

Stevie Hull
picture by Jakki Repellent

Sometimes Steve's Dad drove down from Bond Hill to pick us up—we were still in high school. One night we were hung out to dry and walked to Calhoun St. in Clifton before finding a ride home.

Steve was a study in contrasts—black son of a black mother and father who never seemed comfortable with his race. He hated the terms "Afro-American" and "African American." "I'm black, Goddamnit!" he would say. Steve even made himself into a skinhead, complete with Doc Martins, suspenders, shaved head, and a collection of Screwdriver and other Oi records. I didn't know until years later that his parents had adopted Steve. His brother looked so much like his father and he looked a lot like his mother. Maybe that was one of the things that fired him up and made him tough for some people to like. I don't know, but we had so much fun hating together.

After our Jockey Club days Steve joined the army, and ended up a tank commander in the Gulf War. I remember him talking about the day they were pushing north into Iraq and he looked over and realized that his navigator's head was gone. He got into some trouble for that.

I lost contact with Steve after that, but learned that he couldn't get used to civilian life and re-upped as a Marine, ending up in a special forces unit called FAST. He tried to contact me at one point, but I didn't know it. I spent 2+ years trying to track him down, figuring no one would tell me because he was doing something hush-hush in Afghanistan or Iraq.

In late 2006, I went to my 20th high school reunion, hoping to run into someone who knew Steve's whereabouts. That day I learned that he had died in an apartment fire in January, 2005. Neighbors who were interviewed described him as "a man who lived alone with a cat." I was finally able to locate his parents here in Cincinnati. They were still too overcome with grief to do anything with his ashes, which had been sitting in the front hall in a makeshift shrine since the memorial service. A few weeks later, I was honored to join them for Steve's interment at Spring Grove Cemetery, with military honors. I think about Steve all the time and regret not getting back together with him sooner. At least I now know where he will always be.

—Matt Becher

Rick Sims

I first met Rick Simms in grade school. I was in second grade. He was in third grade. Rick was the brightest student in his class and had knowledge about a lot of things. We used to get a kick out of how uncoordinated he was in gym class and the way he kinda looked like Frankenstein when he walked. It was part of what made him unique.

Rick Sims
photo by Witt

Rick founded the first Cincinnati punk band in 1978 at the age of 17. In those days Rick played guitar, Dave "Hap" Hilton" sang and Phil Ludwig played drums. They had no bass player. Bill wasn't the singer yet. He was like an advisor/manager and lent moral support. I saw their second and last gig (of the original band) at the 4th of July fireworks in 1979 at the Newport Floodwall. It was my introduction into the world of punk rock. Hap announced, "This is our 10-inch disco single 'Pretty Vacant.'"No one really dug it except for the band's friends and some unbiased 5-year-olds dancing enthusiastically in front of the stage. They did punked-up versions of "Wild Thing" (Hap sang, "Wild thing I think I hate you!") "Satisfaction", "No Fun", "1979" (OK) Rick was wearing an army shirt with an artillery belt and a Jim Morrison button. It was a very radical thing to be playing punk rock at an event like that in the late 70's. I really dug it and it changed my perception of rock music.

Rick was a very talented and unique individual whom I'll always remember. I was really shocked when I heard that he had passed away, way too soon at the age of 35. I remember Rick for a lot of things but this one had the most impact. Rest in Peace, Uncle Ricky.

—Snare

Jesse Zimmerman

I first met Jesse at the JC. Him, Paul and Chris and Evan were making a pyramid of empty beer cans on the table. We just started talking and the rest is history. We were very close friends for years. If there was a show at the JC, we were there, if there was not a show, sometimes we still went. We would hang out in the front room. Sometimes we worked the door. He was a very, very talented artist. He graduated from Antonelli College I think, but went to high school at Cincinnati Performing Arts and Withrow, and was even in a couple of "After School Specials". We hung out almost every day. I remember his place in Clifton. A nasty little place. It was efficiency, one big room. We built a castle out of cardboard and created a door. It was cool. When the college kids left we got some furniture and even had the best chair ever as it was like the "Maxell" chair from the old poster. It was great. I remember driving up to Columbus once listening to MDC's the chicken squawk over and over, but we were bored and decided to go to Caesar's creek instead. One time (I am from England) we went to Fairborn to an English grocery store. Half way there Jesse said "why are we going again" I said "potato chips". He never let me live that down. Then there was the time Jesse, Becky and I were camping. We had a tent, beer and chips. We shared and said "care for" when we offered. When we went to sleep, Jesse fell asleep on a picnic table, letting the ladies have the tent. Then we heard screaming, Jesse was woken up by a raccoon next to him on the table eating the chips....That was funny. He was always there to protect me. Sometimes it got him in trouble. I remember having breakfast with Lesley I Gains in the old Clifton Perkins once. Jesse later started doing tattoos. He

Jesse Zimmerman

would practice on me for a 12 pack. He ended up opening a shop in Norwood. He was a very, very talented man. He drew a picture of his parents that looked like a photograph it was so good. I would still like to find out the story behind his passing. Not a day goes by that I don't think of him. At his funeral his mom pulled me aside and said "you know Jesse loved you very much" I said "I know and he always will". I would have given my life for him. He was there with me and Becky and Sheri in good times and bad. He won awards for his tattoos. He is on a pedestal in my memories, and for the people who read these and now him, I am sure they will feel the same. I LOVE YOU JESSE!!!!!

—Cathy Lakes

Ben "The Shred Rat" Shipman

I was looking through my old scrapbook and found a photo of Ben that I had taken with one of those old disc cameras. It was a picture of him during a stage dive at one of those awesome D.O.A. shows at The Jockey Club. I have several shots of him playing guitar with Musical Suicide but that D.O.A. photo really captured the essence of "The Shred Rat". Ben was so into playing in a super cool punk band. Musical Suicide was an intricate part of The Jockey Club history. Their album "Big Fish in A Little Sea" will forever be a classic in the punk genre. Ben wasn't just in a great band but he was also a fan of the music and the people that made up the Cincinnati scene. The thing I remember most is that he was just a really cool guy and enjoyed life and his friends.

—Chuck Byrd

The Freakshow

JOCKEY CLUB
633 YORK STREET
NEWPORT, KY. 41071

Peter Aaron (Wegele)
Jerry Adams
Sean Allen
Neil Aquino, aka The Hockeypunk
Steve "Snare" Arnzen
Jake Ashcraft
Stacy Adkins
Matt Becher
Tim Benz
Bevo
Celene Black
Greg Borman
Teresa Bowling
James Bramlage
Scott Bruno
"Toxic" Bob Butler
Chuck Byrd
"Handsome" Clem Carpenter
Jim Cole
Max Cole
Jim Danehy
Jonathan Dameron
Wendy Darst
Jimmy Davidson, aka Jimmy D
Bentley Davis
Dave Davis

Art Dieck
Chris Donnelly
George DuChaine
Gregory Fernandez
Victor Garcia-Rivera
Margie Garrett
Jan Gerber
Mike Gregory
Brendan Halpin
Laura Harrell
Jacob Heintz
Ric Hickey
Walt Hodge
Bill Igerent
Joey "Shithead" Keithley
Amy Kreitzer
Sarah Kuhl
Cathy Lakes
Bill Leist, aka Billy Blank
Jenny Bennett Leist
Uncle Dave Lewis
Joetta Lickteig
Amy Miller
Brian Moore
Lisa Nichols
J.J. Pearson
Becky Baldock Powell
Heather Prescott
John Rapach
Angie Rawers
Jakki Repellent
Bryce Rhude
Judi Rothenberg
David "Dook" Russell
Witt Schmitz
Allen Scott
Chris Smith
Paul Smith
Dee Snyder

Mike Stocks
Robert "Jughead" Sturdevant
Mark Urschel
Vivien Vinyl
Eerie Von
Spike Vrusho
William D. Waltz
William Gilmore Weber
Betsy Young
Tammy Zienau

Thanks, Shorty.

www.ingramcontent.com/pod-product-compliance
Lightning Source LLC
Chambersburg PA
CBHW070025100426
42740CB00013B/2600